Number Three: Texas A&M Southwestern Studies

ROBERT A. CALVERT *and* LARRY D. HILL
General Editors

PRIVATE BLACK COLLEGES IN TEXAS, 1865–1954

Private Black Colleges in Texas, 1865–1954

BY

MICHAEL R. HEINTZE

TEXAS A&M UNIVERSITY PRESS

College Station

Library of Congress Cataloging in Publication Data

Heintze, Michael R., 1950–
    Private Black colleges in Texas, 1865–1954.

    (Texas A&M southwestern studies; no. 3)
    Bibliography: p.
    Includes index.
    1. Afro-American universities and colleges—Texas—
History.   I. Title.   II. Series.
LC2802.T4H45 1985   378.764   84-40565
ISBN 0-89096-223-5

Contents

List of Illustrations

Artemisia Bowden, ca. 1950
Reuben S. Lovinggood, ca. 1916
Melvin B. Tolson, ca. 1935
Wiley College library, ca. 1947
Wiley College campus, 1945
Bishop College homecoming dance, 1950
Flo Mills Drama Society, Samuel Huston College, 1928
Wiley College Quartet, 1936
Texas College voice recital, ca. 1940
1928 Samuel Huston College men's basketball team
1922 Paul Quinn College football team

List of Tables

Acknowledgments

LIKE most authors, I have accumulated many debts during the research and preparation of this study. I want to express my sincere thanks to the staffs of the Amistad Research Center, the Eugene C. Barker Collection, the Lyndon B. Johnson Library, the United Negro College Fund Archives, and the State Archives of Texas for their assistance in locating manuscript materials. I am also grateful to the librarians of Huston-Tillotson, Bishop, Wiley, St. Philip's, Paul Quinn, Texas, and Jarvis Christian colleges, who enthusiastically supplied me with relevant college and church publications, presidential papers, and valuable suggestions for securing other sources. Courteous and helpful aid also was offered by the librarians of Baylor University, Texas Christian University, Southwest Texas State University, Texas Lutheran College, the University of Texas at Austin, the Austin Presbyterian Theological Seminary, the Crockett Public Library, the Tyler Public Library, the Marshall Public Library, and the Seguin Public Library.

I would like to acknowledge the critical readings and valuable suggestions of my doctoral committee at Texas Tech University, especially those of Dr. Otto M. Nelson and Dr. Joseph E. King. To Dr. Alwyn Barr, I owe a particular debt of gratitude. His efforts to sharpen my literary skill and to improve my critical thinking while directing this study as a dissertation were greatly appreciated. The aid of Dr. Robert A. Calvert of the Texas A&M University history department was also invaluable in the final preparation of the manuscript. Thanks also to Donna Barnes, secretary of the Texas Tech political science department, who patiently typed and retyped the numerous drafts. Two research grants from the American Lutheran Church also facilitated the completion of this study.

This work is dedicated to my wife, Cheryl, and to our sons, Chris and Craig, who were a constant source of encouragement.

PRIVATE BLACK COLLEGES IN TEXAS, 1865–1954

Introduction

OVER the course of the 1980s, most of the private black colleges in Texas have celebrated, or will be celebrating, their hundredth year of service. During these hundred years, historians, educators, and social scientists have viewed, from widely divergent perspectives, the significance of these institutions. Under the scrutiny of such observers, the nation's black colleges have been the subject of much criticism and little acknowledgment. With the exception of black educators such as Booker T. Washington, W. E. B. DuBois, Robert Russa Moton, and others, it has been only in the past twenty-five years that scholars have begun to construct a more judicious assessment of these schools, by examining their accomplishments as well as their weaknesses.[1] To understand better the issues surrounding black colleges in Texas and elsewhere, it seems appropriate to begin this study with a survey of the more significant analyses, on the national and state levels, of the development of these institutions.

Two of the earliest works devoted to examining black colleges came from the pen of W. E. B. DuBois. The first of these, *The College Bred Negro*, which appeared in 1900, surveyed the social and economic conditions of black college graduates in the South. Another report, *The College Bred Negro American*, followed in 1910. In the second study, DuBois evaluated the character and quality of the education offered by black colleges. In both studies, he concluded that the liberal arts curriculum needed to be strengthened throughout the ranks of black colleges.[2]

[1] An excellent bibliographic source on black higher education is Frederick Chambers, *Black Higher Education in the United States: A Selected Bibliography on Negro Higher Education and Historically Black Colleges and Universities*.

[2] W. E. B. DuBois, *The College Bred Negro*, pp. 38–40; Jane E. Smith Browning

These findings came as no surprise, as DuBois had already become the focal point of debate within the black community for espousing these very views. In his famous article "The Talented Tenth" the outspoken champion of liberal arts instruction openly challenged the theories of accommodation and industrial education espoused by Booker T. Washington. While he recognized the need for some practical vocational training, DuBois objected to its racial application, noting:

Education and work are the levers to uplift a people. Work alone will not do it unless inspired by the right ideals and guided by intelligence. Education must not simply teach work—it must teach life. The Talented Tenth of the Negro race must be made leaders of thought and missionaries of culture among their people. No others can do this work and Negro colleges must train men for it. The Negro race, like all other races, is going to be saved by its exceptional men.[3]

His counterpart, Booker T. Washington, also supported the idea that black colleges were genuinely needed, but differed with DuBois's views about their mission and purpose. In 1903, Washington published his controversial article "Industrial Education for the Negro." In it, he contended that the most effective means of uplifting the greatest number of black Americans in the shortest time was through the type of industrial education offered at Tuskegee Institute. While he did not object to liberal arts training, Washington believed the surest path to economic, social, and political equality was to demonstrate, through industrial and agricultural accomplishment, the worthiness of his race. He observed that

One farm bought, one house built, one home sweetly and intelligently kept, one man who is the largest taxpayer or has the largest bank account, one school or church maintained, one factory running successfully, one truck garden profitably cultivated, one patient cured by a Negro doctor, one sermon well preached, one office well filled, one life

and John B. Williams, "History and Goals of Black Institutions of Higher Learning," in *Black Colleges in America: Challenge, Development, Survival*, ed. Charles V. Willie and Ronald R. Edmonds, pp. 79–80.

[3]W. E. B. DuBois, "The Talented Tenth," in *The Negro Problem*, ed. Booker T. Washington et al., pp. 33, 75.

cleanly lived—these will tell more in our favor than all the abstract eloquence that can be summoned to plead our cause.[4]

Although DuBois and Washington disagreed on the primary mission of black colleges, they did agree that black colleges played a vital part in the advancement of their race. Most of the other writers on black colleges during the first half of the twentieth century, most of whom were white educators and social scientists, took a less optimistic view. A 1916 federal government study, designed to gather as much data as possible on the state and nature of black educational institutions, provides an early example of this skepticism. Directed by white sociologist and educator Thomas Jesse Jones, this report found that, while black students were eager for instruction, most of the nation's black colleges remained rather anemic in terms of equipment, facilities, and organization. The study selected Howard University and Fisk University as the best black colleges but noted that they were clearly underendowed. For other well-known institutions such as Bishop College (Texas), Talladega College (Alabama), Meharry Medical College (Tennessee), and Morehouse College (Georgia), Jones reserved more pointed language. These institutions he characterized as colleges in name only, as no more than 10 percent of their enrollments were doing college-level work.[5]

The report also chastised the unsystematic location of these schools. Jones pointed out that competition among the various religious denominations resulted in the establishment of two or more black colleges in such cities as Selma, Alabama; Little Rock, Arkansas; Atlanta, Georgia; New Orleans, Louisiana; Holly Springs and Jackson, Mississippi; Greensboro, North Carolina; Columbia and Orangeburg, South Carolina; and Austin, Marshall, and Waco, Texas. In addition, the 1916 government study faulted the classical curricula offered by these institutions. Not-

---

[4] Booker T. Washington, "Industrial Education for the Negro," in *The Negro Problem*, ed. Booker T. Washington et al., pp. 9–29 (quote, pp. 28–29).

[5] U.S. Department of the Interior, Bureau of Education, *Negro Education: A Study of the Private and Higher Schools for Colored People in the United States*, prepared by Thomas Jesse Jones, Bulletin No. 39, pp. 55–56.

ing that these colleges had an almost "fatalistic belief" in the study of Latin and Greek, the report concluded that most black college leaders concerned themselves more with traditional curricula than with the types of courses needed by their students and community.[6]

In contrast to the Jones report during this period were two important works by Benjamin Brawley and Robert Russa Moton. In his *History of Morehouse College* (1917), Benjamin Brawley investigated Morehouse's founding and early years of development. While acknowledging the hardships involved in launching this institution, Brawley observed that church-related colleges such as Morehouse were invaluable training grounds for black leaders, including ministers, teachers, administrators, and businessmen. Brawley noted that, in its first fifty years of service, Morehouse had been "an efficient school, a Christian home, and the salvation of thousands of people."[7] In 1920, Robert Russa Moton published his autobiography, *Finding a Way Out*. Moton, who was selected as the president of Tuskegee Institute following the death of Booker T. Washington in 1915, declared that black colleges offered "an opportunity to help in the solution of a great problem, the human problem of race, not merely changing the modes of life and the ideals of a race, but of almost equal importance, changing the ideals of other races regarding that race."[8]

In 1928, the Department of the Interior funded a reexamination of its 1916 study of black colleges; this report also proved to be critical. Under the direction of white educator and historian Arthur J. Klein, this report pointed out that black colleges had failed to determine and recognize properly the professional status of their faculty members. The report also noted that in many institutions little or no attempt had been made to apportion academic duties according to training and merit. Accordingly, Klein held that the failure of these colleges to organize and

[6] The two colleges in Waco were Paul Quinn College and Central Texas College (ibid., p. 56).

[7] Benjamin Brawley, *History of Morehouse College*, pp. 9–30, 148–59 (quote p. 159).

[8] Robert Russa Moton, *Finding a Way Out: An Autobiography*, pp. 216–17.

rank properly their faculties led to considerable institutional confusion.[9]

Klein also observed the presence of heavy work schedules, noting that most deans also taught full-time. He concluded that in nearly every black college teachers were laboring under excessive work loads. These tiring schedules, according to the report, led to a lack of energy on the part of the instructors and a corresponding lack of enthusiasm on the part of the students. Similarly, Klein found that the salaries at these schools were woefully inadequate. He noted that most of the schools had no sound basis for establishing salary schedules, which led to the flagrant underpayment of many professors. The report concluded that these problems were further compounded by the fact that these colleges found it difficult to retain their personnel. Klein explained that over half the black colleges experienced a turnover of from one-third to one-half of their faculties every three years.[10]

Other needs were highlighted by Jackson Davis, a white educator and agent for the General Education Board. After visiting ninety-nine black colleges in 1928, Davis observed that "the needs of the Negro colleges do not differ materially from the needs of white colleges in the same stage of development." Davis argued that these schools needed bigger and better libraries, more educational equipment, and dedicated teachers. All these things could be acquired only if the colleges found new sources of income. To do this, Davis advocated that black colleges increase their tuition and seek increased support from the Negro churches, especially the Methodists and Baptists. He also suggested that it might be wise to concentrate upon developing a relatively small number of outstanding institutions as colleges, while supporting others as high schools.[11]

In 1932, the Phelps-Stokes Fund produced a broad-based study of the black colleges it supported. This report offered

[9] U.S. Department of the Interior, Bureau of Education, *Survey of Negro Colleges and Universities*, prepared by Arthur J. Klein, Bulletin No. 7, pp. 40–41.

[10] Ibid., pp. 42–45.

[11] Jackson Davis, "The Outlook for Negro Colleges," *Southern Workman* 57 (September, 1928): 135, 136.

some disturbing suggestions for black colleges. While urging the expansion of local, state, and federal aid for these schools, the report also called for the closing of what it called "inefficient private black institutions" and a greater participation by white educators and politicians in the planning and operation of black education. The report implicitly supported the development of black higher education only if it was firmly in the hands of white administrators.[12]

In 1934, Dwight Oliver Wendell Holmes published *The Evolution of the Negro College,* the nation's first extensive monographic study of black colleges. While Holmes remarked that "gratifying progress" had been made in enrollment, curriculum, and accreditation, he noted that, as a whole, these colleges were "faulty in several important respects." Holmes pointed out that there was intensive and undesirable competition for students, which had caused some colleges to lower their admissions standards. He also felt many of the schools lacked clear-cut objectives concerning curriculum and institutional growth. Furthermore, Holmes observed a continued lack of adequate funding for educational equipment and scholarships. Staff members, he revealed, spent so much time seeking funds that the operation of their institutions often went neglected.[13]

During the same year, white educator William R. Davis's *The Development and Present Status of Negro Education in East Texas* was published. Davis's regional study, which traced the development of all levels of black education, included a chapter on black colleges in which he portrayed the emergence of the private schools as the result of white racism. Because the Texas constitutions of 1866 and 1876 made it clear that the state was concerned only with the education of whites, many missionary and denominational groups shouldered the responsibility for the elementary, secondary, and higher education of black Texans.[14]

[12] Browning and Williams, "History and Goals of Black Institutions of Higher Learning," in *Black Colleges,* ed. Willie and Edmonds, pp. 80–81.

[13] Dwight Oliver Wendell Holmes, *The Evolution of the Negro College,* pp. 208–209.

[14] William R. Davis, *The Development and Present Status of Negro Education in East Texas,* pp. 102–103.

In this study, Davis echoed the observation of earlier authors that their founders had been unsystematic in locating these schools. Five of the six denominational colleges established in this region were situated in cities only sixty miles apart. Davis also indicated that there were too many colleges, which led to unnecessary duplication and competition. In addition, Davis viewed the curricula of these schools as outdated, since they emphasized classical courses, such as Greek and Latin, instead of courses like history, science, and mathematics.[15]

In 1944, the Bi-Racial Conference on Education for Negroes in Texas funded a state study of senior colleges for blacks. T. S. Montgomery, the chairman of the Department of Education at Sam Houston State Teachers College, authored the study, which found positive as well as negative data concerning the quality and purpose of these schools. While he found the purpose of the colleges to be democratic and similar to those of white colleges, Montgomery also concluded that the church-related black colleges in Texas continued to suffer from poor locations, low faculty salaries, poor libraries, and inadequate laboratory facilities.[16]

In 1948, Ridgely Torrence charted the life and achievements of John Hope, who had been president of Morehouse College from 1906 to 1936. He found that Hope had not only introduced many improvements to Morehouse, but had also helped lead the way in creating the Atlanta University Center. Torrence noted that Hope's efforts made Morehouse the "coming Negro college of the South" and set the stage for Atlanta to emerge as "a great, if not the great, educational center for Negroes."[17]

In 1951 Willard Range's *The Rise and Progress of Negro Colleges in Georgia, 1865–1949* was published. Range observed that white Georgians, like most white southerners, opposed black education, especially higher education. When the Georgia legislature refused to establish adequate educational opportunities for the freedmen following the Civil War, the Freedmen's Bu-

---

[15] Ibid., pp. 107–108, 118–19.

[16] T. S. Montgomery, *The Senior Colleges for Negroes in Texas*, pp. 91–92.

[17] Ridgely Torrence, *The Story of John Hope*, pp. 241–61.

reau and the white and black religious denominations were forced to shoulder the responsibility for educating the former slaves. During the late 1800s, the various church bodies constructed a network of black schools and colleges that offered elementary through collegiate training. Range pointed out that these institutions had many problems, such as inadequate financing and limited facilities, but concluded that they played a crucial role in improving living conditions for the black community in Georgia.[18]

Perhaps one of the most sweeping condemnations of black colleges was published in 1968 by Christopher Jencks, a white educator, and David Riesman, a white sociologist. Their book, *The Academic Revolution*, declared that public and private black colleges were "academic disaster areas." The authors abhorred the "authoritarian atmosphere" that had developed in the so-called typical Negro college, with its "intervening trustees, its domineering but frightened president, its faculty tyrannized by the president and in turn tyrannizing the students, and the tendency of . . . all . . . to identify with their persecutors." They also charged that these institutions forced their students to "go through the motions of being prim, disciplined models of Victorian virtue," a pattern which ignored the real qualities of people and resulted in a make-believe atmosphere.[19]

While dishonesty was not unique to black colleges, Jencks and Riesman believed it had become more common in these institutions. They noted many alleged cases of blackmail and fraud, such as college officials profiteering on textbooks or a president borrowing money from an untenured faculty member with no intention of repaying it. The authors also related stories of faculty members using grades to blackmail students into "mowing lawns, sweeping offices, or even providing sexual favors."[20]

---

[18] Willard Range, *The Rise and Progress of Negro Colleges in Georgia, 1865–1949*, pp. 3–20, 66–78, 99–108, 204–21.

[19] Christopher Jencks and David Riesman, *The Academic Revolution*, pp. 425, 426, 433.

[20] Jencks and Riesman elaborated: "This does not mean that sexual relations between faculty and students were or are more common on Negro than on white campuses. We doubt this. What seems to vary, at least according to the second-hand reports we

Jencks and Riesman also found little to commend in the black professional schools. They labeled the two black medical schools, Meharry and Howard, among the worst in the country. The authors speculated that both would have been closed long ago had they not been the principal source of physicians willing to treat black patients. After examining the nation's five black law schools, Jencks and Riesman concluded that they were barely "one jump ahead of the accrediting agencies."[21]

In the years since the rise of the modern civil rights movement, scholars have taken a fresh look at black higher education and black history, displaying greater sensitivity to achievements accomplished in the face of considerable obstacles. Several educators and social scientists have responded specifically to earlier critics. Authors such as Tilden J. LeMelle and Wilbert J. LeMelle have suggested that black colleges had been victimized by the "callous insensitivity of many interested individuals," such as Jencks and Riesman, who failed to comprehend the complexity of the problems facing this special segment of American higher education.[22]

Other revisionists, such as Herman B. Smith, Vernon E. Jordan, Tobe Johnson, Charles V. Willie, and Ronald Edmonds, have emphasized the positive contributions of black colleges. They have pointed out that these schools graduate a majority of the nation's black physicians, lawyers, teachers, and business leaders; assist black communities with a variety of social services; provide an environment conducive to enhancing racial

---

have gotten from both settings, is the basis on which male instructors approach a female student. On a white campus the man is usually at pains to make clear that he is interested in the girl for her own sake and to avoid anything that might give the appearance of blackmail, for he assumes blackmail would both defeat his romantic ambitions and very possibly land him in serious trouble. Negro men who have power seem less concerned about admitting and exploiting it, and girls in turn seem less reluctant to admit that they are using their sexuality for extrinsic purposes" (ibid., p. 427).

[21] Ibid., p. 437.

[22] Tilden J. LeMelle and Wilbert J. LeMelle, *The Black College: A Strategy for Achieving Relevance*, p. 17. See also Allen B. Ballard, *The Education of Black Folk*, pp. 24–25. Revisionist views were foreshadowed by a brief chapter on higher education in Horace Mann Bond, *The Education of the Negro in the American Social Order*, pp. 358–66.

pride and solidarity; and keep alive the dream of an integrated and democratic society.[23]

In recent years, several historical works have added to the revisionist literature on black education. Several studies highlighted the contributions of individual institutions. In *The Story of Spelman College* (1961), Florence M. Read maintained that private black colleges like Spelman were crucial to the development of blacks because, historically, only "limited educational opportunities have been open to the great majority of Negroes." The former Spelman president pointed out that the segregated system of education that developed after the Plessey decision was separate, but never equal.[24]

Edward A. Jones, in his 1967 book, *A Candle in the Dark: A History of Morehouse College*, reiterated that had it not been for the founding of the independent black colleges, most southern blacks would have remained in the grasp of ignorance and the associated ills of disease, crime, and economic dependency. Jones declared that Morehouse was dedicated to the task of "building men: first by enlightening their minds, then by freeing them from the shackles of a psychological conditioning brought about by nearly two hundred and fifty years of slavery."[25] Some recent historical studies have analyzed specific aspects of black education. James M. McPherson, in *The Abolitionist Legacy: From Reconstruction to the NAACP* (1975), examined the role of abolitionists in the struggle for racial equality. While earlier historians had argued that the abolitionists deserted the Negro

[23] Herman B. Smith, "New Roles for Black Colleges," in *Effective Use of Resources in State Higher Education*, pp. 35–36; Carnegie Commission on Higher Education, *From Isolation to Mainstream: Problems of the Colleges Founded for Negroes*, pp. 14–16; Vernon E. Jordan, "Blacks and Higher Education—Some Reflections," *Daedalus* 104 (Winter, 1975): 165; J. John Harris, III, Cleopatra Figgures, and David G. Carter, "A Historical Perspective of the Emergence of Higher Education in Black Colleges," *Journal of Black Studies* 6 (Spring, 1975): 66; Charles V. Willie, "Uniting Method and Purpose in Higher Education," in *Black Colleges*, ed. Willie and Edmonds, pp. 263–70; Tobe Johnson, "The Black College as System," *Daedalus* 100 (Summer, 1971): 798–812.

[24] Florence Matilda Read, *The Story of Spelman College*, pp. 374–75.

[25] Edward A. Jones, *A Candle in the Dark: A History of Morehouse College*, pp. 9–10. See also Rayford W. Logan, *Howard University: The First Hundred Years, 1867–1967*.

after 1870, McPherson found that the majority of these white activists continued to battle for racial equality. The best evidence of their commitment was in education, where abolitionist-inspired groups such as the American Missionary Association helped establish dozens of colleges and universities for freedmen throughout the South. McPherson concluded that much of the continuing debate over the effectiveness of these schools has been unwarranted. Pointing out that these schools provided the majority of educational opportunities for blacks in the two generations following emancipation, the author went on to note that it was the "talented tenth," trained in these institutions, who "led most of the twentieth-century civil rights movements and furnished much of the leadership for the black community."[26]

In his 1978 work, *Schooling for the New Slavery: Black Industrial Education, 1868–1915*, Donald Spivey argued that industrial education had been a "major force in the subjugation of black labor in the New South." Industrial education not only kept blacks in a subservient position, but also provided northern entrepreneurs and southern whites with a ready pool of cheap labor. According to Spivey, industrial training was aimed at building a way of life similar to that which existed before the Civil War, by indoctrinating blacks with certain "social and psychological values necessary to create . . . a recognition of their position in the New South."[27]

Historian Robert G. Sherer, in *Subordination or Liberation? The Development and Conflicting Theories of Black Education in Nineteenth Century Alabama* (1977), found that, even in the face of powerful white support for industrial training and the efforts of Booker T. Washington, most of the state's black educators remained committed to the liberal arts philosophy of the American Missionary Association. This opposition was based upon principles rather than personalities, even though most of the state's black educators perceived Washington as a "symbol

[26]James M. McPherson, *The Abolitionist Legacy: From Reconstruction to the NAACP*, pp. 3, 392–93.

[27]Donald Spivey, *Schooling of the New Slavery: Black Industrial Education, 1868–1915*, pp. ix, 71–79.

of white interests rather than being a truly indigenous black leader."[28]

A review of these studies makes it obvious that there has been a wide range of opinions regarding the quality, mission, and purpose of black colleges. Generally speaking, the black educators, social scientists, and historians have been more sympathetic in their appraisals of black colleges than whites. While acknowledging the problems faced by these schools, black scholars have perceived these institutions as important ingredients in the quest for social, economic, and political independence. During the age of Jim Crow, black colleges provided much of the elementary and secondary schooling for black children and virtually all of the higher education for young black adults. The consensus among the black authors discussed here is that, had it not been for the efforts of these institutions, the status of most black Americans would have improved very little between 1865 and 1954.

White educators, social scientists, and historians, on the other hand, have given far different impressions of black colleges. With few exceptions, most of the white educators and social scientists, especially in the first half of the twentieth century, viewed black colleges in a critical and often paternalistic light. Ignoring or minimizing the schools' accomplishments, they painstakingly scrutinized the faculties, libraries, facilities, endowments, and curricula of black colleges and found them to be little more than pale copies of white institutions. Only in the past three decades have white scholars, especially historians, begun to offer a more balanced appraisal, one which examines the strengths and contributions as well as the shortcomings of black colleges.

This work is the first topical examination of the founding and development of the private, primarily church-related, black colleges in Texas from 1865 to 1954. Such a study is needed to evaluate the significant controversies and problems that confronted black colleges. These issues include institutional mission

---

[28] Robert G. Sherer, *Subordination or Liberation?, The Development and Conflicting Theories of Black Education in Nineteenth Century Alabama*, pp. 146–48.

and purpose, administrative and faculty development, academic and vocational curricula, finances, and student life. This work also compares these institutions with the public black colleges of Texas, as well as other black colleges and universities in the United States. Thus, this study begins within the perspective of recent revisionism, first tracing the origins of the private black colleges in Texas.

1

The Early Years

ON June 19, 1865, federal troops, under the command of General Gordon Granger, landed at Galveston and formally proclaimed an end to the institution of slavery.[1] For several weeks, a wave of excitement and joy swept across the state, as the newly-freed slaves rejoiced:

> Jubilee, jubilee. Oh! Lord.
> Free at last, free at last!
> Thank God A'Mighty
> I'm free at last!
> Free at last, free at last!
> Thank God A'Mighty
> I'm free at last![2]

Such strong emotional outbursts seemed to be quite common. Former slave Millie Williams remembered: "It wuz a pretty sight when the slaves knowed they wuz free. They hug one another and almost tear their clothes off shouting. Some crying for sold husbands and children. They prayed so long and sometimes thought God would never hear po' niggers' prayers. But freedom had come."[3]

Regrettably, black Texans soon discovered that the abolition of slavery did not carry with it any guarantee of social, political, or economic equality. This became apparent during Reconstruction, as white Texans refused to accept blacks as equal citizens

---

[1] *Texas Republican* (Marshall), June 30, 1865.

[2] Thomas R. Frazier, ed., *Afro-American History: Primary Sources*, p. 95.

[3] Federal Writers' Project, *Slave Narratives, A Folk History of Slavery in the United States from Interviews with Former Slaves*, IV: 170; Melvin J. Banks, "The Pursuit of Equality: The Movement for First Class Citizenship Among Negroes in Texas, 1920–1950" (Ph.D. diss., Syracuse University, 1962), p. 2.

and systematically worked to reduce them to a segregated, second-class status as close to slavery as possible. This attitude was evident, for example, in the state's newspapers, which commonly referred to blacks as "niggers," compared them to apes, and published articles emphasizing "white" as a synonym for purity and "black" as the equivalent of wickedness.[4]

Even more troubling were the actions of Texas lawmakers, who between 1866 and 1900 erected an elaborate panoply of segregation laws that effectively robbed blacks of their rights as citizens. Beginning with the Constitution of 1866, laws were passed that prohibited blacks from intermarriage with whites, voting, holding public office, and serving on juries. Legislators also passed statutes that segregated public facilities such as railroad cars, theaters, restaurants, and hotels. Most importantly, they ensured that the state's educational system was kept separate and, knowingly, unequal.[5]

With the rise of these Jim Crow school systems, blacks would be hardpressed to provide their children with meaningful education. Consequently, the burden of starting, operating, and financing basic education for blacks fell to the newly created Freedmen's Bureau, several northern missionary and philanthropic groups, and the black religious denominations. Under the leadership of Lieutenant E. M. Wheelock, a New England Unitarian minister, the Bureau took the lead by establishing a school at Galveston in 1865. By May, 1866, the Bureau had set up more than one hundred schools across the state.[6] The agency found the freedmen extremely eager to acquire educational skills. General J. B. Kiddoo, the Bureau's Assistant Commissioner for Texas in 1866, remarked that the freedmen's "eagerness to learn is a great moral rebuke to the legislative restrictions of this and other states, placed on their being educated, while in slavery."[7]

[4] Alwyn Barr, *Black Texans: A History of Negroes in Texas, 1528–1971*, p. 41.

[5] Ibid., p. 42; William R. Davis, *The Development and Present Status of Negro Education in East Texas*, pp. 11–19.

[6] Alton Hornsby, Jr., "The Freedmen's Bureau Schools in Texas, 1865–1870," *Southwestern Historical Quarterly* 76 (April, 1973): 397–99; Barr, *Black Texans*, pp. 60–61.

[7] U.S. Bureau of Refugees, Freedmen and Abandoned Lands, *Report of Brevet Major General J. B. Kiddoo, Assistant Commissioner for Texas, for the Year Ending December 31st, 1866* (hereafter cited as *Kiddoo Report*), p. 3.

The desire to establish schools for blacks was not shared by most whites in Texas. As William R. Davis observed, "Not only was there a general lack of interest in Negro education on the part of the state, but there [also] existed a rather widespread antagonism to the work of the Freedmen's Bureau in establishing Negro schools." General Kiddoo surmised that white Texans were not particularly happy about these black schools because: "The people of Texas have violent prejudices against teachers from the North being imported to teach the Negroes; they do not consider it compatible with the dignity of the Southern character to teach them themselves, but are willing and anxious to have them taught by their *own race*."[8] Kiddoo's opinion is substantiated by the fact that few white Texans agreed to teach in the black schools and most did what they could to dissuade northern missionaries. In Texas, as in the South in general, the opposition to northern teachers ranged from social ostracism to more blatant harassment in which the missionaries were refused lodging, denied the sale or rental of real estate for schools, insulted, threatened, beaten, tarred and feathered, or even murdered.[9]

As Alton Hornsby, Jr., has noted, whites objected to these northern teachers because they feared education would exacerbate the difficulty of "keeping the nigger in his place." These men and women, sent into the South by such groups as the Freedmen's Aid Society, the American Missionary Association, and the American Baptist Home Mission Society, brought with them the belief that the freedmen were the equals of whites and should be offered the classical form of education. This was in sharp contrast to the feelings of most southerners, who either abhorred the idea of black education or felt such training should be limited to the "rudiments, with the possible addition of manual and vocational training."[10] Most whites believed that educa-

[8] Davis, *Negro Education in East Texas*, p. 33; Freedmen's Bureau, *Kiddoo Report*, p. 3.

[9] Henry Lee Swint, *The Northern Teacher in the South, 1862–1870* p. 130; Barr, *Black Texans*, pp. 61–62.

[10] Hornsby, "Freedmen's Bureau Schools in Texas," p. 39; James M. McPherson, *The Abolitionist Legacy: From Reconstruction to the NAACP*, p. 179; Swint, *The Northern Teacher*, p. 115.

tion would only serve to make the freedmen arrogant, stubborn, and resentful of their rightful place in southern society. They also were convinced that blacks were intellectually inferior to themselves and probably "uneducable." Moreover, white Texans, like most southerners, feared the racial mixing represented by having unmarried white women alone in classes full of blacks. In short, most southern whites considered black higher education to be impossible or foolish, and probably dangerous.[11]

Understandably, the status of black education in Texas at the close of Reconstruction remained rather pathetic. In 1870, the United States Commissioner of Education remarked, "In Texas no school legislation has, so far, succeeded, and no public officers are at work for the organization of schools, her entire population being left to grow up in ignorance save as here and there a private enterprise throws a ray of light upon the general darkness." The following year, the Commissioner described Texas as "the darkest field, educationally, in the United States."[12]

Northern backers of Negro education in Texas soon realized that little headway would be made until the state had a well-trained cadre of black leaders, which included teachers. This realization was compounded by two conditions. First, the missionary groups could not recruit adequate numbers of white instructors to brave the perils of the "violent prejudices" in Texas, in order to spread their denominational gospel and bring education to the black community. Second, the Texas legislature refused to provide sufficient public educational opportunities for its black citizenry.[13] The Freedmen's Aid Society reported in 1877 that "the great want of the schools in Texas is qualified teachers; for those utterly unfit for the work of training the minds and hearts of the youth are now employed for the want of better ones."[14] Consequently, the need for qualified teachers be-

[11] Hornsby, "Freedmen's Bureau Schools in Texas," pp. 398–412; Swint, *The Northern Teacher*, p. 115.

[12] Quoted in Davis, *Negro Education in East Texas*, p. 35.

[13] Frederick Eby, *The Development of Education in Texas*, p. 267; Davis, *Negro Education in East Texas*, p. 101; Freedmen's Bureau, *Kiddoo Report*, p. 3; Hans Peter Nielsen Gammel, *Laws of Texas, 1822–1897*, V: 882; Davis, *Negro Education in East Texas*, p. 101.

[14] Quoted in Davis, *Negro Education in East Texas*, p. 101.

came one of the principal reasons for the founding of the denominational colleges in Texas.

In light of these conditions, white denominational groups set out to establish, in Texas and throughout the South, a network of institutions of higher education, dedicated to the spiritual and educational uplifting of the freedmen. Describing the motives of the missionary groups, Kelly Miller later observed:

> There is no chapter in the educational history of America that is so replete with romantic interest as the foundation of Negro schools and colleges. . . . The Negro in his intellectual and moral nakedness aroused the missionary enthusiasm as nothing else could do. . . . The nation's choicest sons and daughters volunteered for this moral crusade. . . . It was in such a spasm of virtue that the foundation of the higher life of the Negro was laid.[15]

At the same time, black religious denominations, such as the African Methodist Episcopal Church, the Colored Methodist Episcopal Church, and black Baptists, also were actively establishing schools and colleges for freedmen. From their inception, the black church bodies were deeply committed to the Christianization and education of their race. These denominations realized that if blacks were to overcome the illiteracy, poverty, and degradation imposed upon them by two hundred years of servitude, a variety of educational opportunities had to be provided. For instance, the educational program of the African Methodist Episcopal Church was more than a protest against discrimination. It was a "determined effort on the part of Negroes to gain respect for the worth and dignity of their personality by their own efforts." The Colored Methodist Episcopal Church displayed a similar attitude: "The C.M.E. Colleges were founded on the principle that the Christian faith has an obligation to the intellectual life of mankind; that human freedom and dignity, the sacredness of human personality are Christian ideals which must be kept alive in society by a Christian-structured educational program. . . ."[16]

---

[15] Kelly Miller, "The Higher Education of the Negro Is at the Crossroads," *Educational Review* 72 (December, 1926): 272.

[16] Sherman L. Greene, Jr., "The Rationale Underlying the Support of Colleges Maintained by the African Methodist Episcopal Church," *Journal of Negro Education* 29

Paul Quinn College

The first of these schools, Paul Quinn College, was founded in Austin in 1872, by a small group of circuit-riding preachers of the African Methodist Episcopal Church (AME). The purpose of Paul Quinn College was to develop clergymen and "train the newly emancipated Negro slaves to assume the duties and responsibilities of citizenship."[17] Apparently the school could not attract adequate support in Austin, for, after operating in a local AME church for five years, the school was relocated in Waco, where it struggled to survive as a trade school. Here freedmen were offered courses in blacksmithing, carpentry, tanning, saddlery, and other skills.[18]

As additional AME districts were organized in the Southwest, more money became available to improve the size and quality of the college. In addition, the school received another boost in 1880 when Bishop Richard H. Cain became president. His charm and ability brought increased support for the college. In 1881, two acres of the Garrison Plantation in east Waco were purchased. The following year, twenty more acres were added. Upon this site a three-story building was completed in 1882. When Cain delivered the formal opening address on April 4, 1882, he stated that elementary, secondary, and college courses would be offered and remarked that classical education had been brought "to the very doors of the people."[19]

Upon reviewing the literature connected with the early days of Paul Quinn, one finds a considerable amount of confusion concerning the accepted date of founding for the school. Some authors, as well as recent Paul Quinn catalogs, suggest that the college was "founded" in 1872. Other writers and several

---

(Summer, 1960): 319; C. D. Coleman, "The Christian Methodist Episcopal Church: The Rationale and Policies upon Which Support of Its Colleges Is Predicated," ibid., p. 316.

[17] Greene, "Colleges Maintained by the African Methodist Episcopal Church," p. 320; Phillip McClennon Harvey, ed., A Brief History of Paul Quinn College, 1872–1965, p. 25; Eldon Stephen Branda, ed., The Handbook of Texas: A Supplement, III: 711.

[18] Paul Quinn College, Catalog, 1978, p. 19; Branda, Handbook of Texas, III: 711.

[19] Ronald L. Lewis, "Cultural Pluralism and Black Reconstruction: The Public Career of Richard H. Cain," Crisis, February, 1978, p. 64; Harvey, History of Paul Quinn College, p. 25; Paul Quinn College, Catalog, 1887, p. 21, and 1978, p. 19.

government studies suggest that Paul Quinn was "chartered" in 1881. The conflict seems to be a semantical one, depending upon one's interpretation of the terms "founded" and "chartered." While Paul Quinn was not officially chartered until 1881, it seems certain that the school was put into operation in 1872. Thus, Paul Quinn has the distinction of being the first black college in Texas, as well as the first black-owned and black-operated institution west of the Mississippi River.[20]

Paul Quinn College was sponsored by one of the oldest black organizations in America—the African Methodist Episcopal Church. Since the majority of the black colleges throughout the South were founded by predominantly white, northern denominations, the work of the AME Church was significant. The AME Church arose in the late 1700s as a protest against segregation and repression within the Methodist Episcopal Church.[21] The leading personality in this drive for a new religious organization was Richard Allen. Allen was born on February 14, 1760, as a slave on the William Chew plantation, near Germantown, Pennsylvania. He later moved to Delaware with his master, who gave Allen and his brother the opportunity to purchase their freedom for sixty pounds of silver and gold currency, or $2,000 in continental paper money. By 1777, Richard and his brother had raised the money and were freed. Allen then served as a teamster in the Revolutionary War and, in 1782, became the first black to be licensed as a Methodist Episcopal minister in America.[22]

Angered by the segregationist attitudes of the Methodists, Allen withdrew his membership from Philadelphia's St. George Methodist Episcopal Church in 1787 and began to seek out

---

[20] Branda, Handbook of Texas, III: 711; Greene, "Colleges Maintained by the African Methodist Episcopal Church," p. 320; Harvey, History of Paul Quinn College, p. 25; Dwight Oliver Wendell Holmes, The Evolution of the Negro College, p. 144; U.S. Department of the Interior, Bureau of Education, Survey of Negro Colleges and Universities, prepared by Arthur J. Klein, p. 856; Paul Quinn College, Catalog, 1978, p. 19.

[21] Bishop Reverdly Ransom, Preface to History of A.M.E. Church (Nashville: AME Sunday School Union, 1950), p. 53; L. L. Berry, A Century of Missions of the African Methodist Episcopal Church, 1840–1940, p. 27; Carter G. Woodson, The History of the Negro Church, pp. 72–78; Holmes, Evolution of the Negro College, p. 139.

[22] James H. Smith, Vital Facts Concerning the African Methodist Episcopal Church; Its Origins, Doctrines, Government, Usages, Polity, Progress (A Socratic Exposition), p. 178; Berry, A Century of Missions, p. 31.

other dissatisfied parishioners. Eventually, sixteen delegates from Pennsylvania, Delaware, Maryland, and New Jersey met in Baltimore, in 1816, and united their congregations under the banner of this new denomination. Allen won election as its first bishop, and he served in this capacity for fifteen years, until his death in 1831.[23]

Before the Civil War, the AME Church, confining its activities to northern states, had approximately 20,000 members. Following the war, the ranks of the AME Church swelled to over 75,000, as missionary workers fanned out across the South. In addition to recruiting religious converts, the AME Church pioneered in the field of education. Union Seminary and Farm, established in 1847, near Columbus, Ohio, became the first black institution of higher learning founded in America. The school later merged with Wilberforce University, which the AME Church purchased from the Methodist Episcopal Church in 1863. After the war, the AME Church placed colleges in six southern states.[24]

The AME Church named most of its schools for prominent church leaders, and Paul Quinn was no exception. The Waco school was named after one of the most beloved bishops and missionaries of the AME Church. Paul Quinn was born on April 10, 1788, and grew up in Bucks County, Pennsylvania. He became an AME Church minister in 1812 and, after several pastorates, was appointed Bishop and General Missionary for the Western States in 1844. For the next twenty-eight years, he served his faith in the vast expanse of the American frontier, until his death in 1873.[25]

Wiley College

Wiley College was founded in Marshall in 1873, through the efforts of the Freedmen's Aid Society of the Methodist Episcopal Church.[26] The Freedmen's Aid Society was organized in

[23] Smith, *Vital Facts Concerning the AME*, p. 139.

[24] Greene, "Colleges Maintained by the African Methodist Episcopal Church," pp. 319–20; Holmes, *Evolution of the Negro College*, p. 144. For a brief survey of early AME activity in Texas, see H. T. Kealing, *History of African Methodism in Texas*, pp. 1–35; Holmes, *Evolution of the Negro College*, p. 140.

[25] Smith, *Vital Facts Concerning the AME*, p. 140.

[26] Ernest Berglund, *History of Marshall*, p. 50. Originally the school was called

Cincinnati, Ohio, August 7–8, 1866. It sought to bring "relief and education" to the freedmen and to cooperate with the Missionary and Church Extension Societies of the ME Church.[27] More specifically, at its organizational meeting the society enumerated the following justifications for its work:

1. The progress of the missionary work of the Methodist Episcopal Church in the South has developed inviting openings for schools among Freedmen and demonstrated that such schools are essential to its highest usefulness among that people.

2. The Aid Commissions, with their own schools to maintain, have not the means to support others thus required by our missionary work. . . .

3. Several leading denominations, [have] organized societies . . . within themselves, by which they are greatly strengthening their respective missionary efforts. . . .

4. The Missionary and Church Extension Societies of the Methodist Episcopal Church, . . . do not meet this special educational want of the Freedmen. . . .[28]

While these were solid, businesslike reasons for embarking on so noble a mission, other motives such as Christian idealism also shaped the goals of the society. In its *Annual Report* for 1875, the society reminded Christians that, although the Civil War had ended slavery, much work was still ahead if the struggle to uplift the freedmen was to succeed.

To have emancipated and left these millions in ignorance and degradation would have been a work of doubtful philanthropy, and would have partaken more of the character of crime than of charity. To neglect the preparation of this people would be to perpetuate the wrongs inflicted by slavery, increase the peril to the nation, bring disgrace upon the Church, and provoke the just judgements of heaven. Giving free-

---

Wiley University, but in 1929, the name was changed to Wiley College. See Lloyd K. Thompson, "The Origins and Development of Black Colleges in East Texas" (Ph.D. diss., North Texas State University, 1976), p. 30.

[27] Freedmen's Aid Society, *Annual Report*, 1866, p. 13. The list of initial officers (p. 14) included: President, Rev. Bishop Davis W. Clark; Vice-Presidents, Major General Clinton B. Fisk, Grant Goodrich, and Rev. I. W. Wiley; Treasurer, Rev. Adam Poe; Corresponding Secretary, Rev. J. M. Walden; General Field Superintendent, Rev. R. S. Rust; and Recording Secretary, Rev. J. Morrison Reid.

[28] Ibid., pp. 13–14.

dom, and preparing its recipients for it, must go hand in hand, else this blood-bought boon is not worth the terrible price it cost.[29]

In the field, the Freedmen's Aid Society sought to meet the educational needs of blacks by promoting education and, where possible, providing teachers and preachers with the basic training necessary to take up the task of educating and evangelizing the masses. With the help and guidance of the Freedmen's Bureau, schools were established where they were most needed. By 1869, the society had created fifty-nine elementary schools, spread over nine states. These schools employed 105 teachers and ministered to more than 2,000 students.[30]

In addition to these elementary schools, the Freedmen's Aid Society also organized a large number of institutions of higher education. By 1878, the society had founded twenty colleges, seminaries, or medical schools, located in eleven southern states. The combined enrollment of these institutions in 1878 was 2,940. The number of pupils engaged in college-level work, however, comprised only 29 percent of that figure. Students doing work above the normal school level were listed as: academic, 275; collegiate, 75; medical, 50; law, 25; and Biblical, 400.[31]

Wiley College was named for one of the Freedmen's Aid Society's foremost figures, Bishop Isaac D. Wiley. Born in Lewistown, Pennsylvania, on March 29, 1825, Wiley grew up in a comfortable, middle-class environment, helping with the family's grain business. At the age of ten, Wiley joined the Methodist Sunday School, where he experienced what he called a "tremendous religious feeling." Wiley gained membership in the church at fourteen, became a youth leader, and committed himself to a life of spreading the gospel. Subsequently, he became a minister in the ME Church and later served as a missionary in China and as a pastor in New York, New Jersey, and Pennsylvania.[32]

[29] Freedmen's Aid Society, *Annual Report*, 1875, p. 4; *Methodist Review* 68, Fifth Ser. (1866): 329.

[30] Freedmen's Aid Society, *Annual Report*, 1871, pp. 9–10, and 1873, p. 4; Holmes, *Evolution of the Negro College*, p. 105.

[31] Freedmen's Aid Society, *Annual Report*, 1875, p. 7; Holmes, *Evolution of the Negro College*, p. 105.

[32] Richard S. Rust, ed., *Isaac W. Wiley*, pp. 2–4, 8; Thompson, "Black Colleges in East Texas," p. 34.

When the Civil War erupted, Wiley became a staunch supporter of the Union war effort. He defended the actions of the federal government, "urged a vigorous prosecution of the war, encouraged young men to enlist . . . and inspired the desponding with courage and hope." At the war's end, Wiley pressed for the church to become involved in the education and Christianizing of the freedmen. Thus, it was not surprising that Wiley appeared as one of the charter members of the Freedmen's Aid Society, and went on to serve as its vice-president and president. Wiley's biographer, Richard S. Rust, characterized Wiley as an energetic, resourceful leader, who "spent a great deal of time in the service of the society; delivered addresses in laying cornerstones for our buildings; dedicated school edifices; made speeches at our anniversaries; and was ever ready for any good word and work he could give in behalf of an organization he so highly prized. . . ." In light of Wiley's service to the Methodist Church and blacks throughout the South, it seems appropriate that the first Methodist Episcopal college for freedmen west of the Mississippi should bear his name.[33]

Tillotson College

Tillotson College was chartered in Austin during February of 1877, under the name Tillotson Collegiate and Normal Institute, and opened to students in January, 1881. Founded by the American Missionary Association (AMA), Tillotson provided elementary, secondary, and college training for blacks in the Austin area. The college was only one of several benevolent projects undertaken by this missionary organization. The association had involved itself for many years in the struggle for racial equality, first as an abolitionist group, then as a relief agency during the Civil War, and finally as an educational organization.[34]

The American Missionary Association was founded in 1847,

---

[33] Rust, *Wiley*, pp. 119, 121–22, 123; Berglund, *History of Marshall*, p. 50.

[34] Tillotson College, *Catalog*, 1934, p. 14; Texas, Secretary of State, Charter Division, *Charter of Tillotson Collegiate and Normal Institute*, Charter No. 803; Walter Prescott Webb and H. Bailey Carroll, eds., *The Handbook of Texas*, II: 780; Eby, *Education in Texas*, p. 276; Holmes, *Evolution of the Negro College*, p. 76.

as the result of a merger of several northern missionary groups. These included the Amistad Committee, a group of philanthropists and abolitionists organized in New York during 1839 to protect the legal rights of a shipload of Africans who had mutinied enroute to America; the Union Missionary Society, an antislavery group based in Hartford, Connecticut; and the Committee for the West Indian Missions, which, in 1844, began the operation of missions for newly freed blacks in Jamaica. Two years later, the Western Evangelical Missionary Society for Work Among the American Indians was added. This group had been founded in 1843 for the purpose of furthering missionary work among the Indians of the Minnesota territory.[35]

The new organization was an independent, nonsectarian corporation, committed to the removal of caste limitations wherever they were found. Its members shared several religious and social beliefs. These included a belief in the basic equality of human beings, the Christian belief in the brotherhood of man, and a belief in the sinfulness of slavery.[36] Describing its philosophy, the AMA stated:

As a missionary association having in view the intellectual and religious growth of men, especially of the people of color and particularly the emancipated, and those who in the providence of God, and the march of events, are speedily to be emancipated, we claim that our colored brother should be treated in all respects as a man and a citizen by the churches, by the Government, and the people. . . .

Before and after the Civil War, the AMA worked to establish schools of higher education for blacks. Beginning in 1858, the AMA founded eight colleges, including Atlanta University, Fisk University, and Hampton Institute.[37]

In 1875, Rev. George Jeffrey Tillotson, a retired Congregationalist minister from Hartford, Connecticut, embarked upon

[35] Holmes, *Evolution of the Negro College*, pp. 76–78; Fred L. Brownlee, *New Day Ascending*, p. 21.

[36] Brownlee, *New Day Ascending*, p. 21; Holmes, *Evolution of the Negro College*, p. 78.

[37] Mabel Crayton Williams, "The History of Tillotson College, 1881–1952" (M.A. thesis, Texas Southern University, 1967), p. 11; Holmes, *Evolution of the Negro College*, pp. 187–88.

a tour of the Southwest for the AMA, charged with recommending a site for another college. Born in Farmington, Connecticut, Tillotson through his paternal grandmother was descended "through an unbroken line of ancestry from Alfred the Great of England and from Hugh Capet of France."[38] Though from a family of worldly political leaders, Tillotson's lifework gravitated toward the religious realm. He earned degrees from Yale College and the Yale Divinity School, where he was Phi Beta Kappa. After his ordination, he remained an active minister until his retirement in 1875. He had always been a strong opponent of slavery and a vocal supporter of black education, beliefs he demonstrated by living a very modest lifestyle in order to give money to further the work of the AMA.[39]

Traveling with Rev. Gustave D. Pike, Tillotson arrived in Austin in 1875. Both were impressed by the view from atop a steep hill overlooking the Colorado River. Tillotson felt this location was ideal for another college. He then raised over $16,000 and purchased several acres of land in east Austin, upon which Tillotson Collegiate and Normal Institute was established.[40]

Bishop College

Bishop College was founded in Marshall in 1881 by the American Baptist Home Mission Society. Chartered in 1885, Bishop became the first Baptist college for blacks in the Southwest. Since more blacks belonged to the Baptist denomination than any other, the society became a leading force in the establishment of black schools. It was founded in 1832, to assist in evangelizing the West. Little is known of its efforts from 1832 to 1862, but with the start of the Civil War the Home Mission Society became interested in the plight of southern blacks and emerged as a prominent group in spreading the gospel and edu-

---

[38] *American Missionary* 60 (1895): 98.

[39] Ann Hollinshead, "The Hill That Was Good," p. 1, Addendum: Huston-Tillotson College, Temporary Box No. 2, Amistad Research Center, New Orleans; Jones, "Tillotson College From 1930–1940," p. 3.

[40] Rev. Gustave D. Pike to Rev. E. B. Wright, February 8, 17, 24, 1876, Archives, Huston-Tillotson College, Austin; *American Missionary* 36 (1882): 140, and 49 (1895): 98.

cation in the South. By 1865, it had sent sixty-eight missionaries into twelve southern states.[41] The Home Mission Society felt this work to be crucial, as "a whole race had suddenly been liberated from the bonds of servitude, but . . . were still in the bondage of ignorance." By 1881, the society had succeeded in establishing five colleges, including Morehouse College, Benedict College, and Bishop College.[42]

The drive to found a college for black Baptists in Texas was spearheaded by a white educator, Nathan Bishop. Bishop was born on August 12, 1808, in Vernon, New York. As did most youth of his time, Bishop grew up on a family farm, where his parents instilled in him a keen sense of responsibility, self-reliance, and Christian virtue. Bishop graduated from Brown University, and in 1838 became the superintendent of public schools in Providence, Rhode Island. He exhibited uncommon skill and wisdom in his work and was credited with revolutionizing the Providence school system. Bishop's ideas for buildings and curricula became models used in many parts of the country. In 1851, he was named the superintendent of Boston's public schools. Harvard University acknowledged his contributions to education by awarding Bishop a Doctor of Laws degree in 1855.[43]

After his retirement in 1858, Bishop devoted the remaining twenty-two years of his life to helping his fellow man. Using the wealth he had accumulated during his career, Bishop extended a helping hand to the young, the old, the poor, and the ignorant. His interests were not confined to any single group. Bishop supported women through contributions to Vassar College, Civil War refugees, freedmen and poor whites of the South, Indians, and a number of other missionary ventures. As one of Bishop's last projects, he supported the founding of a black Baptist college west of the Mississippi. He already had given large sums of

[41] Bishop College, *Catalog*, 1897, p. 1; McPherson, *The Abolitonist Legacy*, pp. 149, 154; Holmes, *Evolution of the Negro College*, pp. 120–21.

[42] Ullin Whitney Leavell, *Philanthropy in Negro Education*; John M. Ellison, "Policies and Rationale Underlying the Support of Colleges Maintained by the Baptist Denomination," *Journal of Negro Education* 29 (Summer, 1960): 330.

[43] Melvin J. Banks, "Bishop College Founded by an Earlier Social Activist," *Bishop Herald*, April, 1975, p. 10.

money to other black colleges in the South, which had prompted criticism from southern whites. Bishop remained unmoved, declaring: "I have been blamed for giving so many thousand dollars to the benefit of colored men. But I expect to stand side by side with these freedmen on the day of judgment. Their Lord is my Lord. They and I are brethren. And I am determined to be prepared for that meeting."[44]

In choosing a site for a college in Texas, Baptists were mindful that the majority of the state's black population lived in the eastern portion of the state. Dr. Rufus C. Burleson, president of Baylor University, expressed concern for the need to evangelize and educate more of the former slaves in this region. As the chairman of the Committee on Colored Population for the Baptist General Convention of Texas, Burleson appealed to Bishop in 1872 for assistance in building a black Baptist college, saying: "We want a grand college for teachers and preachers of the colored race. Can not you give twenty-five thousand dollars to start this enterprise?"[45] Several years later, Bishop notified Burleson that he would comply, but before the money could be sent, Bishop died. His wife, Carolina Caldwell Bishop, also supported the idea and later contributed $10,000 to the American Baptist Home Mission Society to begin such a school.[46]

The society dispatched Dr. S. W. Marston, the district secretary, and Reverend A. R. Griggs, pastor of New Hope Baptist Church of Dallas, to select an appropriate site in the Southwest. After visiting Dallas, Houston, Austin, Marshall, Texarkana, Little Rock, and Shreveport, they settled on Marshall, because of the enthusiasm of the East Texas Baptists, the dense black population there, and the presence of a black Baptist high school called Centennial College.[47] Local Baptist supporters raised

[44] Ibid.

[45] Caesar Francis Toles, "The History of Bishop College" (M.A. thesis, University of Michigan, 1947), p. 9; Lawrence D. Rice, *The Negro in Texas, 1874–1900*, p. 321.

[46] Melvin J. Banks, "Nine Dedicated Men Translate Nathan Bishop's Dream to the Reality of a Great Bishop College," *Bishop Herald*, Fall, 1976, p. 9; Bishop College, *Catalog*, 1881, p. 4; Toles, "History of Bishop College," p. 9. E. C. Evans maintains that Bishop gave $20,000 and that his wife gave an additional $30,000 (E. C. Evans, *The Story of Texas Schools*, p. 215); Arthur J. Klein also credits Bishop with donating $20,000 (*Survey of Negro Colleges and Universities*, p. 810).

[47] Melvin J. Banks, "They Lighted the Lamp!" *Bishop Herald*, March, 1976,

$1,600 and purchased the ten-acre estate of the Holcomb family for what was temporarily named South-Western Baptist College. In 1880, forty more acres were added from the donation made by Mrs. Bishop. The college was then renamed Bishop College. The process was completed when Centennial College merged with Bishop, thus giving the new institution the nucleus of its first student body.[48]

Guadalupe College

Guadalupe College was founded in 1884 by a group of black Baptists who had previously organized the Guadalupe Baptist Association.[49] A black-owned and black-operated institution, Guadalupe College was established on five acres of land near the county courthouse in Seguin. The association purchased the property for ten thousand dollars from the Catholic Church, which had operated a school there.[50] In 1914, the college was relocated on the western edge of the city, on a site donated by San Antonio philanthropist George W. Brackenridge.[51]

While the American Baptist Home Mission Society conducted most of the educational work sponsored by Baptists, other schools such as Guadalupe were governed by independent boards. Beginning in 1870, several state conventions of Negro Baptists began to establish schools in areas where the Home Mission Society had not been active. In most cases, these colleges were poorly financed and ill-equipped and reflected the

---

pp. 6–7. Toles points out that in Harrison County alone there were 17,000 black citizens, as opposed to only 8,000 whites ("History of Bishop College," p. 7).

[48] Banks, "They Lighted the Lamp!" p. 7; Rice, *The Negro in Texas*, p. 232; Toles, "History of Bishop College," p. 12.

[49] Barr, *Black Texans*, p. 103. The *Handbook of Texas* (I: 742), gives the name of the school as Guadalupe Colored College.

[50] Guadalupe College, *Prospects and General Outlook: The Guadalupe College As Others See It*, p. 5; Guadalupe College, *Catalog*, 1892, p. 1; U.S. Department of the Interior, Bureau of Education, *History of Education in Texas*, prepared by J. J. Lane, p. 118; Barr, *Black Texans*, p. 103. Rice (*The Negro in Texas*, p. 233), states that the site was bought for $5,000.

[51] Marilyn Sibley, *George W. Brackenridge: Maverick Philanthropist*, pp. 167–68; Bruce Alden Glasrud, "Black Texans, 1900–1930" (Ph.D. diss., Texas Tech University, 1969), p. 250.

economic limitations faced by blacks in the late nineteenth century.[52]

Guadalupe College sprang from an intradenominational squabble between the white Home Mission Society and black Baptist groups in Central and South Texas. Its founding resulted directly from the society's decision to establish Bishop College in Marshall. Black Baptists in the central and southern portions of the state were disappointed that the school had not been placed within their regions. To provide local educational opportunities for their youth, they established Hearne Academy in 1881, followed by Houston Academy and Guadalupe College in 1884. All three began as little more than elementary and industrial training schools, but their supporters hoped that at least one of them eventually would become a liberal arts college.[53]

In light of the developing rivalry between these two Baptist educational systems, the black Baptist state convention voted in 1888 to divide its monetary support between Hearne and Houston academies and between Bishop and Guadalupe colleges. Central Texas Baptists then appealed to the Home Mission Society to do the same. The society countered with an alternate scheme. It would support only one liberal arts college in each state and would assist other schools only if they were maintained at the academy or high school level. These schools would then serve as feeders for the colleges.[54]

The society's plan kindled widespread controversy. Some black leaders began to question the "blackness" of Bishop College, noting that it was controlled by a white organization, the Baptist Home Mission Society. They contended that blacks had the ability to run their own institutions, as at Guadalupe College, and called upon all black Baptists to support them. They opposed the idea of limiting the black Baptist schools to the high school level, seeing it as an unfavorable reflection upon the ability of blacks.[55]

---

[52] Holmes, *Evolution of the Negro College*, pp. 148–49.
[53] Lane, *History of Education in Texas*, p. 118; Melvin J. Banks, "Revival for Survival," *Bishop Herald*, Spring, 1979, p. 9.
[54] Banks, "Revival for Survival," p. 9.
[55] Ibid.

The split came in 1893, when black and white Baptists gathered for the state's Baptist Missionary and Educational Convention. Guadalupe College supporters attending the San Antonio meeting offered a petition proposing Guadalupe College be recognized as an independent institution of higher learning and calling for the convention to commit one-half of its educational budget to the development of this college. The petition was dismissed on the grounds that (1) it did not allow time for thoughtful deliberation, (2) the resources of the convention were too meager to support two colleges, (3) the need for two colleges had not been proven, (4) a number of higher-quality high schools and academies were needed in strategic locations around the state, and (5) the supporters of Guadalupe College had denied the convention any role in the business of the college. As a result, the Seguin delegation walked out of the meeting and, on October 13, 1893, formed the General Missionary Baptist Convention of Texas. The new denomination then gave its full support to Guadalupe College.[56]

Mary Allen College

Mary Allen Seminary was founded in 1886 in Crockett, on 10 acres of land provided by local citizens and an adjoining 260 acres donated by James Snydor of Illinois. The Presbyterian Board of Missions for Freedmen of the Presbyterian Church, U.S.A., established the school for Negro women. The school was named after Mary E. Allen, wife of the board's secretary. Mrs. Allen had toured the Southwest, where she was appalled to find the majority of black women almost entirely illiterate. Thereafter, she worked to convince the Freedmen's Board to establish a school for women in Texas.[57]

Largely through the efforts of Samuel Fisher Tenney, pastor of the First Presbyterian Church of Crockett, the Freedmen's Board picked Crockett as the site of the college. The decision of

[56] Ibid.

[57] "History of Mary Allen Junior College," n.d., Archives, Crockett Public Library, Crockett, Texas, p. 1; Board of Missions for Freedmen of the Presbyterian Church in the United States of America, *Annual Report*, 1888, p. 20.

the board was prompted by its desire to ameliorate the deplorable conditions faced by many black women in East Texas and the hope of evangelizing large numbers of Negroes in the so-called Black Belt of Texas.[58]

While the Presbyterian Church did not found or operate as many institutions as the other northern denominational boards, it did succeed in developing several noteworthy colleges. The Presbyterians began their commitment to black education in 1865, with the formation of the Committee of Missions for Freedmen of the Presbyterian Church. The Committee of Missions sought to set up schools in the South that would be closely affiliated with their churches. By 1871, the Presbyterians operated forty-five schools, with an enrollment of more than forty-five hundred students.[59]

In 1883, the church reorganized its agency into the Presbyterian Board of Missions for Freedmen. Although it was plagued by indebtedness, the board managed to found and support five reputable colleges in four states. The board also had ties with Lincoln University in Pennsylvania, which the Presbyterians had helped found in 1854 as Ashmun Institute.[60]

Texas College

Texas College was organized in 1894, on 101 acres of land just north of Tyler. The school opened its doors in January, 1895, and received an official charter in 1907, under the auspices of the Colored Methodist Episcopal church.[61] In 1909, the college was renamed Phillips University, in honor of the exceptional

---

[58] Board of Missions for Freedmen of the Presbyterian Church in the United States of America, *Annual Report*, 1888, p. 20; Albert Amistead Aldrich, *History of Houston County*, p. 114; Webb and Carroll, *Handbook of Texas*, II: 153; Davis, *Negro Education in East Texas*, p. 105.

[59] Holmes (*Evolution of the Negro College*, p. 130) notes that the congregational support for these schools was rather weak and, consequently, in 1871, the Committee was deeply in debt.

[60] Ibid., pp. 131–34, 187–89.

[61] "Texas College History," Allen C. Hancock Papers, Texas College, Tyler; Texas College, *Catalog*, 1916, p. 8. After 1954, the CME was renamed the Christian Methodist Episcopal Church (Thompson, "Black Colleges in East Texas," p. 87).

service rendered to the institution by a CME Bishop, Henry Phillips. Because of objections from college supporters, the school took back its original name, Texas College, in 1917.[62]

Texas College became the state's third black-controlled institution to be founded by a black denomination. The CME Church became, in some ways, the southern counterpart of the African Methodist Episcopal Church. When the national Methodist Church had split over the issue of slavery in 1845, the southern branch had formed the pro-slavery Methodist Episcopal Church, South. On the eve of the Civil War, this faction included nearly all white, southern Methodists and some 207,000 slave communicants. At its annual meeting in New Orleans in April, 1866, the ME Church, South, decided that freedmen should be allowed to form their own church body. The decision was prompted by the dissatisfaction of blacks with their inferior status in the denomination, which had led to a decline in the black membership in the church from 207,000 in 1860 to 78,000 in 1865. Most of the blacks who had left had joined either the AME Church or the AME Zion Church.[63]

By 1870, blacks had formed five state conferences. At the 1870 meeting of the ME Church, South, the black delegates requested and received permission to proceed with their plans to create a new national conference. Later that year, black Methodists met and adopted the title Colored Methodist Episcopal Church in America.[64] It is noteworthy that the split was a peaceful one, leaving no ill will on either side. Over the years, the ME Church, South, maintained amiable relations with the

[62] Texas College, *Catalog*, 1917, p. 6. As an example of his talents of persuasion, Phillips is said to have gathered more than $35,000, in three fund-raising rallies, for the construction of an office, dormitory, and classroom facility. Completed in 1909, the building was named Phillips Hall ("Texas College History," Hancock Papers, pp. 3–4; Texas College, *Catalog*, 1925, p. 7).

[63] C. H. Phillips, *The History of the Colored Methodist Episcopal Church in America: Its Organization, Subsequent Development and Present Status*, pp. 23, 25; Evans, *The Story of Texas Schools*, p. 219; Woodson, *History of the Negro Church*, p. 195; Thompson, "Black Colleges in East Texas," pp. 87–88.

[64] Othel Hawthorne Lakey, *The Rise of Colored Methodism: A Study of the Background and the Beginnings of the Christian Methodist Episcopal Church*, p. 81; Phillips, *History of the Colored Methodist Episcopal Church*, pp. 26, 34–35; Woodson, *History of the Negro Church*, p. 174.

CME Church and even cooperated with it in several educational endeavors.[65]

The CME Church began its educational program in 1873, by establishing five colleges in different states among the freedmen. The doctrine of the CME Church was similar to other denominations, because it founded colleges with the conviction that "Christian faith has an obligation to the intellectual life of mankind; [and] that human freedom, dignity, and the sacredness of human personality are Christian ideals which must be kept alive . . . by a Christian-structured educational program."[66]

St. Philip's College

In March, 1898, the Protestant Episcopal Church established St. Philip's College in San Antonio. St. Philip's was one of only four institutions of higher education for blacks founded by the Episcopal Church. These schools ultimately fell under the control of the American Church Institute for Negroes, which was created in 1906 to promote the educational activities of the Episcopal Church. St. Philip's was unusual because its founders did not aspire to see their college become a center for liberal arts instruction. Instead, St. Philip's began as a vocational institution and remained one for most of its history.[67]

The person most closely associated with the creation of St. Philip's was the Reverend James Steptoe Johnston. The son of a plantation owner, Johnston was born on June 9, 1843, in Jefferson County, Mississippi. Although an Episcopalian, Johnston attended a Presbyterian school, Oakland College, near his home. Expelled during his sophomore year for pranksterism, he then enrolled in the University of Virginia. The Civil War interrupted

[65] Phillips, *History of the Colored Methodist Episcopal Church*, pp. 25–26; Holmes, *Evolution of the Negro College*, p. 147; Thompson, "Black Colleges in East Texas," pp. 90–91.

[66] Phillips, *History of the Colored Methodist Episcopal Church*, pp. 62, 77; Evans, *The Story of Texas Schools*, p. 219; C. D. Coleman, "The Christian Methodist Episcopal Church," p. 316.

[67] Clarence W. Norris, Jr., "St. Philip's College: A Case Study of a Historically Black Two-Year College" (Ph.D. diss., University of Southern California, 1975), pp. 58, 63; Holmes, *Evolution of the Negro College*, p. 135.

his studies, and in 1861 Johnston enlisted in the Confederate Army. After the war, he studied law until 1867, when he took over his father's plantation. Finding agriculture not to his liking, Johnston decided to devote his life to the Episcopal Church. He was ordained in 1869 and served in Mississippi, Kentucky, and Alabama. In 1888, Johnston was elected bishop for the Missionary District of Western Texas.[68]

In his new capacity, Johnston became involved in efforts to bring education to blacks in Texas. He knew that his own denomination was far less committed to black education than others. In 1900, he noted:

Other bodies of Christians are more alive than our own to their responsibilities in this matter. The Congregationalists give $360,000 a year through their splendid system of primary schools, academies, colleges, and one university—Fisk—in which they have invested $2,000,000. The Presbyterians, North, are giving $250,000 annually. The Methodists and Baptists, each $200,000. Our own church is giving only $60,000. . . .[69]

He was convinced that more Christian-oriented schools must be established. In 1895, Johnston looked to San Antonio as an excellent place for such an institution. Although San Antonio had black public schools, they were of poor quality and narrow curriculum. In addition, a black Episcopal church, St. Philip's, had recently been organized and was flourishing. Bishop Johnston began his efforts in 1897, when he helped organize a girls' sewing class in the church rectory. Boys also attended the Saturday classes but were engaged in art projects. The success of this venture spurred church members to establish a permanent institution, St. Philip's School. In 1898, Johnston purchased a lot behind the church for four hundred dollars and commissioned the construction of a two-room schoolhouse. Upon completion, it became St. Philip's Industrial School, which initially offered courses in cooking, sewing, and housecleaning.[70]

[68] Lawrence L. Brown, *A Brief History of the Church in West Texas*, p. 19; Everett H. Jones, *Bishop James Steptoe Johnston: A Biographical Sketch*, p. 7.

[69] Norris, "St. Philip's College," pp. 43–44.

[70] Ibid., pp. 52–54; Brown, *Church in West Texas*, p. 28; Norris, "St. Philip's College," pp. 54–58.

Samuel Huston College

In 1900, the Freedmen's Aid Society founded its second college in Texas. The act capped a twenty-four-year struggle that began in 1876, when Andrews Normal School was opened in Dallas. Failing to attract sufficient support there, Methodist leaders moved the school to Austin. In 1883, Richard S. Rust, secretary for the Freedmen's Aid Society, purchased six acres of land on the east side of Austin. Shortly afterward, Samuel Huston—a wealthy landowner from Marengo, Iowa, for whom the college was later named—got the enterprise off the ground by donating nine thousand dollars. Another Methodist supporter, H. S. White of Romeo, Michigan, contributed a 500-volume library. In the early 1890s, T. C. Hartzell, who succeeded Rust as secretary, authorized work on the buildings to begin. The stone foundation of one building had been completed when funds ran out in 1893. It was sixteen years before the structure could be finished.[71]

In 1898, Bishop J. W. Hamilton ordered the basement enclosed and, two years later, sent Dr. Reuben S. Lovinggood, a professor at Wiley College, to open the school. When Lovinggood and his wife arrived, the college facilities were unbelievably crude. All the black educator found was a five-room basement that was completely unfurnished and vacant, except for several pigs and goats that slept there and a number of chickens that roosted in the rafters. There was no kitchen, dining hall, dishes, or furniture. Lovinggood opened the school with eight students, who had to use trunks and old wooden boxes for desks. The courses were rudimentary at first, but, as time passed, Lovinggood raised funds and materials from the surrounding community and began the expansion of the school's physical plant and curricula. By 1905, a few college-level courses were being offered.[72]

[71] Evans, *The Story of Texas Schools*, p. 217; U.S. Bureau of Education, *Survey of Negro Colleges and Universities*, p. 836; Webb and Carroll, *Handbook of Texas*, II: 539. A publication by the U.S. Bureau of Education (*History of Education in Texas*, p. 121) lists Samuel Huston as coming from Ohio.

[72] *Waco Messenger*, December 14, 1934; *Houston Informer*, April 18, 1931; J. Mason Brewer, ed., *An Historical Outline of the Negro in Travis County*, p. 47; Alton Hornsby,

Butler College

Like the establishment of Guadalupe College, the founding of Butler College resulted from independent action on the part of local black Baptists.[73] The East Texas Baptist Association founded Butler College in Tyler in 1905. The school was originally named East Texas Normal and Industrial Academy and offered only elementary courses and a few classes in sewing. Upon the death of its first president, C. M. Butler, who served the school for nineteen years, the board of trustees voted to change the name of the institution to Butler College.[74]

Jarvis Christian College

The last of the black denominational colleges to be founded in Texas was Jarvis Christian College. The Christian Women's Board of Missions of the Disciples of Christ established the school in 1912 in the small East Texas town of Hawkins. Like most of the northern denominations, the Disciples of Christ began their work among blacks by sending missionaries into the South with the advancing Union armies. By 1872, the number of communicants had grown to the point that the church felt the need for an educated corps of black ministers to help carry on the process. Thus, the church decided to provide its converts with some form of general and religious education. In 1875, they established their first school, the Southern Christian Institute, in Hemingway, Mississippi. In all, five schools, patterned after the Southern Christian Institute, were founded in different states by the Disciples of Christ.[75]

Jr., "Negro Education in Texas, 1865–1917" (M.A. thesis, University of Texas, 1962), pp. 143–44.

[73] Stephen J. Wright, "Some Critical Problems Faced by the Negro Church-Related Colleges," *Journal of Negro Education* 29 (Summer, 1960): 335–37. No Butler College records remained after it closed in 1972.

[74] U.S. Bureau of Education, *Negro Education*, II: 588; Evans, *The Story of Texas Schools*, p. 215; Davis, *Negro Education in East Texas*, p. 106; Webb and Carroll, *Handbook of Texas*, I: 257.

[75] Disciples of Christ, *Survey of Service: Organizations Represented in the International Convention of the Disciples of Christ*, pp. 161, 171, 177; Grant K. Lewis, *The American Christian Missionary Society and the Disciples of Christ*, pp. 18–19; Jarvis

Jarvis Christian College traces its roots back to 1910, when Major and Mrs. J. J. Jarvis of Fort Worth donated 456 acres near Hawkins for the establishment of a black college. Their commitment to such a missionary endeavor resulted from the active membership of Mrs. Jarvis (Ida) on the Christian Women's Board of Missions, which she had served several times as state president. Moreover, she and her husband already actively supported the white Disciples institution, Texas Christian University. In recognition of their gift, the new college was named Jarvis Christian Institute.[76]

Colleges in Name Only

In addition to the institutions already discussed, a number of other so-called colleges offered educational opportunities for blacks. These schools, however, never provided college-level work. While it seems certain they all hoped to rise to such a stature, each of these institutions failed to do so for lack of funding, personnel, or other obstacles.

One of the earliest of these was Centennial College, which was founded by black Baptists in Marshall. The school provided high school training between 1875 and 1881, before merging with Bishop College.[77] The black Baptist Missionary and Educational Convention founded Hearne Academy in 1881. In 1909, Hearne Academy moved to Fort Worth, where it continued its elementary and secondary instruction under the name Fort Worth Industrial and Mechanical College.[78] In 1885, black Baptists founded another elementary and secondary school, which

Christian College, *Catalog*, 1922, p. 2; Winfred Ernest Garrison and Alfred T. DeGroot, *The Disciples of Christ, A History*, pp. 477–79.

[76]Virgil A. Sly, "Between Dawn and Dusk at Jarvis," *World Call* 16 (April, 1934): 6; Jarvis Christian College, *Catalog*, 1913, p. 4, and 1929, p. 8; W. W. Phares, "Mrs. Ida Jarvis—An Appreciation," *World Call* 19 (June, 1937): 29; Disciples of Christ, *Survey of Service*, p. 177; E. B. Byrnum, *These Carried the Torch: Pioneers of Christian Education in Texas*, pp. 44–47.

[77]Banks, "They Lighted the Lamp!" pp. 6–7.

[78]U.S. Department of the Interior, Bureau of Education, *Negro Education: A Study of the Private and Higher Schools for Colored People in the United States*. Report prepared by Thomas Jesse Jones, Bulletin No. 39, II: 592; Rice, *The Negro in Texas*, p. 231.

they named Houston Baptist College.[79] From 1901 to 1928, the black General Baptist Convention of Texas provided pre-college instruction in Waco at Central Texas College.[80]

Similar training was offered at Conroe-Porter Industrial College, which was opened in 1903 by a black private stock company.[81] A local black Baptist association established Brenham Normal and Industrial College in 1905, but the institution offered mostly elementary courses.[82] In 1906, R. L. Smith, the president and founder of the Farmers' Home Improvement Society, created a school in Ladonia called the Farmers' Improvement Society Agricultural College.[83] In 1913, white Baptist ministers in Austin founded St. John's Industrial Institute and Orphanage, which specialized in elementary and domestic training. During the same period, in Oakwood, black Baptists established Boyd Industrial Institute, which operated until 1919, when a fire destroyed the campus. Mexia was selected in 1925 by the Primitive Baptist Church as the site for St. Paul Industrial College.[84] Finally, around the turn of the century, the Northeast Texas Christian Convention established in Palestine an elementary school which was named Christian Theological and Industrial College.[85]

Institutional Purposes

The statements of purpose of the church-related black colleges are significant for a number of reasons. Such statements

---

[79] *Houston Post*, May 7, 1905; U.S. Bureau of Education, *Negro Education*, II: 578.

[80] U.S. Bureau of Education, *Negro Education*, II: 586; Barr, *Black Texans*, p. 160; William Malcolm Batts, "What the General Baptists of Texas (Negro) Want Educationally, With Suggestions for Improvement of the Educational Program" (M.A. thesis, Prairie View A&M University, 1946), p. 9.

[81] J. B. Raynor to John H. Kirby, November 29, 1904, John Henry Kirby Collection, Box 38, File R-1, Houston Metropolitan Research Center, Houston Public Library; U.S. Bureau of Education, *Negro Education*, II: 602.

[82] U.S. Bureau of Education, *Negro Education*, II: 600; Barr, *Black Texans*, p. 160.

[83] U.S Bureau of Education, *Negro Education*, II: 575; Rice, *The Negro in Texas*, pp. 110–11.

[84] St. John Regular Missionary Baptist Association, *Minutes*, 1915, pp. 78–9; Missionary Baptist General Convention of Texas, *Annual Report*, 1916, pp. 123, 127–30, and 1922, p. 66; Glasrud, "Black Texans, 1900–1930," p. 252.

[85] U.S. Bureau of Education, *Negro Education*, II: 601.

are among the earliest descriptions of what these colleges stood for and what they hoped to accomplish. Most importantly, they provide valuable clues to each school's priorities with respect to religious, professional, and vocational training.

In article II of its charter, Paul Quinn College was described as an institution designed to educate black youth in the "liberal and manual arts and sciences." The Board of Trustees, in its by-laws and regulations, went on to describe the school's prime function as teacher training.[86] The charter of Wiley College declared, "The object of said corporators is to establish and perpetuate an institution of learning wherein may be afforded opportunities to all, without distinction of race, condition, sex, or religious antecedents, to acquire a liberal education."[87] In the catalog of Tillotson College, the following statement is made: "It is the aim of Tillotson College to provide unexcelled training for scholarship and character for all who desire either a general or cultural college education or special preparation as elementary or high school teachers."[88]

Bishop College stated its purposes as the "education of colored men and women for teachers, and colored men for preachers of the gospel." The 1882 catalog went on to underscore the religious emphasis of the college:

No system of education can properly be considered complete that does not provide for religious culture. Bishop College has a distinctly religious design, which is kept steadily in view in the daily educational work. It is desired that they who come to receive the benefits of the school, should not only acquire a thorough education in secular knowledge, but that they should leave it intelligent, sensible and earnest Christian men and women.[89]

According to an early catalog, the mission of Guadalupe College was to "awaken a warm educational interest among Colored people of the South West, giving special prominence to the *Normal* and *Theological* training."[90]

[86] Harvey, *History of Paul Quinn College*, p. 26.
[87] Quoted in Roy H. Lanier, "Church-Related Colleges for Negroes in Texas" (M.A. thesis), pp. 26–37.
[88] Tillotson College, *Catalog*, 1934, p. 14.
[89] Bishop College, *Catalog*, 1882, p. 14.
[90] Guadalupe College, *Catalog*, 1892, p. 1.

The purposes of Texas College are evident in the following passage: "It was the aim of the founders of this school to make it possible for the Negro youths to have the advantage of a liberal Christian education in order that they might be better prepared to lead and serve their people and at the same time meet and successfully grapple with the problems of a complex civilization." The deep religious convictions of the CME school are seen in another statement: "The general atmosphere of the institution is Christian and no acts are countenanced on the part of anyone that would not be in accord with a well ordered Christian home. Daily devotions are observed with mid-week prayer meetings, Sabbath School and preaching regularly on the Sabbath."[91]

The purposes of St. Philip's College were expressed in a more vocational tone:

It is the purpose of St. Philip's to impart to the Negro girl intellectual, moral, and industrial training so that she might be prepared to render the greatest and most effective service possible to the community to which she may go. . . . The student is also required to follow, at least one vocation, so as to be prepared, if need be, to earn an independent and respectable livelihood, as well as to be able to contribute toward the higher economic standard of home life.[92]

In a similar vein, Jarvis Christian College declared its purpose was to "produce men and women especially trained for leadership, not only in the industrial world, but in the professional world as well."[93]

It is clear from such statements that these institutions held many of the same purposes and goals. In each instance, the founders pledged their schools to the moral and religious development of their students. In addition, the founders wanted to provide classical and, in some cases, vocational training that would enable their men and women to be useful, productive citizens. They were convinced that, "just as religion without education was an empty shell, education without religion would impart only information without conscience."[94]

[91] Texas College, *Catalog*, 1918, pp. 6, 7.
[92] Quoted in Norris, "St. Philip's College," p. 109.
[93] Jarvis Christian College, *Catalog*, 1922, p. 11.
[94] McPherson, *The Abolitionist Legacy*, p. 151.

Early Conditions

Little information is available concerning the physical characteristics and early operation of the private black colleges in Texas. That which does exist gives us some idea of the painful, poverty-ridden conditions in which these colleges were launched. In the beginning, many of the schools had no facilities at all. Paul Quinn offered its first classes during 1872 in the Metropolitan AME Church of Austin. Similarly, St. Philip's College first operated in the rectory of St. Philip's Episcopal Church. When Samuel Huston College formally opened in 1900, it did so in the basement of a partially finished building. The fact that it took sixteen more years to complete the structure testifies to the college's financial problems.[95]

Some institutions that had facilities were not in much better shape. Texas College opened in 1895 with three students, in what was described as a "rude shanty." In 1912, Jarvis Christian College began with seven pupils and one instructor in the remains of an old logging camp. The Jarvis campus was significantly enhanced during that same year when the first "little cabin" was built.[96] In the case of Tillotson College, the school's opening was delayed from 1877 to 1881, until enough money could be raised to construct Allen Hall, the college's first building. In such stark settings, one can only imagine the hardships endured by the faculties. Early teachers at Wiley College received praise for their "peculiar sacrifices because of conditions."[97]

It is obvious that during their formative years, these institutions served primarily as elementary schools. In 1878, W. H. Davis, the second president of Wiley College, noted: "Although the school began with a very low grade of scholarship, or al-

[95] Harvey, *History of Paul Quinn College*, p. 25; Norris, "St. Philip's College," pp. 57–58; Lanier, "Church-Related Colleges for Negroes," p. 34; Brewer, *The Negro In Travis County*, p. 47.

[96] Lanier, "Church-Related Colleges for Negroes," p. 33; Sly, "Between Dawn and Dusk at Jarvis," p. 7; Disciples of Christ, *Survey of Service*, p. 177; Lanier, "Church-Related Colleges for Negroes," p. 35; Clifford H. Taylor, Jr., "Jarvis Christian College: Its History and Present Standing in Relationship to the Standards of the Texas State Department of Education and the Southern Association of Colleges and Secondary Schools" (B.D. thesis, Texas Christian University, 1946), pp. 7–8.

[97] Tillotson College, *Catalog*, 1934, pp. 13–14; Wiley College, *Catalog*, 1949, p. 17.

most no scholarship, a very respectable scholarship has been attained by some of its pupils. A few of the most advanced are . . . ready for the [college] Preparatory course of our College. . . . A University it is called. More properly speaking it aspires to be a University." In a similar observation made in 1881, the first president of Tillotson College, W. E. Brooks, wrote: "Our courses of study embrace all from the Grammar Dept. to the full four years course. We have students in all save the College proper.—two in [the] 2nd year Preparatory—& several in the 1st & large classes in the Grammar & Normal."[98]

Reviewing the founding of the denominational black colleges in Texas, several observations can be made. First, although the physical conditions varied, the founding process was very similar with all the denominations. Perhaps the most noticeable difference in the process was that the colleges founded by black religious denominations were owned and operated by blacks, while those established by northern church bodies were at first controlled by whites. Second, it should be noted that these colleges developed out of the same missionary spirit which prompted the establishment of the other black colleges around the country. Third, the goals of the white and black denominations were also basically the same, in that they sought to evangelize the freedmen and hasten their quest for equality in American society, by providing Christian educational opportunities.

Although eleven such colleges were founded in Texas, that is not an extraordinarily large number when compared with other states. In 1932, a total of 109 public and private black colleges operated in the United States. While Texas led all states with eleven denominational colleges, other states with large black populations also had significant numbers of private institutions. These included: Georgia, North Carolina, and South Carolina with eight apiece; Tennessee with seven; and Louisiana and Mississippi with six each.[99]

In terms of public black colleges, Texas with two, Prairie

[98] W. H. Davis, "Wiley University, Marshall, Harrison County, Texas," November 9, 1878, Archives, Wiley College, Marshall; W. E. Brooks to Reverend M. E. Krieby, December 9, 1881, Addendum: Huston-Tillotson College.

[99] Holmes, *Evolution of the Negro College*, pp. 187–89.

View State College (1878) and Houston Colored Junior College (1927), was about average. What may explain the larger number of private schools in Texas is the fact that the state's public colleges were so late—1878 and 1927—in getting started. Comparing the number of private and public institutions makes it clear that state governments were not providing sufficient educational opportunities for their black citizens. In 1932, for example, there were seventy-four private colleges for blacks in the nation, compared with only thirty-five public institutions. More importantly, of the 23,036 students enrolled in 1932 in black colleges, 13,598, or 59 percent, pursued their studies at denominational colleges and universities.[100] There is little question that the private black colleges in Texas and elsewhere provided blacks with vitally needed training on all educational levels. Had it not been for the efforts of these colleges, a majority of the nation's black youth probably would have remained illiterate.

[100] Ibid.

2

Curriculum

THE curricula of the private black colleges in Texas changed markedly between 1872 and 1954. Like most black colleges, the Texas schools found themselves embroiled in a continuing controversy over the direction of their curricula. When the missionaries of the American Missionary Association, the Baptist Home Mission Society, and others, fanned out across the South in the late 1860s, they had a common goal—to establish colleges and universities for the freedmen. The early aim of these institutions was to uplift the ex-slaves by training ministers and teachers who would then go out and spread the benefits of Christianity and education to their race. Since most of these white missionaries had received their training in northern colleges that offered the so-called New England or classical form of study, it was not surprising that they founded black denominational colleges which also followed this format.[1]

Missionary leaders soon realized, however, that classical college training, involving the study of Greek and Latin, was of limited use to most freedmen. The poor quality of public black education, characterized by an almost complete lack of public black high schools, meant that few black students were qualified for college study. The denominational bodies addressed this situation by combining New England–styled preparatory divisions with their college curricula.[2]

By 1880, most private black colleges were organized into elementary, intermediate or grammar, secondary, and college

[1] Willard Range, *The Rise and Progress of Negro Colleges in Georgia, 1865–1949*, p. 67.

[2] Board of Missions for Freedmen of the Presbyterian Church in the United States of America, *Annual Report*, 1892, p. 16; *American Missionary* 49 (1895): 100; James M. McPherson, *The Abolitionist Legacy: From Reconstruction to the NAACP*, pp. 203–207.

departments. The three R's, geography, and history received emphasis in the elementary and grammar grades. Secondary courses were normally divided into two categories: (1) college preparatory, which included Latin, Greek, rhetoric, literature, mathematics, and science courses; and (2) normal, which emphasized geography, civics, basic English, and teaching methods. While there were some variations in the college divisions of the denominational schools, classical studies, including Latin, Greek, mathematics, science, philosophy, modern language, and theology, were common everywhere.[3]

Although such training seemed impressive and desirable to many blacks, and most missionaries thought it worthwhile, opposition to classical instruction began to grow in the 1880s. For a variety of reasons, southern and northern whites worked to undermine the efforts of the northern missionaries and to control the future of Negro education. First, critics pointed out that since the vast majority of freedmen were completely illiterate, it was foolish even to offer classical education to the former slaves. "Mandy, is yo' did yo' Greek yit?" was a popular witticism of the period that prompted laughter in many white circles.[4]

The real reasons whites opposed formal college training for blacks, however, went much deeper. These reasons began to surface after the so-called Compromise of 1877, which ended Reconstruction by removing federal troops from the South and clearing the way for a general wave of repression in the southern states. In the post-Reconstruction South, blacks found themselves being systematically disenfranchised and forced to accept a subservient, segregated, second-class status. In general, whites sought to eliminate classical higher education for blacks and to replace it with vocational or industrial training.[5]

[3] McPherson, *Abolitionist Legacy*, pp. 203–207; *American Missionary* 49 (1895): 100–101.

[4] Allen B. Ballard, *The Education of Black Folk: The Afro-American Struggle for Knowledge in White America*, p. 9; Horace Mann Bond, *The Education of the Negro in the American Social Order*, p. 362; Virgil A. Clift, Archibald W. Anderson, and Gordon H. Hullfish, *Negro Education in America: Its Adequacy, Problems and Needs*, p. 44; Range, *Negro Colleges in Georgia*, pp. 67–68.

[5] Jane E. Smith Browning and John B. Williams, "History and Goals of Black Institutions of Higher Learning," in *Black Colleges in America: Challenge, Development, Survival*, ed. Charles V. Willie and Ronald R. Edmonds, p. 72; Kenneth M. Stampp, *The*

The reasoning or rationalizations for this policy were many. Chief among them was the belief that blacks were inferior to whites and thus best suited for vocational, rather than liberal arts, instruction. This claim of inferiority became the subject of many scientific and social science discussions throughout the late nineteenth and early twentieth centuries.[6] Typical of such racist attitudes was an article by James B. Craighead. Writing in 1884 in *Popular Science Monthly*, Craighead postulated that the African race was a subhuman species, incapable of attaining the intellectual sophistication of whites. Craighead believed that the Negro was unsuited for higher learning and argued that blacks held the mistaken notion that it was education that gave whites their superiority over other peoples. He argued that "as Eve was induced to think that if she and Adam could eat of the forbidden fruit they would be as gods, so the ordinary African thought if his child could only read, write, and cipher, he would be in every way the equal of the Caucasian." Craighead maintained that a black should be afforded only enough education to "calculate the amount of his wages, and to verify the entries and summings of his passbook."[7]

In the 1886 issue of *North American Review*, white author Edmund Kirke noted that in the "nature of things" most blacks became house servants, farm workers, or industrial laborers. He concluded it was a disservice to offer blacks educational opportunities outside their station. Instead, he advocated only basic education for the black masses, with a possibility of higher learning for those who displayed uncommon ability. Kirke considered this to be only a remote possibility, since he perceived blacks as possessing only childlike intellectual abilities. It was Kirke's conviction that, in order to become solid citizens, Negroes must accept their societal position as semiskilled laborers.[8]

Era of Reconstruction, 1865–1877, pp. 210–11; Ballard, *Education of Black Folk*, pp. 11–12.

[6] Interview with Dr. Melvin J. Banks, Bishop College, Dallas, Texas, July 23, 1979; Browning and Williams, "History and Goals of Black Institutions of Higher Learning," in *Black Colleges*, ed. Willie and Edmonds, p. 72.

[7] James B. Craighead, "The Future of the Negro in the South," *Popular Science Monthly*, November, 1884, pp. 41–43.

[8] Edmund Kirke, "How Shall the Negro be Educated?" *North American Review*, November, 1886, pp. 424, 426.

George M. Fredrickson and John S. Haller, Jr., pointed out in 1971 that such white attitudes concerning black inferiority were based not only upon cultural concepts constructed during the seventeenth and eighteenth centuries, but also upon nineteenth-century scientific and social science research. According to Fredrickson and Haller, scholars in both Europe and America conducted extensive studies during the late 1800s which attempted to determine the relative qualities of man, establish racial hierarchies, and even justify race legislation. Spurred on by the philosophies of Charles Darwin and Herbert Spencer, research in anthropometry, phrenology, craniometry, and medicine reinforced notions that the Caucasian race was a superior species, while the black race was an inferior survivor of evolutionary and hereditary development. Haller observed that behavioral scientists also supported this concept of a racial hierarchy. On one hand, social scientists believed that the white race had developed to its advanced state as the result of its superior ability to adapt to a changing environment. These so-called social environmentalists abandoned this concept, however, when examining the nonwhite races. In the case of blacks, most social scientists concluded that negative hereditary factors played a more important role than the environment. Fredrickson and Haller pointed out that scientists and social scientists of the period further agreed that alleged failures in these earlier stages of evolution had restricted the brain size and quality of nonwhite peoples and that the environment no longer played a significant part in human evolution.[9]

As a result, the white race had continued to advance biologically and socially, while evolution had come to an end in Negroes. Haller noted that such racially oriented concepts of natural selection carried an ominous forecast for the future of the black race. Negroes were seen not only as beings fitted solely for manual labor but also as freakish survivors of the past, "mentally incapable of shouldering the burdens of complex civilization and

[9] George M. Fredrickson, *The Black Image in the White Mind: The Debate on Afro-American Character and Destiny, 1817–1914*, pp. 74–82, 84–96, 231–33, 246–55; John S. Haller, Jr., *Outcasts from Evolution: Scientific Attitudes of Racial Inferiority, 1859–1900*, pp. ix, 3–68, 209–10.

slowly deteriorating structurally to a point when, at some time in the future, they would become extinct, thus ultimately solving the race problem."[10]

Another type of rationalization for industrial education dealt with economics. It involved the role southern and northern whites visualized for blacks in the post–Civil War southern economy. The end of the Civil War had marked an end to southern slavery. In the late nineteenth century, northern investors seized upon the opportunity to extend their operations southward. In rapid succession, northern capitalists gained a financial foothold in many of the South's railroad, coal, iron, steel, cotton, and cottonseed oil companies. The northern industrialists agreed with most southern whites that cheap black labor was a key factor in the expansion of these industrial and agricultural concerns.[11]

Blacks also recognized the vital role they were expected to play. Viewing this period, W. E. B. DuBois observed that the last decade of the nineteenth and the first decade of the twentieth centuries were more significant for blacks than the Reconstruction years: "This was the age of triumph for big business, for industry, consolidated and organized on a worldwide scale, and run by white capital with colored labor. The Southern United States was one of the most promising fields for this development, with . . . a mass of cheap and potentially efficient labor."[12]

In economic terms, both southern whites and northern businessmen sought to guarantee for themselves a stable and efficient black labor force. This attitude was subsequently articulated by numerous political, educational, and business leaders of the late nineteenth century. Among such figures was J. L. M. Curry, a former confederate and pro-slavery congressman, who between 1881 and 1903 championed the so-called New South Movement. Curry and others hoped to rebuild the South along industrial lines and place the Negro in a controlled labor status. Curry believed that the former slaves should be educated, but only along lines that would serve white purposes. He suggested

---

[10] Haller, *Outcasts from Evolution*, p. ix.

[11] Donald Spivey, *Schooling for the New Slavery: Black Industrial Education, 1868–1915*, Contributions in Afro-American and African Studies, no. 38, pp. 71–75.

[12] Quoted in Spivey, *Schooling for the New Slavery*, pp. 75–76.

that a system of education was needed to remove the "intemperance, dissipation, laxity of morals, low standards of character, and false views of religion" exhibited by blacks. At the same time, Curry felt such a system of education should instill in Negroes the virtues of cleanliness, moral character, and discipline. In addition, a system of manual training would indoctrinate blacks with certain social and psychological values that would encourage them to accept their second-class position in the New South.[13]

As a trustee and general agent for the Peabody Fund and as the first president of the Conference of Southern Education, Curry exercised considerable influence upon black education. His ideas won applause from an assortment of national figures, including industrialists John D. Rockefeller and Andrew Carnegie, and educators like Booker T. Washington and Robert Curtis Ogden. Curry's thoughts also gained support from several prominent regional figures, including northern journalists Amory T. Mayo and Walter Hines Page, the demagogue and white-supremacist governor Charles Aycock of North Carolina, and from college presidents such as Edwin A. Alderman of Tulane University and Paul Barringer of the University of Virginia.[14]

Considering the prevailing racial attitudes in the late nineteenth century, it is not surprising that the ideas of men like Curry found expression in the establishment of industrial training schools. The man who created the prototype for such schools was General Samuel Chapman Armstrong. Born in Hawaii in 1839, Armstrong was the son of Scotch-Irish missionary parents from New England. As a boy, he was impressed that his father had far greater success training the Hawaiian natives in handicrafts than in literature.[15] During the Civil War, Armstrong joined the Union forces and rose to the rank of brevet brigadier general. Toward the end of the war, he commanded detachments of

---

[13] Ibid., pp. 76–79.

[14] Ibid., pp. 11, 76–79, 82; Clift, Anderson, and Hullfish, *Negro Eduation in America*, p. 41.

[15] Edith Armstrong Talbot, *Samuel Chapman Armstrong: A Biographical Study*, pp. 3–40; J. H. Dillard, "The Negro Goes to College," *World's Work* (1928): 337; J. C. Hemphill, "Problems of Negro Education," *North American Review* (July, 1886): 438–39; Basil Mathews, *Booker T. Washington, Educator and Interracial Interpreter*, p. 46; Range, *Negro Colleges in Georgia*, p. 69.

newly-freed Negro troops and administered to the needs of thousands of black refugees who flocked to the advancing Union armies. In 1867, Armstrong left the military and became the principal of Hampton School, which he then reorganized in 1868 into Hampton Institute. Drawing upon his childhood and military experiences, Armstrong established Hampton as a coeducational school for young Negroes, specializing in handicrafts, agriculture, and homemaking. In addition to vocational courses, he stressed the virtues of thrift, discipline, and self-reliance. By the end of the century, significant numbers of black students had graduated, and Hampton had become, in the minds of most whites, the model for black higher education.[16]

Subsequently, foundations such as the General Education Board, the Peabody Fund, the Slater Foundation, and the Phelps-Stokes Fund contributed large sums for the establishment of similar vocational programs throughout the South. The federal government also gave impetus to the movement with the passage of the Morrill Act of 1890, which assisted states in founding land-grant colleges for blacks, based upon industrial or agricultural formats. As a result, the private black colleges faced a rival educational model and a growing number of institutional competitors backed with federal, as well as white philanthropic, support.[17]

The movement toward vocational training created a national controversy. A significant portion of the black academic community, as well as most northern missionary groups, resisted the swing toward universal vocationalism and continued to back the early liberal arts ideals of their colleges. Consequently, as the controversy and debate grew over the definition, purpose, and needs of the nation's black colleges, a dualistic type of liberal arts–vocational curriculum emerged in most of these institutions.[18]

[16] Talbot, *Samuel Chapman Armstrong*, pp. 97, 119; Mathews, *Booker T. Washington*, p. 46; Browning and Williams, "History and Goals of Black Institutions of Higher Learning," p. 73.

[17] Henry Allen Bullock, *A History of Negro Education in the South*, pp. 117–46; Browning and Williams, "History and Goals of Black Institutions of Higher Learning," p. 74.

[18] Browning and Williams, "History and Goals of Black Institutions of Higher Learning," pp. 75–76.

Symbolic of this ideological debate were the thoughts of two noted black educators, Booker T. Washington and W. E. B. DuBois. Washington, the founder and president of Tuskegee Institute, emphasized the concept of industrial education, while DuBois, a noted scholar and social activist, advocated liberal arts instruction. Neither man doubted the necessity of black colleges. They agreed that black colleges were valuable because they were distinctive, made a general contribution to humanity, and taught their students important social, cultural, and religious values. They did not agree, however, upon the content of the curricula these colleges should offer. Washington reasoned that vocational training should be stressed since its benefits would more readily affect the lives of the majority of black citizens. DuBois, as previously mentioned, desired to develop a professional corps of black leaders, the so-called "talented tenth," which would then take the lead in uplifting his race.[19]

A closer examination of each man's life, however, reveals a considerable amount of overlap in their views on education. Booker T. Washington was born a slave in Franklin County, Virginia, during 1856. After the Civil War, Washington attended Hampton Institute, where he was deeply influenced by Samuel Chapman Armstrong. A model student, Washington was later sent, by Armstrong, to establish a similar industrial school farther south. Washington accomplished this in 1881, with the founding of Tuskegee Institute in Macon County, Alabama.[20]

Washington rose to national prominence in 1895, when he delivered his famous address to the Cotton States Exposition in Atlanta, Georgia. In his speech, Washington articulated his belief that blacks should remain in the South and strive to achieve for themselves a place in American society. This could be done if blacks prepared for a way of life that was compatible with their existing status and abilities. Washington's appeal for racial toleration and industrial training was clear:

[19] Ibid.; Louis Harlan, "The Secret Life of Booker T. Washington," *Journal of Southern History* 37 (August, 1971): 393–95; W. E. B. DuBois, "The Talented Tenth," and Booker T. Washington, "Industrial Education for the Negro," in *The Negro Problem*, ed. Booker T. Washington, et al., pp. 33–75, 9–29, respectively.

[20] Mathews, *Booker T. Washington*, p. 62; Clift, Anderson, and Hullfish, *Negro Education in America*, p. 48.

For those of my race who depend on bettering their condition in a foreign land or who underestimate the importance of cultivating friendly relations with the Southern white man, who is their next-door neighbor, I would say: "Cast down your bucket where you are"—cast it down in making friends in every manly way of the people of all races by whom we are surrounded.

Cast it down in agriculture, mechanics, in commerce, in domestic service, and in the professions. . . . No race can prosper till it learns that there is as much dignity in tilling a field as in writing a poem.[21]

In the years following his Atlanta speech, Washington became a national celebrity. His notions about industrial training were accepted by some blacks, heralded by many northern philanthropists, and warmly received by most whites. Southern whites especially welcomed Washington's apparent acceptance of segregation and the white supremacy it implied.[22]

It must be noted that Washington saw vocational education neither as a surrender to white domination nor as the only educational avenue, but rather as the most realistic approach to the immediate economic, social, and political problems of blacks. He argued that Negroes could achieve equality in American society by simply adhering to the white man's Puritan ethic of hard work and sacrifice. Although Washington conceded that some formal schooling was necessary for the development of basic skills, he seemed convinced that liberal arts training held little tangible value for the majority of his race. This attitude was clear in his leadership of Tuskegee Institute, where he steadfastly refused to organize a liberal arts curriculum. Yet it is important to note that he regularly employed the liberal arts graduates of Fisk University to teach in the primary department of the Alabama school. This philosophical overlap also appeared in his so-called "dovetailing" of certain academic fields, such as mathematics, with vocational courses in agriculture, carpentry, and blacksmithing. Thus, while Washington realized the value of at least some "higher education," he remained convinced that the best hope for his largely rural and illiterate race rested with vo-

---

[21] Booker T. Washington, *Up From Slavery: An Autobiography*, pp. 154–55.

[22] Clift, Anderson, and Hullfish, *Negro Education in America*, p. 50; Herbert Aptheker, ed., *A Documentary History of the Negro People in the United States*, p. 755.

cational training. The master of Tuskegee perceived that only after the general condition of Negroes improved, through manual training, would the appropriateness of liberal arts training be enhanced.[23]

Unlike Washington, W. E. B. DuBois was a northerner, born in 1868 in Great Barrington, Massachusetts. While Washington attended classes at Hampton, DuBois graduated with a liberal arts degree from Fisk University in 1888 and from Harvard University in 1890. After studying two years abroad at the University of Berlin, DuBois returned in 1895 to receive a Ph.D. in history from Harvard.[24] Throughout his academic career, he distinguished himself as a teacher, poet, scholar, novelist, and social activist. In all, DuBois produced a dozen important books and more than a hundred pamphlets, articles, and essays. He gave freely of his time to the National Association for the Advancement of Colored People (NAACP) and served for two decades as the editor of its news organ, *The Crisis*.[25]

DuBois first attracted national attention at the turn of the century, when he began to criticize Washington's philosophy of universal vocational education. DuBois did not object to vocational training as one part of a broader educational picture, but he vigorously opposed using it as the primary solution to black social and economic problems. He admitted that the majority of black men and women were engaged in agricultural and industrial jobs, but he maintained that liberal arts training was as vital to the improvement of his people as vocational training. The object of "true education," DuBois declared, was not to make men carpenters, but to make carpenters men.[26]

[23] David E. Washington, ed., *Selected Speeches of Booker T. Washington*, p. 57; Louis R. Harlan, *Booker T. Washington: The Making of a Black Leader, 1856–1901*, pp. 275–80; Harlan, "Secret Life of Booker T. Washington," p. 394; Louis R. Harlan, "Booker T. Washington Biographical Perspective," *American Historical Review* 75 (October, 1970): 1584–85; Elliot M. Rudwick, *W. E. B. DuBois: A Study in Minority Group Leadership*, p. 62.

[24] Rudwick, *W. E. B. DuBois*, pp. 18–30; Francis L. Broderic, *W. E. B. DuBois: Negro Leader in a Time of Crisis*, pp. 1–32.

[25] Rudwick, *W. E. B. DuBois*, pp. 39–53, 94–120, 151–52, 165–78, 191–92; Rayford W. Logan, ed., *W. E. B. DuBois: A Profile*, p. 294.

[26] W. E. B. DuBois, "The Talented Tenth," p. 63; Rudwick, *W. E. B. DuBois*, pp. 64–69.

In *The Souls of Black Folk* (1903), DuBois lashed out at the "Atlanta Compromise," characterizing it as a program of "industrial education, conciliation of the South, and submission and silence." DuBois asserted that Washington was the leader of "not one race, but two—a compromiser between the South, the North, and the Negro." He argued that Washington's vocationalism represented little more than the old slave attitudes of adjustment and submission, hung against the modern backdrop of the industrial revolution. He also viewed the economic program of the Tuskegee leader as a "gospel of Work and Money," that overlooked the "higher aims of life." He accused Washington of asking blacks to surrender, at least temporarily, their political power, insistence on civil rights, and quest for higher education, in favor of concentrating all their energies on industrial education, the accumulation of wealth, and the conciliation of the South.[27] This course of action, in DuBois's mind, had brought disastrous results, as the South was responding to Washington, not with cooperation, but with Jim Crow laws that were intended to segregate and subjugate blacks.[28] Washington's refusal to combat this trend openly led DuBois to comment:

> Manly self-respect is more than lands and houses. A people who voluntarily surrender such respect or cease striving for it are not worth civilizing. . . . I hold these truths to be self-evident, that a disfranchised working class in a modern industrial civilization is worse than helpless. . . . It will be diseased, it will be criminal, it will be ignorant, it will be the plaything of mobs, and it will be insulted by caste restrictions.[29]

In order to reach intellectual, social, and political equality, DuBois felt, blacks must have the opportunity of acquiring a liberal arts education. He based this belief upon his concept of a "talented tenth," which posed for education "the problem of developing the Best of his race that they may guide the Mass away from the Worst, in their own and other races." He envisioned the talented tenth as a small corps of exceptional men who

[27] W. E. B. DuBois, *The Souls of Black Folk*, pp. 79, 86, 87–88.
[28] Rudwick, *W. E. B. DuBois*, pp. 68–69; Broderick, *W. E. B. DuBois*, p. 62; Basil T. Mathews, "The Continuing Debate: Washington vs. DuBois," in *W. E. B. DuBois: A Profile*, ed. Logan, p. 185.
[29] Mathews, "The Continuing Debate," pp. 185–86.

would be trained in liberal arts subjects such as education, theology, science, law, and business. This intellectual elite would then lead the masses of its race out of the shadows of poverty and social inequality. "Men we shall have," DuBois insisted, "only as we make manhood the object of the work of schools— intelligence, broad sympathy, knowledge of the world that was and is, and of the relation of men to it—this is the curriculum of that Higher Education which must underlie true life."[30]

Although both Washington and DuBois commanded large blocks of support within the black community, most whites, including prominent philanthropists and businessmen, favored the founder of Tuskegee. Consequently, by the opening of the twentieth century, industrial education had become visible in most black colleges in America, and Washington was regarded as the dominant black leader of his time. Vocationalism seemed strongest in the public black colleges, however; in the private black colleges, vocationalism shared the academic spotlight to varying degrees with liberal arts courses. Apparently for idealistic as well as religious reasons, the majority of the denominational colleges quietly continued to build their liberal arts offerings, while accepting the rising popularity of vocational training. Such attempts to address simultaneously the philosophies of both Washington and DuBois were clearly visible in the church-related black colleges of Texas.

Development of Liberal Arts Curricula

Statements in the early catalogs of the private colleges indicate firm commitment to liberal arts instruction. The Bishop College catalog of 1882 stated that the primary responsibility of the college was the preparation of teachers and ministers. In its 1887 catalog, Paul Quinn College acknowledged, "Our aim is to give students a liberal education and such training . . . as will make them happy and useful in life."[31]

[30] W. E. B. DuBois, "The Talented Tenth," pp. 33–34.
[31] Caesar Francis Toles, "The History of Bishop College" (M.A. thesis, University of Michigan, 1947) p. 30; Paul Quinn College, *Catalog*, 1887, p. 23; Texas College, *Catalog*, 916, p. 8.

The 1920 catalog of Wiley College outlined the chief purpose of the institution as furnishing "a place for the young Negro men and women of the Southwest to obtain a liberal and Christian education that will fit them for leadership." Samuel Huston College emphasized that its "broad liberal program" was intended to promote the "all-around development of Christian youth" and listed the following aims:

1. To develop Christian character.
2. To stress student-participation in college management.
3. To lead the student into a deep reverence for truth and a genuine appreciation for the scientific approach to life situations.
4. To provide broad general education for all students and lay a foundation for graduate or professional training.
5. To prepare students for definite life tasks.
6. To prepare leaders who will serve the people and cooperate in the community.[32]

While recognizing the importance of vocational training, the 1922 catalog of Jarvis Christian College pointed out that "no race can permanently endure without its professionally trained men and women."[33]

Because of their strong classical tone, the curricula of these colleges stressed ancient languages, such as Greek and Latin, and modern languages, such as French, German, and Spanish. The emphasis on foreign languages was so strong that other fields, such as English, history, science, and mathematics, received less attention.[34] For example, the required college, or "classical," course listings for students at Guadalupe College during 1892 placed their greatest emphasis upon the study of Latin and Greek:

FRESHMAN YEAR

Solid Geometry, Higher Algebra, Virgil, Cicero, De Senectute and De Amicitia, Homer, Greek Prose Composition, Livy, Horace, New Testament Greek, Physiology, German, Botany.

[32] Wiley College, *Catalog*, 1920, p. 14; Samuel Huston College, *Student Handbook*, n.d., p. 8.

[33] Jarvis Christian College, *Catalog*, 1922, p. 11.

[34] William R. Davis, *The Development and Present Status of Negro Education in East Texas*, pp. 117–19.

SOPHOMORE YEAR
Trigonometry, Surveying, Tacitus, Homer's Odyssey, Physics, Rhetoric, Demosthenes, General History, New Testament Greek.

JUNIOR YEAR
Analytical Geometry, De Corona, Chemistry, Astronomy, Logic, French, Psychology, Zoology, History of Civilization.

SENIOR YEAR
Geology, Butler's Analogy, Political Economy, Mental and Moral Philosophy, Evidence of Christianity, International Law, English Literature, Art Criticism.[35]

Many whites and some blacks questioned the virtue of such abstract courses, but the private colleges tended to champion them well into the 1920s. The 1924 catalog of Bishop College defended its program in Greek, declaring:

The aim of this department [Greek] is to give the student a mastery of the essentials of inflection and syntax as will remove from the beginner and seeker after Greek the difficulties that will hinder him from understanding the Greek Language, and shut him off from a people gifted in the instinct for beauty and the power for creating beautiful forms, and of all things which they created, their own language is the most beautiful. We speak of their language as a dead language, when in fact their language is far more alive than those languages which contain little worth reading. . . .[36]

Eventually, as job opportunities expanded, the private colleges began to realize the need for more diverse courses. The continued criticism of classical curricula, combined with the need for more specialized professional training, led the colleges to reevaluate their academic programs. During the 1920s and 1930s, these institutions reconstructed their curricula to include the same types of liberal arts courses found in white colleges and universities. Table 1 illustrates how this process took place at Wiley College between 1892 and 1950. In 1892, 43.9 percent of the courses required for a Bachelor of Arts degree were in an-

[35] Guadalupe College, *Catalog*, 1892, p. 3.
[36] Davis, *Negro Education in East Texas*, p. 119.

TABLE 1
Bachelor of Arts Curriculum Requirements for Wiley College, 1892, 1920, 1930, and 1950

Curriculum Requirements In Semester Hours	YEAR 1892	1920	1930	1950
Education	0	18*	24*	27*
English	6	24	18	21
Ancient Languages	24	12	0	0
Modern Languages	12	12	12	12
Mathematics	12	12	6	6
Philosophy	6	18	0	0
Science	8	18	12	6
Social Science	8	24	12	12
Theology	6	2	4	3
Electives	0	0	30	27
Percent Ancient and Modern Languages of Total Requirements	43.9	17.6	10.1	10.2

SOURCE: Wiley College, *Catalog*, 1892, p. 15; 1920, p. 34; 1930, p. 38; 1950, p. 46.

*Required for state teaching certificate.

cient and modern languages. This figure dropped to 17.6 percent by 1920 and then fell to just over 10 percent in 1930 and 1950. By 1930, required courses in the ancient languages had been eliminated. As Wiley moved away from its narrow classical format, it expanded its offerings in English, history, psychology, sociology, and education.

Because teaching was one of the prime job opportunities for blacks and because the State Board of Education began to demand specific education courses for teaching certification, the expansion of education offerings among all the black colleges became commonplace. In the late nineteenth and early twentieth centuries, there had been little uniformity in the teacher preparation provided by either black or white colleges. Generally, anyone with two or more years of college study could teach.

Consequently, a major shift occurred in the 1920s when the State Board of Education handed down guidelines requiring education courses in methods, observation, and practice teaching. Nearly every black college carried a statement in its catalog regarding these requirements:

Elementary Permanent—An applicant who has satisfactorily completed the second year of college work in a Texas State normal college, and who has specialized in the materials of elementary education, including a minimum of thirty-six recitation hours of practice teaching, in the elementary grades, under the supervision of a critic teacher, shall be entitled to receive a permanent elementary certificate.

High School Permanent—A permanent high school certificate shall be granted to a student who has satisfactorily completed a four year course leading to a degree, in a Texas State normal college or in any university, senior college, or normal college, classified as first class by the State Superintendent of Public Instruction; provided, that this work shall include four courses in education, one of which shall consist of study of methods, observation of methods, and practice in teaching, one of which shall bear upon high school teaching.[37]

At first glance, it might seem that there was a uniform improvement in the education programs of the private colleges. In a report surveying the state's black senior colleges in 1944, however, the Bi-Racial Conference on Education for Negroes in Texas discovered many differences. The best department of education, in terms of faculty preparation, course organization, and library holdings, was found to be at Tillotson College. The conference found the department of education at Jarvis Christian to be the weakest, lacking any clear, definite aims. The 1944 study believed the Hawkins school, which had only one instructor in education and limited library materials, did not possess the facilities or staff to maintain even a minimal teacher education program.[38]

Texas, Wiley, Bishop, and Samuel Huston colleges fell between these extremes. The Bi-Racial Conference felt that these

[37] Tillotson College, *Catalog*, 1934, pp. 33–34; Jarvis Christian College, *Catalog*, 1941, p. 20; Texas College, *Catalog*, 1942, p. 31; Wiley College, *Catalog*, 1939, p. 25.
[38] T. S. Montgomery, *The Senior Colleges for Negroes in Texas*, p. 61.

schools tailored their education programs to their institution's philosophy, location, and facilities. At Texas College, where library materials were limited, the department compensated by not confining its work merely to courses in techniques and observations. Instead, education courses cut across all fields of study, interpreting the problems of education in terms of language, literature, and social and natural sciences. The study of the child and parent, in the context of their surrounding culture, was also emphasized. Wiley and Bishop directed their education programs toward the functional training of teachers for rural schools. The conference found the faculties to be energetic and competent but considered the libraries weak. Samuel Huston emphasized secondary school training, rather than either elementary or rural.[39]

By comparison, the departments of education in the public black colleges in Texas were slightly stronger. Prairie View offered specialized teacher training for urban, rural, secondary, and elementary schools. Its library was considered the best of all the black college libraries, although inadequate to deal with the large number of students taking education courses. The conference also gave Houston College high marks but noted that it was primarily geared toward preparing instructors for urban schools.[40]

Similar difficulties were found among the science departments of the private colleges. Wiley, Texas, and Tillotson colleges had solid, but limited, science offerings in biology, chemistry, and physics. The other institutions, however, suffered from inadequate facilities, space, laboratory equipment, periodicals, and reference books. Jarvis Christian was able to "provide sound training in hardly more than biology and chemistry on the first year level." Bishop College did not offer a single major in a specific field of science. By contrast, the 1944 report found that Prairie View, with its emphasis upon agriculture, prenursing, and home economics, had a well-developed, though overcrowded, science program.[41]

[39] Ibid., pp. 56–61.
[40] Ibid.
[41] Ibid.

Perhaps the strongest academic areas in the curricula of the independent colleges were their social science and humanities offerings. Nearly all the colleges offered majors in religion, philosophy, history, and sociology. Library holdings in these fields were usually more adequate than in others, but still less abundant than those in most white colleges. Forged in a spirit of deep Christian piety, the private schools offered extensive courses in theology and required each of their students to take from three to six semester hours of religion for graduation. In addition, all of these institutions expected their students to participate in the numerous religious opportunities of the colleges, which included daily devotions, evening vespers, Sunday school, and chapel services.[42]

Reviewing the academic departments of these colleges, it is clear that some programs were stronger than others. Determining the best college, in terms of overall academic curricula, however, is difficult. Comparisons of the quality of faculties, staffs, and facilities of these institutions run the risk of being subjective and should therefore be approached cautiously. Perhaps a better measure of the growth and relative quality of the private black colleges can be found in their dates of recognition by state and national accrediting bodies. Accreditation by the Texas Department of Education and the Southern Association of Colleges was eagerly sought by all these schools, for it denoted an acceptable level of institutional ability and performance. For a college to receive an "A" rating from the State Department of Education, numerous requirements had to be met. For example, in 1923, the state ruled that all colleges had to demand at least fourteen high school credits of applicants. They also had to maintain not fewer than seven separate departments in the liberal arts and sciences and operate them independently of their preparatory departments. All faculty members were expected to have college degrees. In return, instructors were to be paid at levels comparable with those in "standard institutions" and could be

[42]Ibid.; Willie Lee Glass, interview with author, Tyler, April 4, 1981; Wiley College, *Catalog*, 1920, p. 35, 1928, p. 38, and 1950, p. 46; Samuel Huston College, *Student Handbook*, n.d., pp. 15–16; Guadalupe College, *Catalog*, 1892, p. 15; Paul Quinn College, *Catalog*, 1937, p. 13; Texas College, *Catalog*, 1916, p. 9.

asked to teach no more than twenty class hours per week. Class size was not to exceed thirty students, and libraries were supposed to contain a minimum of five thousand volumes. Finally, each college was required to receive an annual income of at least $20,000 from tuition or endowment, offer adequate scientific equipment, provide proper "hygienic" living conditions, and prepare its graduates to enter recognized graduate and professional schools.[43]

Among the private black colleges in Texas, Tillotson, Wiley, Samuel Huston, Bishop, and Texas colleges were the first to meet these standards. The Texas Department of Education recognized the work of Bishop and Wiley in 1901. The two Marshall schools held this distinction exclusively for over two decades, until accreditation was extended to Tillotson in 1925, Samuel Huston in 1927, and Texas College in 1932. The Southern Association, which did not begin accrediting black colleges until 1930, granted "B" ratings to Bishop College in 1931 and to Texas and Tillotson in 1933. "A" ratings were received by Wiley in 1933, Samuel Huston in 1934, Tillotson in 1943, and Texas and Bishop in 1948.[44]

Jarvis Christian acquired state junior college accreditation in 1928 and senior college status in 1941. The Southern Association did not grant the Hawkins institution an "A" rating, however, until 1950. Similarly, St. Philip's College was accredited by the state in 1927 but was not recognized by the Southern Association until 1951. While Guadalupe, Paul Quinn, and Butler colleges received state recognition in 1929, 1933, and 1949, respectively, none of them was granted accreditation by the Southern Association.[45] Thus, in terms of accreditation, it appears that

[43] Texas, *Laws, Rules and Regulations Governing State Teachers Certificates*, Bulletin No. 289, 1923, p. 222.

[44] *Houston Informer*, December 16, 1933; "Texas College History," 1951, Allen C. Hancock Papers, Texas College, Tyler, p. 8; Tillotson College, *Catalog*, 1934, p. 13, and 1945, p. 13; Huston-Tillotson College, *Catalog*, 1978, p. 8; Walter P. Webb and H. Bailey Carroll, *The Handbook of Texas*, II: 539; Roy H. Lanier, "Church-Related Colleges for Negroes in Texas" (M.A. thesis, Hardin-Simmons University, 1950), pp. 81–82, 91; Lloyd K. Thompson, "The Origins and Development of Black Religious Colleges in East Texas" (Ph.D. diss., North Texas State University, 1976), p. 84.

[45] Jarvis Christian College, *Catalog*, 1967, p. 24; Clarence W. Norris, Jr., "St. Philip's College: A Case Study of a Historically Black Two-Year College" (Ph.D. diss.,

Wiley, Bishop, Tillotson, Texas, and Samuel Huston matured at about the same time and presented the best academic programs among the private institutions.

Development of Vocational Curricula

While Samuel Chapman Armstrong and Booker T. Washington attracted national attention for their work at Hampton and Tuskegee, similar efforts were taking place in the black denominational colleges in Texas. The first vocational courses appeared in their curricula around 1880 and were offered more because of realistic needs than because of any doctrinaire philosophy. First, since a majority of the students attending these institutions came from underdeveloped agricultural or industrial backgrounds, groups like the American Missionary Association felt vocational courses would be of immediate value to many. While the AMA was among the first to provide both liberal arts and vocational education, all the major denominations soon acknowledged the advantages of providing at least limited vocational training. Second, because most students had received little prior formal education, the initial demand for college courses was small. Therefore, the black colleges stressed elementary and later secondary studies, along with vocational training, in an effort to attract students and prepare them for higher levels of study. Third, the early vocational classes served the vital function of helping to sustain these colleges physically. Students in these courses often raised crops and livestock to feed the students and faculty, constructed many college buildings, handcrafted furniture for the dormitories and classrooms, and served in countless campus custodial and maintenance positions. Thus, while the overriding concern of the private colleges continued to be the development of their liberal arts curricula, they also realized the appropri-

---

University of Southern California, 1975), pp. 116, 214; *Waco Messenger*, June 2, 1933, December 14, 1934; Lavern C. Wood, interview with author, Paul Quinn College, Waco, July 13, 1979; Eldon Stephen Branda, *The Handbook of Texas: A Supplement*, III: 129; E. C. Evans, *The Story of Texas Schools*, p. 215; Anne Brawner, "Guadalupe College: A Case History in Negro Higher Education, 1884–1936" (M.A. thesis, Southwest Texas State University, 1980), p. 71.

Grant Hall, Paul Quinn College, circa 1889. The second major building constructed at the college, this three-story structure served as a dormitory and classroom building. Courtesy Paul Quinn College.

Bishop Hall, circa 1900. This building served as a dormitory for women at Bishop College. Courtesy Bishop College.

Left: Richard Allen, circa 1800, the founder and first bishop of the African Methodist Episcopal Church. Courtesy Paul Quinn College. *Right*: Paul Quinn, circa 1870. Quinn served as bishop and missionary for the African Methodist Episcopal Church. Courtesy Paul Quinn College.

Left: Rev. George Jeffrey Tillotson, circa 1875. A retired Congregationalist minister from Hartford, Connecticut, Tillotson was employed by the American Missionary Association to select a site in Texas for an AMA college. Courtesy Huston-Tillotson College. *Right*: Nathan Bishop, circa 1870. This New England educator contributed ten thousand dollars toward the establishment of Bishop College. Courtesy Bishop College.

Administration building, Guadalupe College, circa 1920. The structure was destroyed by fire in 1936. Courtesy Texas State Archives.

Left: Rev. James Steptoe Johnston, founder of St. Philip's College, circa 1890. Courtesy St. Philip's College. *Right*: Samuel Huston, circa 1900. The Iowa philanthropist donated nine thousand dollars to aid in the founding of Samuel Huston College. Courtesy Huston-Tillotson College.

Jarvis Christian College, circa 1912. The college first began its classes in these remains of an old logging camp. Courtesy Jarvis Christian College.

J. J. Jarvis (*left*) and Ida Jarvis (*right*), circa 1900. The couple donated 456 acres of land near Hawkins for the founding of a college for blacks by the Disciples of Christ. Courtesy Jarvis Christian College.

Samuel Huston College campus in 1916. This was the second black college established in Texas by the Freedmen's Aid Society of the Methodist Episcopal Church. Courtesy Huston-Tillotson College.

Student body of Samuel Huston College in 1900, including both normal and college departments. Courtesy Huston-Tillotson College.

Paul Quinn College art class in 1916. Courtesy Paul Quinn College.

Bishop College education class in 1947. Courtesy Bishop College.

Chemistry class, St. Philip's College, in 1951. Courtesy St. Philip's College.

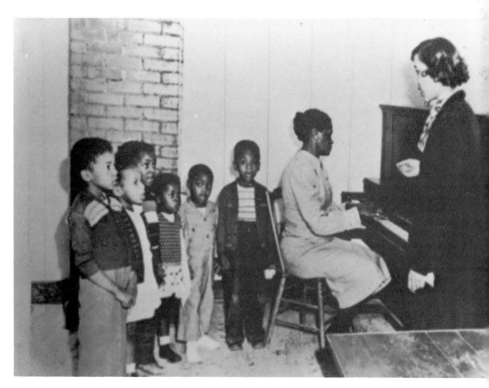

Jarvis Christian College nursery school in 1951. Courtesy Jarvis Christian College.

Jarvis Christian College library, circa 1950. Courtesy Jarvis Christian College.

French class, Jarvis Christian College, circa 1950. Courtesy Jarvis Christian College.

ateness of vocational education.[46] Consequently, most of the colleges offered two types of curricula. One, in the liberal arts, ranged from elementary through college level. The other,.which was vocational, was usually separated from the academic departments and limited to elementary- and secondary-level courses.[47]

Some of the early catalogs of these colleges illustrate clearly the types of vocational offerings and the practical significance which was attached to them. The 1887 catalog of Paul Quinn College noted that its industrial department offered elementary courses in agriculture, carpentry, printing, cutting, sewing, and needlework. Of these, Paul Quinn considered its courses in agriculture the most important, because the successful operation of the "college garden" proved to the world that a "little money and much energy, when rightly directed, will make a good school." In addition, Paul Quinn students, regardless of their major or educational level, were expected to contribute at least one hour of work a day in the fields or on the college grounds. The catalog suggested this activity provided the student with "needed exercise and training in useful employments." At the same time, such labor gave the campus a "decided home-like appearance," which made the students feel they were among friends and were an important part of the college community. For those who objected to the mandatory work period, the Paul Quinn catalog warned, "The student who enters our school with a disposition to evade work, finds that the tide flows the other way, and soon takes up the line of march." The vocational program at Paul Quinn was evidently as beneficial for the school as it was for the students. In fact, the catalog remarked that without this feature, "it would be impossible for us to run our school."[48]

In the late 1880s and early 1890s, Wiley College offered industrial courses, which included printing, shoemaking, farming,

[46] *American Missionary* 47 (1893): 191–92, and 50 (1896): 277–78; Robert G. Sherer, *Subordination or Liberation? The Development and Conflicting Theories of Black Education in Nineteenth Century Alabama*, p. 145.

[47] Allen C. Hancock, interview with author, Texas College, Tyler, July 18, 1979; George H. Chandler, interview with author, Wiley College, Marshall, July 20, 1979; Banks interview.

[48] Paul Quinn College, *Catalog*, 1887, pp. 23–24.

gardening, typing, shorthand, cooking, sewing, and housekeeping: The Wiley catalog for 1887 characterized these courses as "highly creditable to beginners," indicating their elementary level, and noted that their "healthy influence on the workers is quite discernable, and will render skillful the hand for some useful occupation in future life." Wiley students from all educational departments were required to devote at least one hour of work per week to the needs of the campus grounds, gardens, or orchards. Apparently there were no exceptions, for the catalog for 1891 declared: "If a little start in an education disqualifies a young man or woman for manual labor, making them feel above honest work, then they had better remain where they are, for this is a world of work and God says 'he that will not work neither shall he eat.'"[49]

Students at Mary Allen Seminary were taught "practical housekeeping," which included cooking, dressmaking, millinery, and "other useful arts." In 1892 Guadalupe College officials organized a vocational program around courses in elementary carpentry, sewing, cutting, and crocheting. In order to "secure industrial habits and good health, and to keep the price of schooling down," the college required each student to do a "certain amount" of work each day, keeping the grounds and facilities in order.[50]

The evolution of vocationalism in the private black colleges of Texas can be charted through the enrollment statistics and vocational curriculum offerings for selected years between 1900 and 1954. As Table 2 indicates, the enrollments of the Texas college in 1915 remained overwhelmingly at the elementary and secondary levels. Of a combined enrollment of 2,189 in the private institutions, 1,351 (61 percent) were enrolled in elementary classes, 706 (32 percent) in secondary studies, and only 132 (6 percent) in college courses. A similar situation existed in the black public college, Prairie View. Out of a total enrollment of

[49] Wiley College, *Catalog*, 1887, p. 26, and 1891, pp. 5, 10, 58–63; Chandler interview.

[50] Board of Missions for Freedom of the Presbyterian Church in the United States of America, *Annual Report*, 1888, p. 21; Guadalupe College, *Catalog*, 1892, pp. 15–16.

TABLE 2
Enrollments in Private and Public Black Colleges in Texas, 1915

Institution	Classification			Sex		Total
	Elementary	Secondary	College	Male	Female	
Bishop	176	153	42	93*	102*	371
Butler	122	28	0			150
Guadalupe	57	29	0	38	48	86
Jarvis Christian	14	0	0			14
Mary Allen	88	27	0		115	115
Paul Quinn	213	57	13			286
St. Philip's	68	5	0			73
Samuel Huston	267	92	18	55†	63†	377
Texas	35	75	3	38	72	110
Tillotson	135	70	18	95	128	223
Wiley	176	170	38	89*	119*	384
Prairie View	115	437	0	130	422	552

SOURCE: U.S. Department of the Interior, Bureau of Education, *Negro Education: A Study of the Private and Higher Schools for Colored People in the United States*, by Thomas Jesse Jones, Bulletin No. 39, II:572–601.
* Figures represent only those students above the elementary level.
† Figures represent only those students above the seventh-grade level.

TABLE 3
Vocational Courses Offered in Private and Public Black Colleges in Texas, 1915

Institution	Courses for Women						Level	
	Cooking	Domestic Service	Dress-making	Laundry	Millinery	Sewing	Elementary	High School
Bishop	X					X	X	X
Butler						X	X	X
Guadalupe	X	X		X		X	X	X
Jarvis Christian	X	X		X		X	X	X
Mary Allen	X					X	X	X
Paul Quinn	X					X	X	X
St. Philip's	X					X	X	X
Samuel Huston	X		X			X	X	X
Texas	X		X			X	X	X
Tillotson	X					X	X	X
Wiley	X				X	X	X	X
Prairie View			X		X	X	X	X

Courses for Men

	Agriculture	Broom Making	Carpentry	Iron-works	Manual Training	Mattress Making	Printing	Shoe-making	Tailoring	Type-setting
Bishop	X				X					
Butler					X		X			
Guadalupe				X					X	
Jarvis Christian	X		X							
Mary Allen										
Paul Quinn	X		X				X			
St. Philip's										
Samuel Huston									X	
Texas	X		X		X					
Tillotson					X					
Wiley	X		X		X		X	X	X	X
Prairie View	X	X	X	X		X		X	X	

SOURCE: U.S. Department of the Interior, Bureau of Education, *Negro Education: A Study of the Private and Higher Schools for Colored People of the United States*, prepared by Thomas Jesse Jones, Bulletin No. 39, II:572–601.

552, Prairie View had 115 (21 percent) elementary students, 437 (79 percent) secondary students, and no college students.

With the majority of the state's black students at the lower rungs of the educational ladder, the curricula of these colleges reflected a preponderance of elementary and secondary vocational courses. Table 3 shows that courses offered for women included laundry, sewing, cooking, millinery, dressmaking, and domestic service. The most popular of these was sewing, which was offered in every college, while cooking was offered in all but two, Butler and Prairie View. The colleges with the largest number of offerings for women were Guadalupe and Jarvis Christian, which offered classes in cooking, sewing, laundry, and all forms of domestic service.

Course offerings for men were even more numerous, including agriculture, broom making, carpentry, ironworks, mattress making, printing, typesetting, tailoring, shoemaking, and a broad category called manual training, which included such things as woodwork, furniture construction, mechanical drawing, domestic art, and bricklaying. The most common of these courses were agriculture, manual training, carpentry, and tailoring. Wiley College exhibited the most extensive vocational program among the private colleges, with classes in agriculture, carpentry, manual training, printing, typesetting, and tailoring. Bishop College had the least extensive, listing only manual training. Prairie View, the state-supported black college, showed the widest curriculum for men of all, with unique courses in ironworks, broom making, shoemaking, and mattress making.

Between 1915 and 1927, the course of vocationalism in Texas shifted from principally elementary courses to mostly work at the high school and college level. Enrollment statistics for 1927 illustrated a sharp decline in the number of elementary students and an increase in high school and college enrollments. Table 4 shows that out of the total private college enrollment of 2,016 only 179 (9 percent) were in elementary grades, while 614 (30.5 percent) were in secondary classes, and 1,219 (60.5 percent) were enrolled in college courses.

With this change in the student bodies, college administrators were free to restructure some vocational courses and

TABLE 4
Enrollments in Private and Public Black Colleges in Texas, 1927

| | Classification | | | |
Institution	Elementary	Secondary	College	Total
Bishop	0	123	316	439
Butler*				
Guadalupe*				
Jarvis Christian	80	60	14	154
Mary Allen*				
Paul Quinn	0	75	177	252
St. Philip's[†]	0	29	32	61
Samuel Huston	0	0	201	201
Texas	60	174	107	341
Tillotson	39	67	20	126
Wiley	0	86	352	438
Prairie View	0	372	559	931

SOURCES: U.S. Department of the Interior, Bureau of Education, *Survey of Negro Colleges and Universities*, prepared by Arthur J. Klein, Bulletin No. 7, pp. 795–881; Clarence W. Norris, Jr., "St. Philip's College: A Case Study of a Historically Black Two-Year College" (Ph.D. diss., University of Southern California, 1975), p. 137.

*Figures not available for Butler, Guadalupe, and Mary Allen colleges.

[†] St. Philip's figures are for 1929.

delete others. For men and women, the reshaping of vocational curricula took different paths. Industrial courses for men were being phased out (see Table 5). Of the eight colleges represented, only Bishop, Jarvis Christian, Texas, and Paul Quinn colleges still offered such coursework.

Vocational courses for women, however, continued to increase in number and educational level. By 1928, all the private colleges developed high school programs and St. Philip's College even offered college credit for some of its courses. Only Jarvis Christian and St. Philip's continued to carry any elementary classes. As their vocational programs moved to the secondary and collegiate plane, many of the colleges began to consolidate their household-related offerings under the heading of home economics. At the same time, business-related courses appeared. Bishop,

TABLE 5
Vocational Courses Offered in Private and Public Black Colleges in Texas, 1928

Institution	Courses for Women						
	Commercial	Cooking	Domestic Service	Dress-making	Home Economics	Nurse Training	Sewing
Bishop	X						X
Butler*							
Guadalupe*							
Jarvis Christian		X	X				X
Mary Allen*							
Paul Quinn					X		
St. Philip's		X	X	X	X		
Samuel Huston					X		
Texas	X			X	X		X
Tillotson	X	X	X		X		
Wiley	X	X		X			X
Prairie View					X	X	

Courses for Men

	Agriculture	Carpentry	Iron-works	Manual Training	Mechanical Arts	Printing	Tailoring
Bishop				X			
Butler*							
Guadalupe*	X						
Jarvis Christian				X			
Mary Allen*							
Paul Quinn		X	X				
St. Philip's					X		
Samuel Huston							
Texas	X			X			
Tillotson							
Wiley							
Prairie View	X				X		

SOURCES: U.S. Department of the Interior, Bureau of Education, *Survey of Negro Colleges and Universities*, prepared by Arthur J. Klein, Bulletin No. 7, pp. 795–881; Wiley College, *Catalog*, 1928, p. 14; Texas College, *Catalog*, 1927, p. 9; Clarence W. Norris, Jr., "St. Philip's College: A Case Study of a Historically Black Two-Year College" (Ph.D. diss., University of Southern California, 1975), pp. 125–28.
*Information not available for Butler, Guadalupe, and Mary Allen colleges.

Tillotson, and Wiley each provided several commercial courses in typing, shorthand, and bookkeeping. The state school, Prairie View, offered nursing training and home economics. Among the private schools, Wiley and Tillotson had the broadest programs for their women, programs encompassing both home economics and secretarial science.

As Tables 4 and 5 indicate, the private colleges in Texas were much closer to being true colleges. This process, which began in the early 1900s, accelerated in the 1930s and 1940s. Between 1925 and 1942, most of the black colleges terminated their elementary and high school programs in the liberal and vocational arts.[51] At the same time, they modified their existing vocational curricula. Reviewing the organization of vocational and terminal curricula for ten of these colleges offers several striking observations. By 1942, men's vocational programs, which had been declining, had almost completely disappeared. Only Paul Quinn and St. Philip's continued their vocational offerings. Of the two, Paul Quinn had the broadest curricula, offering Bachelor of Arts and Bachelor of Science degrees in tailoring, manual arts, and mechanical arts.[52]

Furthermore, the private colleges continued to stress their vocational classes for women, by elevating them to collegiate status. Table 6 shows that all the colleges had vocational majors in home economics, including courses in clothing, food preparation, home nursing, child care, consumer economics, interior decoration, and home management. Terminal or non-degree courses were also offered by Wiley, Samuel Huston, and St. Philip's. These included commercial courses in typing, shorthand, and cosmetology.[53] The continued emphasis upon vocational curricula for women made it clear that career opportuni-

---

[51]"The Inauguration of Earl Wadsworth Rand, Seventh President of Jarvis Christian College," 1976, Jarvis Christian College Archives, Hawkins; Davis, *Negro Education in East Texas*, p. 104; Toles, "History of Bishop College," p. 100; Webb and Carroll, *Handbook of Texas*, II: 781; U.S. Bureau of Education, *Survey of Negro Colleges and Universities*, pp. 795–881; Norris, "St. Philip's College," pp. 138, 181.

[52]Paul Quinn College, *Catalog*, 1942, pp. 72–88.

[53]*Waco Messenger*, May 4, 1934; Montgomery, *Senior Colleges for Negroes in Texas*, pp. 45–46; Jarvis Christian College, *Catalog*, 1939, pp. 16–17; Wiley College, *Catalog*, 1944, pp. 15, 27; Norris, "St. Philip's College," p. 177.

ties for black women remained more limited than they were for white females.

While the private colleges eliminated their vocational programs for men and streamlined their offerings for women, the public black schools, Prairie View and Houston, created even larger vocational curricula. Under pressure from the state legislature, Prairie View expanded its offerings to include eight separate majors in agricultural education, general agriculture, home economics, nursing education, industrial engineering, stationary engineering, building construction, and industrial education. Prairie View also provided no fewer than fifteen areas of terminal study. Houston College, which was founded in 1927, offered majors in home economics, tailoring, and business-related terminal studies.[54]

Between 1945 and 1954, vocationalism exhibited a brief resurgence, as thousands of black veterans returned from the Second World War. While most veterans were interested in pursuing traditional college majors, many sought degree and nondegree vocational education. As a result, there were wild fluctuations in college enrollments. Most veterans attended either Prairie View or Houston College, the public black institutions, which provided the widest variety of vocational classes. Consequently, the enrollment of these two institutions skyrocketed (see Table 7). Prairie View's student population grew from 1,420 in 1942 to 2,662 in 1954. Even more impressively, the enrollment of Houston College rose from 273 in 1942 to 2,779 in 1954. In keeping with its growth, the college was renamed Texas State University in 1947 and Texas Southern University in 1951.[55]

The demand for vocational training also affected the private colleges. Paul Quinn, which maintained its vocational degree program throughout the late 1940s and early 1950s, experienced an 87 percent increase in its enrollment. St. Philip's, which became a municipal junior college during this period, saw a phenomenal 356 percent increase in its enrollment. Several other schools responded to this demand by quickly resurrect-

[54] Montgomery, *Senior Colleges for Negroes in Texas*, pp. 45–46.
[55] *Texas Almanac*, 1942–56.

TABLE 6

Organization of Vocational and Terminal Curricula of Ten Black Colleges in Texas, 1942–43

Institution	Degrees	Division	Majors	Terminal Curricula
Bishop	B.A., B.S., B. of Music	Vocational, Professional	Home Economics	Clerks, File Clerks, Stenographers, Office Assistants, Tailoring, and Cleaning and Pressing
Houston *	B.A., B.S.	Applied Science, Business	Home Economics, Tailoring	
Jarvis Paul Quinn	B.A., B.S. B.A., B.S.	Vocational Education	Home Economics Home Economics, Industrial Arts, Manual Arts, and Mechanical Arts	
Prairie View	B.A., B.S., B. of Music, M.S.	Home Economics, Mechanical Arts	Agricultural Education, General Agriculture, Home Economics, Nursing Education, Industrial Education, Building Construction, Stationary Engineering, and Industrial Education	Auto Mechanics, Broom Making, Mattress Making, Carpentry, Laundering, Machine Shop, Painting, Decorating, Plumbing, Steam Fitting, Printing, Shoe Repair, Tailoring, and Garment Making

	Associate	Vocational	(Two Year) Secretarial Science, Clothing, Food Preparation, and Homemaking	
St. Philip's				Manual Arts, Mechanical Arts
Samuel Huston	B.A., B.S.	Fine and Practical Arts	Home Economics	Secretarial (Two Years)
Texas	B.A., B.S.	Home Economics	Home Economics	
Tillotson	B.A., B.S., B. of Home Economics	Home Economics	Home Economics	
Wiley	B.A., B.S.	Applied Arts	Home Economics	Cosmetology (One Year) Commercial (Two Years)

SOURCES: T. S. Montgomery, *The Senior Colleges for Negroes in Texas*, pp. 45–46; Paul Quinn College, *Catalog*, 1942, pp. 72–88; Clarence W. Norris, Jr., "St. Philip's College: A Case Study of a Historically Black Two-Year College" (PhD. diss., University of Southern California, 1975), pp. 177, 187.

*Name was changed to Texas State University for Negroes in 1947 and then to Texas Southern University in 1951.

TABLE 7

Biennial Enrollments for Private and Public Black Colleges in Texas, 1942–54

Institution	Enrollment by Year							Percent Increase or Decrease
	1942	1944	1946	1948	1950	1952	1954	
Bishop	318	231	864	1138	558	368	512	+61%
Butler	275	189	300	387	205	216	203	−26%
Huston-Tillotson*						765	545	
Jarvis Christian	163	136	205	200	129	130	203	+24%
Mary Allen	112	143	144	191	368	211	54	−51%
Paul Quinn	230	70	325	767	530	292	425	+87%
Prairie View	1420	1243	1507	2060	2305	2509	2662	+87%
St. Philip's	101	113	113	336	336	361	461	+356%
Samuel Huston*	310	270	469	616	560			
Texas	430	519	863	772	836	711	676	+57%
Texas Southern†	273	456	1746	2032	2185	2219	2779	+919%
Tillotson*	465	502	589	615	616			
Wiley	367	500	744	573	653	617	598	+63%

SOURCE: *Texas Almanac, 1942–56.*
*Samuel Huston and Tillotson colleges merged in 1952.
†Formerly named Houston College.

ing male vocational courses on their campuses. Texas College added agriculture, cabinetmaking, carpentry, tailoring, sheet-metal work, and auto mechanics.[56] Wiley and Bishop instituted classes in agriculture, while Jarvis Christian added courses in agriculture and "industrial trades" to its curriculum. These private colleges, consequently, experienced significant enrollment increases, which ranged as follows: Jarvis Christian, 24 percent; Texas, 57 percent; Bishop, 61 percent; Wiley, 63 percent; and Paul Quinn, 87 percent.[57] While it is difficult to ascertain, in spe-

[56] Ibid.

[57] John P. Jones, interview with author, Texas College, Tyler, July 19, 1979; William H. Ammons, interview with author, Texas College, Tyler, July 17, 1979; Texas College, *Catalog*, 1949, pp. 10–13; Banks interview; Wiley College, *Catalog*, 1945, pp. 27–28;

cific numbers, the effect of these new courses upon enrollment, it seems reasonable that the addition of vocational courses was a positive factor in the postwar growth these colleges enjoyed.

Curriculum-Related Service Programs

The locus of the "ebony tower," unlike some of its ivory counterparts, was firmly fixed within the black community. In addition to striving for academic excellence, the nation's black colleges always placed a strong emphasis upon the concept of service. To learn and go forth and serve was a common formulation of the goals of these institutions. The types of services black colleges provided included extension and adult education, propagation of democratic ideals, financial aid to needy students, instruction in vocational arts, furtherance of racial understanding, attention to ethics and values, and contributions by alumni to society. Black colleges, historically, viewed academic excellence and community service as one, providing an appreciation of the relationship between the curriculum and the world beyond the campus.[58]

All of the private black colleges in Texas developed programs that brought them into effective interaction with their communities. While each had its own priorities and levels of involvment, many participated in similar kinds of projects. Bishop, Texas, Tillotson, and Wiley operated nursery schools for the children of working mothers. Religious conferences for area ministers were regular occurrences at Jarvis Christian and Bishop colleges. For many years, Jarvis and Bishop colleges also offered well-organized community health programs, which included the services of part-time physicians and dentists, as well as clinical services for babies and area school children.[59]

One of the better service programs, among these schools, was found at Texas College. In cooperation with the Community

---

Jarvis Christian College, *Catalog*, 1945, p. 21; Toles, "Bishop College," p. 109; *Texas Almanac*, 1942–56.

[58] Gregory Kannerstein, "Black Colleges: Self-Concept," in *Black Colleges*, ed. Willie and Edmonds, p. 31.

[59] Montgomery, *Senior Colleges for Negroes in Texas*, p. 49.

Council of Tyler, the college helped to sponsor projects in home improvement, create a city library for blacks, and establish a day-care center. Working with the public black schools of Smith County, Texas College provided leadership and guidance by organizing regular educational workshops and supplying hundreds of student teachers. Vocational students also assisted the people of the community by repairing tools, reworking old furniture, and mending clothes.[60]

The broadest and most far-reaching community service program emerged at Bishop College. During the 1940s, leaders of the Marshall school sought to develop "mutually helpful relationships between the college and the homes, churches, farms, and the various community service agencies of East Texas."[61] In a report to the board of trustees in 1944, President Joseph J. Rhoads stressed the mutual benefits of the undertaking:

> Briefly, it is community service in which Bishop students and faculty participate, in vital cooperative relationships with other community leaders and agencies; but its supreme immediate purpose is that of relating life and learning in the general educational processes of the college. Obviously that is more significant than merely learning certain manipulative skills by engaging in helpful activities . . . ; it is more than "Learning by doing." It is Liberal Education.[62]

The Bishop service program was the outgrowth of a local self-help effort, known as the Ebenezer Community Project. Located three and one-half miles northwest of Marshall, the Ebenezer project began inauspiciously in 1939, with the organization of a Community Council in the Ebenezer Baptist Church. The council's first action was to varnish the church pews and place an electric clock in the chapel. The following year, the students and faculty of the college decided to participate in the project and established the Bishop College–Community Relations Program in East Texas.[63]

---

[60] Ibid.

[61] Ibid.

[62] Joseph J. Rhoads, "Interim Report to the Board of Trustees of Bishop College, In Re: College-Community Relations," July 1, 1944, p. 3; Melvin J. Banks Papers, Bishop College, Dallas.

[63] Ibid., pp. 3–4; Montgomery, Senior Colleges for Negroes in Texas, p. 50.

Working with the rural inhabitants, the faculty and staff set out to improve the quality of life for the people of the surrounding settlements and to provide Bishop students with experience in applying their educational skills. These goals were realized through supervised observations; student teaching and preaching; community surveys, conferences, and workshops; basic instruction in agricultural and mechanical arts for the farm home; and the participation by Bishop students in the improvement of family and community life. In addition, the college operated a year-round garden and canning unit; farm, poultry, and swine projects; a rural laboratory; a rural school hot lunch service; a rural community center and farm shop; and a nursery school. College officials even helped organize cooperative medical and dental services. Through the unselfish efforts of the faculty, political forums were held twice each month on Sundays, during which Bishop professors delivered lectures and led discussions about current issues and events.[64]

The Bishop College–Community Relations Project proved to be quite successful, both for the people of this rural area and for the students of the college. Specific accomplishments of the program for the community included:

1. The abolition of illiteracy among Negroes in the community.
2. The purification of the domestic water supply of the 75 Negro families.
3. The improvement of livestock and chickens.
4. Building sanitary toilets.
5. The cultivation of year-around gardens.
6. The erection of a community center and farm shop on the church-school campus.[65]

The program also benefited students by giving them practical experience. Business and accounting majors learned much about their intended life's work by serving in the cooperative commu-

[64] Montgomery, *Senior Colleges for Negroes in Texas*, p. 50; Rhoads, "Interim Report," pp. 3–29; Banks interview. Bishop College helped farmers ease their dependence upon cotton through the introduction of other cash crops such as tomatoes and cucumbers, which garnered $20,000 to $30,000 a year from a business in canned vegetables (Banks interview).

[65] Montgomery, *Senior Colleges for Negroes in Texas*, p. 50.

nity store or helping with the record-keeping of the canning unit. Education and theology majors also received valuable opportunities in the schools and churches of the area. Finally, vocational students applied their knowledge of home economics in areas ranging from cooking, canning, and sewing, to health and prenatal care.[66]

There is little doubt that the service programs of the private black colleges made a significant contribution to their students and communities. Although they did not individually possess the resources to operate community service programs as large as that of Prairie View A&M, as a group they did accomplish equally meaningful results.[67]

Conclusion

On the whole, the development of vocational and academic curricula in the private black colleges of Texas paralleled that in other black institutions. Like the Texas schools, most black colleges elsewhere were first established to offer classical training. Then during the 1880s, they began to adopt vocational courses. This was done more because of a perceived need and sense of service than because of influence by the industrial philosophy of Booker T. Washington. Willard Range, in his study of Negro colleges in Georgia, noted that during the late nineteenth century schools such as Atlanta University, Morehouse College, Spelman College, Clark University, Atlanta Baptist Seminary, and Paine Institute all "initiated students into the manual labor required on the grounds, buildings, farm dining hall, and kitchen." The same vocational duties were required of students attending Tillotson, Wiley, Bishop, Texas, and Paul Quinn colleges during the same period. Furthermore, as in the Texas

---

[66] Banks interview.

[67] Prairie View, through the State Extension Service, had, in 1943, a staff of eighty-nine home and county agents in fifty-six counties. The program enlisted the support of some seven thousand local leaders and communicated with more than forty-seven thousand families. Its major emphasis was vocational agriculture and home economics (Montgomery, *Senior Colleges for Negroes in Texas*, p. 51).

schools, Range found that the most common vocational courses offered in Georgia were sewing, cooking, nursing training, agriculture, printing, metalwork, and woodwork.[68]

Robert G. Sherer, in his analysis of the origins and conflicts of black education in nineteenth-century Alabama, observed that while most of the black colleges in that state developed vocational courses in the 1880s, Talladega College was unique in being committed to "some job-training from the first." Sherer pointed out that students of the AMA institution "worked repairing Swayne Hall and farming the land bought with it in 1867." He also noted that home economics and carpentry were offered almost immediately. This was different from the development of its sister school in Texas, Tillotson College, which opened in 1881 but did not offer vocational courses until 1888.[69]

While most black denominational colleges offered at least some elementary vocational work, they did not necessarily emphasize it. Instead, the majority of these colleges kept their vocational offerings separate from their liberal arts curricula. With the exception of women's courses, such as home economics, vocational courses were never enthusiastically developed. This was clearly the case in Texas, where male vocational courses were phased out during the 1930s and where women's courses were narrowed to degree programs in home economics and secretarial science. A similar decline in vocationalism was seen at schools like Howard University, Talladega College, Morehouse College, and others.[70] Only in the nation's public black colleges and universities did Booker T. Washington's philosophy continue to flourish.

Several factors played a role in the inability of vocational courses to gain acceptability among the private institutions. To begin with, purchasing and maintaining the equipment for vocational courses was extremely expensive. Willard Range observed, "Machinery and tools for shop instruction were costly

[68] Range, *Negro Colleges in Georgia*, pp. 70–71.

[69] Sherer, *Subordination or Liberation?* pp. 79–112, 144; *American Missionary* 49 (1895): 98.

[70] Rayford W. Logan, *Howard University: The First Hundred Years*, pp. 100, 116, 142–43; Sherer, *Subordination or Liberation?* p. 146.

and for all their approval and philanthropy neither the whites of the North or South were willing to increase the bounty sufficiently for this most expensive of all forms of education."[71]

More important, however, were the attitudes of these institutions. Founded in the classical tradition of white New England colleges, the black institutions ideologically opposed industrial education. Fearing that industrial training would prevent blacks from achieving social, economic, and political equality, most black denominational colleges in Texas refused to relinquish their efforts to construct strong liberal arts curricula. In the same vein, Willard Range noted that after 1900 black colleges in Georgia quietly began to abandon their trade courses. Like other black colleges around the country, they reverted to "their first love of a liberal arts curriculum and satisfied the advocates of the trade system with a few courses carried on in tumbledown shops." Reviewing this process in Alabama, Robert Sherer declared: "That most black educators in Alabama did not follow Washington's lead despite all his national prominence and connections has implications for understanding race relations and black history beyond Alabama. . . . This opposition often centered on principles, e.g., the importance of liberal educations, not just personalities."[72]

[71] Range, *Negro Colleges in Georgia*, p. 74.
[72] Ibid., p. 78; Sherer, *Subordination or Liberation?* p. 148.

3

Administration and Faculty

THE authors of most institutional studies, in addition to examining the curricula and philosophies of black colleges, have made efforts to understand their administrators and faculties. Without these dedicated men and women, few black colleges could have survived, let alone developed. In light of their prominent roles, this chapter will focus upon three aspects of these staffs in Texas. The continued white control of most black denominational colleges during the 1880s and 1890s stirred considerable controversy among black and white supporters of these schools. Consequently, a discussion of the issues surrounding racial composition of staffs in the black colleges will accompany an analysis of the racial makeup of the Texas schools. Next, sketches of the more outstanding black college presidents in Texas will emphasize both their common problems and their individual achievements. Finally, a review of the black college faculties will include discussions of salaries, levels of preparation, and the contributions of noteworthy professors.[1]

Racial Composition

As the tide of Reconstruction ebbed and as segregation laws emerged, blacks turned their interests inward toward the two in-

[1] Most studies of black colleges tend to be arranged chronologically, by presidential administrations, or topically, with a single chapter devoted to an outstanding figure. Such studies include Edward A. Jones, *A Candle in the Dark: A History of Morehouse*; Florence M. Read, *The Story of Spelman College*; Robert G. Sherer, *Subordination or Liberation? The Development and Conflicting Theories of Black Education in Nineteenth Century Alabama*; Addie Louise Joyner Butler, *The Distinctive Black College: Talladega, Tuskegee, and Morehouse*; George Ruble Woolfolk, *Prairie View: A Study in Public Conscience*. One of the few studies that provides a chapter on students and faculty is Willard Range, *The Rise and Progress of Negro Colleges in Georgia, 1865–1949*.

stitutions that offered them some opportunity for power—the church and the school. Many blacks appreciated the monetary and physical sacrifices of the white denominations but felt it was time for their race to assume the positions of religious and educational leadership. While most black churches acquired Negro pastors by 1890, changes in the racial composition of the missionary schools took much longer to effect and provoked a smoldering debate that divided both black and white communities.[2]

Many of the leaders within the white missionary societies were reluctant to give up control of their schools. Some believed that blacks were not mature enough to administer institutions of higher education. This paternalistic attitude was paralleled, however, by a genuine concern to maintain high academic standards in these institutions. Since there were not enough qualified black teachers and administrators available to operate all the denominational schools, the missionary leaders honestly felt that a change from white to black control should take place in an orderly, measured manner, and probably over a long period of time.[3]

The black community was divided over the issue. Arguments for black control of the northern denominational colleges were supported by the fact that several black denominations were already running such institutions. The African Methodist Episcopal Church (AME), African Methodist Episcopal Zion Church (AME Zion), and black Baptists had founded several colleges, as well as secondary and elementary schools, during the 1880s and early 1890s. These examples of black self-direction added weight to the reasoning of black clergymen, alumni, and younger people who wished to see their race control all black colleges. Other blacks in communities served by the missionary schools, however, opposed the drive for black control. Parents of school-age children generally objected to the idea of employing teachers on the basis of skin color and rejected arguments that only black instructors could achieve true rapport with black stu-

[2]James M. McPherson, *The Abolitionist Legacy: From Reconstruction to the NAACP*, pp. 262–68.
[3]Ibid., p. 269.

dents. Moreover, they considered white teachers to be better trained, more experienced, and better disciplinarians than black instructors.[4]

Each denomination approached the change from white to black control independently and at its own pace. In view of the divisions within its membership, the American Missionary Association decided in 1877 to move slowly on the issue. By 1895, only 12 of the AMA's 141 secondary school teachers were black. It was not until after 1905 that the AMA began to make significant changes in its college personnel. Meanwhile, the Baptist and Methodist churches, which had much larger black memberships, were forced into more immediate action. Of the two, the Methodists acted first. In 1868, the official report of the Freedmen's Aid Society noted: "Teachers for the freedmen must eventually be furnished by their own race. We must aid them in establishing good schools for the training of teachers and preachers and then as soon as possible deliver these institutions over to them for permanent support."[5] By 1915, 10 of the 23 Methodist colleges had black presidents and 71 percent of the faculties were black.

The Baptist schools, however, experienced a bitter power struggle. Young black Baptist leaders, called separatists, opposed the white, northern Home Mission Society. Black cooperationists, on the other hand, recognized the value of white support and desired to work with the society. The clash between these two opposing groups became so intense that several new Baptist conventions were spawned during the 1890s. In Texas, for example, the split between cooperationists, who supported Bishop College, and separatists, who backed Guadalupe College, led to a breakup of the state convention in 1893. In spite of such problems, the Home Mission Society continued to support several colleges and gradually moved toward black personnel. By 1915, about half the teachers, as well as two of the presidents, in the society's eight colleges were black. The Board of Missions

[4] Ibid., pp. 268–72.
[5] James S. Thomas, "The Rationale Underlying Support of Negro Private Colleges by the Methodist Church," *Journal of Negro Education* 29 (Summer, 1960): 254.

of Freedmen of the Presbyterian Church followed the pattern of the Methodists by beginning to phase out white instructors during the 1890s.[6]

The racial composition found in the staffs of the black denominational colleges in Texas reflected their founding bodies' attitudes, which generally followed one of two patterns. The colleges established by black religious denominations used black personnel in all administrative and teaching positions from the beginning. These included Texas College, a Colored Methodist Episcopal school; Paul Quinn College, an African Methodist Episcopal institution; and Butler and Guadalupe colleges, which were black Baptist enterprises. All-black staffs were employed in spite of the fact that few blacks in the late nineteenth century held advanced degrees. These colleges accepted teachers and administrators with limited training in an effort to have what they considered racially appropriate personnel.[7]

This was not surprising; it was consistent with the attitudes of the black religious denominations. Shunned or ignored by white denominations, many blacks joined together to found their own denomination in order to fulfill their religious needs independently and to acquire respect for their race. Black church bodies were dedicated to securing for their people the "full benefits of Christian fellowship" and "all of the rights, privileges, and benefits of American citizenship." Consequently, from the time of their inception, the CME, AME, AME Zion, and black Baptist denominations set their own goals and relied upon their own leadership to attain those goals.[8]

[6] McPherson, *Abolitionist Legacy*, pp. 273–92; Board of Missions for Freedmen of the Presbyterian Church in the United States of America, *Annual Report*, 1892, p. 16.

[7] U.S. Department of the Interior, Bureau of Education, *Negro Education: A Study of the Private and Higher Schools for Colored People in the United States*, prepared by Thomas Jesse Jones, Bulletin No. 39, II: 576–77, 587–90; Paul Quinn College, *Catalog*, 1891, p. 13; Allen C. Hancock, interview with author, Texas College, Tyler, July 18, 1979.

[8] Sherman L. Green, "The Rationale Underlying the Support of Colleges Maintained by the African Methodist Episcopal Church," p. 319, C. D. Coleman, "The Christian Methodist Episcopal Church: The Rationale and Policies Upon Which Support of Its Colleges is Predicated," pp. 313–14, and John M. Ellison, "Policies and Rationale Underlying the Support of Colleges Maintained by the Baptist Denomination," pp. 335–36, all in *Journal of Negro Education* 29 (Summer, 1960).

In contrast, the black colleges founded by predominantly white religious and missionary bodies began with overwhelmingly white faculties and staffs. The transition from white to black control in Texas followed no set timetable, but generally occurred between 1890 and 1930. The Methodist colleges—Wiley and Samuel Huston—were among the first to have black personnel. Wiley College installed its first black president, the Reverend I. B. Scott, in 1894, and exhibited its first all-black faculty in 1918. Samuel Huston College initiated its activities in the fall of 1900 with a totally black staff. St. Philip's College, an Episcopal school, elected Artemisia Bowden, a black, as its first president in 1902 and developed a black faculty shortly afterward. Jarvis Christian College, founded in 1913 by the Disciples of Christ, employed black teachers and administrators from the beginning. The Board of Missions for Freedmen of the Presbyterian Church started replacing whites with black staff members at Mary Allen Seminary during 1924. At Tillotson College, the change also arrived in 1924, with the selection of J. T. Hodges as president. The Tillotson faculty remained predominantly white, however, until the mid-1930s. In 1929 the Baptist Home Mission Society made Joseph J. Rhoads the first black chief executive of Bishop College. That same year, the Bishop faculty became entirely black when the last remaining white instructors retired.[9]

Administrators

The presidents of the black colleges in Texas were the most salient and often most imposing personalities in the daily life and operation of their institutions. The advancement these colleges achieved and the calamities they averted often resulted directly from the aggressive and pragmatic leadership of their chief executives. Reviewing the administrations of these men and women

[9] U.S. Bureau of Education, *Negro Education*, II: 594, 601; James G. Fleming and Christian E. Burckel, *Who's Who in Colored America: An Illustrated Directory of Notable Living Persons of African Descent in the United States*, 1950, 7th ed., p. 45; "History of Mary Allen Junior College," Crockett Public Library Archives, Crockett; Tillotson College, *Catalog*, 1935, pp. 6–9; Caesar Francis Toles, "The History of Bishop College" (M.A. thesis, University of Michigan, 1947), pp. 62, 78.

yields several observations. Most striking is that their collective leadership reflected a uniformity, rather than uniqueness, of style. Each president had distinctive qualities and possessed particular goals, but the demands of the job usually forced him or her into patterns of operation similar to those of other presidents. This leadership model was a highly centralized, direct-control style of command, in which the president monitored the individual and collective activities of students, faculty, and staff.[10]

The justifications for a centralized power structure in black colleges flowed from the common problems they faced. Educators such as Charles V. Willie, Marlene Y. MacLeish, and Tobe Johnson have pointed out that the two most significant determinants in the style of black college presidents were the "hostile, threatening, and nonsupportive environmental conditions surrounding black colleges" and the constant shortage of money. "The more hostile and threatening the environment," the easier it was for presidents to legitimize the centralization of power. Furthermore, the resources of black colleges remained so meager and the margin for error so small that black administrators simply could not afford mistakes. Consequently, they approached institutional change very cautiously and kept a wary eye on how and where the budget was expended.[11]

Faced with small enrollments, limited funds, overworked and underpaid staffs, and apathy or even hostility from the white community, black college presidents consciously chose to take a large share of the decision-making responsibilities for themselves. They exercised power to differing degrees, but most seemed to be guided by the ideal of furthering the quality of their school. Critics have suggested, however, that many presidents exhibited more concern about their personal ambitions for power than the safety of their institutions. White sociologists Christopher Jencks and David Riesman have declared, for example, that black college presidents ran their institutions as if

[10]Charles V. Willie and Marlene Y. MacLeish, "The Priorities of Presidents of Black Colleges," in *Black Colleges in America: Challenge, Development, Survival*, ed. Charles V. Willie and Ronald R. Edmonds, pp. 132–34.

[11]Ibid., p. 133; Tobe Johnson, "The Black College as System," *Daedalus* 100 (Summer, 1971): 801.

the colleges were their own "personal property." Ann Jones, a white professor who taught at a black college, characterized the president of her institution as a "paternalistic dictator."[12]

It is worth noting, however, that the majority of authors examining black higher education have concluded that, though black college presidents remained visibly in control, it was not for self-serving reasons. Black educator Tobe Johnson has maintained that black administrators exercised tight-fisted control for the sake of preserving their institutions. He has pointed out that they served as a buffer between the college and the hostile environment that surrounded it. Johnson has postulated that black college presidents were probably no more autocratic than many of the officials who governed the so-called "prestigious white schools" during the late nineteenth century.[13]

In the final analysis, the leadership model of the black college president was a complex one. On the one hand, these men and women appeared to be ingenious, pragmatic, and notoriously optimistic. Yet, they were also cautious, conservative, and sometimes authoritarian. Although they approached their occupations in much the same manner, they achieved rather varied results. Whether through skill, luck, or circumstance, a select number left an indelible stamp upon their institutions.

Prior to 1954, each of the private black colleges in Texas had one or more presidents who emerged as exceptional leaders. Some achieved respect as a result of their ability to handle diverse problems over an extended period of time. Others won recognition because they guided their institutions successfully through a major crisis. A brief sketch of each one's career will highlight the personalities and accomplishments of these men and women.

Among the early presidents of Paul Quinn College, Bishop Richard Harvey Cain was renowned for his efforts to save the fledgling AME school. As a South Carolina state senator, United States Congressman, newspaper editor, African Methodist Epis-

---

[12] Christopher Jencks and David Riesman, *The Academic Revolution*, pp. 48–49; Ann Jones, *Uncle Tom's Campus*, p. 119; Willie and MacLeish, "Presidents of Black Colleges," p. 133.

[13] Johnson, "Black College as System," pp. 800–801.

copal bishop, and college president, Cain influenced the lives of countless freedmen. He was born to free black parents on April 12, 1825, in Greenbriar, Virginia. Sometime between 1835 and 1840, his family moved to Cincinnati, Ohio, where he labored on the steamboats that plied the Ohio and Mississippi rivers. Deeply religious, he joined the Methodist Episcopal Church in 1841 and was licensed to preach in 1844. Cain found himself frustrated by racial prejudice in the Methodist Church and decided to join the African Methodist Episcopal Church in 1848. After being ordained the following year, he attended Wilberforce University before taking a pastorate in Brooklyn, New York.[14]

Cain's assertive personality and strong beliefs about racial equality primed him for the more radical individuals he encountered in New York. In the late 1850s a wave of black awareness expressed itself in the appearance of several colonization groups. Cain became interested in the African Civilization Society, which devoted efforts to the civilization and evangelization of Africa, the founding of a new republic on the West Coast of Africa, and the promotion of cultural pride among Afro-Americans. Cain soon developed firm friendships with black activists such as Martin R. Delany and Henry Highland Garnet. For the rest of his life, Cain maintained a twin commitment to the establishment of a positive identification with Africa and the belief that education held the key to the improvement of his race.[15]

In 1862, the AME Church promoted Cain to elder and, in 1865, sent him to work in the newly freed South Carolina Conference. There Cain succeeded in winning thousands of new converts. In Charleston alone, it was reported that Cain brought ten thousand into the AME fold. Cain became too much of a social activist, however, to confine his efforts to church work. Seeking to protect the freedmen from exploitation, Cain decided to

[14] Ronald L. Lewis, "Cultural Pluralism and Black Reconstruction: The Public Career of Richard H. Cain," *Crisis* (February, 1978): 57; Maurine Christopher, *Black Americans in Congress*, pp. 87–88; James H. Smith, *Vital Facts Concerning the African Methodist Episcopal Church; Its Origins, Doctrines, Government, Usages, Polity, Progress*, p. 142; William J. Simmons, *Men of Mark: Eminent, Progressive and Rising*, pp. 866–67.

[15] Christopher, *Black Americans in Congress*, p. 88; Lewis, "The Public Career of Richard H. Cain," p. 58.

enter politics. In 1868, he served as a delegate to the South Carolina State Constitutional Convention, where he crusaded for the incorporation of political rights for blacks and unrestricted, state-supported education. Following the adoption of the new constitution, Cain was elected to a two-year term in the state senate. At the same time, he purchased the *South Carolina Leader*, one of the first black newspapers in the state. Renaming it the *Missionary Record*, Cain used the paper not only to "scold and cajole" black Carolinians into political awareness, but also to wage unrelenting editorial warfare against corruption in the state government.[16]

Cain later won elections for two terms to the United States Congress, first in 1873 and then again in 1877. Like his black colleagues in the House, Cain fought for the passage of the Civil Rights Act of 1875. Then, when the Compromise of 1877 removed federal troops from the South and southern Democrats regained control of state governments, Cain witnessed the erosion of many of the civil rights reforms he had helped create. As the shadow of Jim Crow descended upon the nation, any optimism he held for racial equality faded. Embittered, Cain again turned his interests toward the concept of African colonization. He subsequently spent several years supporting the unsuccessful efforts of the American Colonization Society and the Liberian Exodus Joint Stock Steamship Company.[17]

In 1879, Cain left South Carolina and politics, when he was selected as AME bishop for the Texas-Louisiana Conference and president of Paul Quinn College. For the remainder of his life, Cain devoted himself to church duties and the education of black youth. The AME bishop estimated in 1881 that 700,000 black citizens in Texas and Louisiana had to depend upon their own meager resources for the education of their children. Since the states proved unwilling to provide adequate schools, Cain recognized the necessity for creating alternative educational opportunities. He hoped to accomplish this by transforming a

[16] Simmons, *Men of Mark*, p. 867; Christopher, *Black Americans in Congress*, pp. 88–89; Lewis, "The Public Career of Richard H. Cain," p. 59.

[17] Lewis, "The Public Career of Richard H. Cain," p. 59; Simmons, *Men of Mark*, p. 869.

struggling AME school in Waco into an institution of higher education.[18]

Although Paul Quinn College had been established in 1872, the school was still more dream than reality. After operating in an Austin AME church, the college was moved in the late 1870s to Waco, where it battled to survive as a trade school. The arrival of Richard H. Cain marked a turning point for the college. His personal charm, as well as his leadership qualities, brought renewed support for the college. In 1881, Cain, with AME and local backing, purchased two acres of the Garrison Plantation on the east side of Waco. The following year, twenty more acres were added. Upon this site a two-story brick structure was completed in 1882. President Cain acquired the money for this building through a "Ten Cents a Brick" campaign in which families of AME congregations purchased bricks at ten cents for the building.[19] When Cain delivered the formal opening address on April 4, 1882, he happily declared that education had been brought "to the very doors of the people." He noted that the college would provide elementary, secondary, and college courses which emphasized the classics. Although Paul Quinn would continue to offer industrial courses, no mention of such courses was made.[20]

The survival of the first black college in Texas was gained by the single-minded determination of Richard H. Cain. Moreover, the spirit and philosophy of the institution bore his proud impression. For example, Cain saw to it that all administrative and faculty positions were held by blacks. Cain believed that his race was destined to occupy a prominent place in the nation and maintained that blacks must seize the initiative and educate themselves because "all the elements in this nationality must be self sufficient . . . each adding strength to the whole." Cain preached that blacks must have enough national pride to develop their own educational institutions and added, "Not only

[18]Christopher, *Black Americans in Congress*, p. 96; Lewis, "The Public Career of Richard H. Cain," pp. 63–64; Simmons, *Men of Mark*, p. 867; and Smith, *Vital Facts Concerning the African Methodist Episcopal Church*, p. 142.

[19]Paul Quinn College, *Catalog*, 1978, p. 19.

[20]Lewis, "The Public Career of Richard H. Cain," p. 64; Paul Quinn College, *The Tiger* (Annual), 1927, p. 6; Paul Quinn College, *Catalog*, 1978, p. 19; Simmons, *Men of Mark*, pp. 867–68.

must Afro-Americans control their own institution, it must be staffed with a *faculty of distinguished colored gentlemen* teaching all courses both practical and theoretical."[21]

During the Great Depression, Paul Quinn was again fortunate to have a president who could lead it through another crisis with energy and imagination. A. S. Jackson, a native of Waco, served as president from 1932 to 1939. Raised in poverty, Jackson spent much of his childhood helping to support his family as a bootblack. After graduating from Paul Quinn, Jackson went on to distinguish himself in the work of his church, serving as the commissioner of education for the AME Church and as chairman of the local board of trustees of Paul Quinn College.[22]

Jackson faced depressing conditions when he succeeded President Dean Mohr. Not only was Paul Quinn laboring under the weight of a $42,000 debt, but the economic chaos caused by the Depression had drastically reduced enrollment. From an average student body of 250 in the 1920s, the enrollment had plummeted to 125 in 1930. In addition, the buildings, grounds, and furnishings of the AME institution were in almost total disrepair.[23]

With the college in such dire straits, just keeping it in operation would be an accomplishment. Yet A. S. Jackson established much higher goals. Taking office in June, 1933, Jackson set as his priority the complete renovation of the physical plant. As money was in short supply, he accomplished this feat by rebuilding or repairing as much of the campus as possible with student and staff labor. In the basement of the men's dormitory he created a repair shop, which was used in the restoration of chairs, desks, and dressers. Students and staff also volunteered to patch up and paint the campus buildings. Trees and shrubs were brought from nearby farms to dress up the campus. Jackson knew that his efforts not only revived a tired, old campus, but also built a new sense of pride in the faculty and students.[24]

[21] Lewis, "The Public Career of Richard H. Cain," p. 64.

[22] Paul Quinn College, *The Tiger*, 1927, p. 6; *Waco Messenger*, June 9, 1933.

[23] *Waco Messenger*, June 23, 1933; *Texas Almanac*, 1931, p. 282; McClennon Phillip Harvey, ed., *A Brief History of Paul Quinn College, 1872–1965*, p. 37.

[24] *Waco Messenger*, June 23 and July 14, 1933.

Jackson believed that if the college were to survive, it must have new sources of income and must develop a better academic program. Throughout his tenure in office, Jackson made himself available to AME groups all over the state. Traveling to large and small communities, he always stressed the importance Paul Quinn represented to black education in Texas and the need to support it. In 1935, Jackson organized a special fund-raising group, composed of alumni and friends. The organization, which Jackson called the Progressive Club, helped in many ways—by holding development drives for library books, donating trees and shrubbery, and appealing to the state Department of Education for an improved accreditation. The Progressive Club also helped sponsor a weekly fifteen-minute radio program on station WACO. Hosted by Jackson himself, the show broadcast the virtues of Paul Quinn College and raised the recognition level of the school. Entertainment was often provided by the Paul Quinn Quartet Club. At the same time, Jackson improved the academic quality of the school by insisting faculty members return to graduate school. In spite of limited funds, Jackson also arranged for the creation of more senior-level courses.[25]

The efforts of A. S. Jackson proved quite successful. At the end of his first four-year term, he had managed to pay $10,500 on the college debt and had increased the student enrollment to over three hundred. The college board of trustees was so impressed with his leadership that they broke with college tradition and reelected Jackson for a second term. The Texas Department of Education also rewarded Jackson by granting Paul Quinn a four-year senior college accreditation in 1938.[26] Such recognition acknowledged the fact that A. S. Jackson not only had saved Paul Quinn from extinction but also had strengthened its academic and financial position beyond previous levels.

Among the presidents who served Wiley College, none did so with more distinction than Matthew Winfred Dogan. The board of trustees and the Methodist Episcopal Church placed

[25]Waco Messenger, July 21, 1933, February 8, 1935, and August 25, 1933; Paul Quinn College, Catalog, 1937, p. 19.
[26]Waco Messenger, May 28, 1937, April 23, 1938.

complete confidence in Dogan, who guided Wiley through almost half a century of diverse problems, from 1896 to 1942.[27]

Dogan was born to slave parents on December 21, 1863, in Pontotoc, Mississippi. Between 1879 and 1884, he attended Rusk College in Holly Springs, Mississippi. There he received Bachelor of Arts and Master of Arts degrees. Dogan later earned a Ph.D. from Walden College and a Doctor of Divinity degree from New Orleans College. In 1889, at the age of twenty-six, Dogan became a professor of mathematics at Central Tennessee College, in Nashville. The diminutive scholar displayed a wide variety of talents and interests outside the classroom by working with such groups as the National Convention of Colored Men. He also lectured and wrote articles for the Methodist Church. His magnetism and ability led a friend to observe, "The man has thunder, and he's not afraid to unleash it."[28]

When the Board of Education of the Methodist Church asked Dogan to take over the presidency at Wiley in 1896, the college was little more than an elementary school. Of an enrollment of 350, well over 90 percent were in elementary, preparatory, or industrial courses. In order to make Wiley a respected institution of higher learning, Dogan sought to recruit better students, attract more financial aid from the church and the local community, improve public relations, and upgrade the college facilities.[29]

Changes did not occur overnight, but Dogan soon made Wiley one of the leading private black colleges in Texas. In 1930, Wiley became one of the first black colleges in the state to eliminate its elementary and secondary programs. Dogan also helped improve the quality of the Wiley faculty. When he took control in 1896, over half the faculty held no college degree of any type. By 1915, nearly all had B.A. degrees, and four held master's degrees. Dogan alone had a doctorate. In 1933, the faculty in-

[27] Wiley College, *Catalog*, 1976, p. 13.

[28] Thomas Yenser, ed., *Who's Who in Colored America: A Biographical Dictionary of Notable Living Persons of African Descent*, 4th ed., p. 161; Effie Kaye Adams, *Tall Black Texans: Men of Courage*, p. 185.

[29] Wiley College, *Catalog*, 1892, p. 14; Adams, *Tall Black Texans*, p. 186.

cluded two doctoral and twelve master's degrees in its ranks. By 1945, those figures had increased to three Ph.D.'s and twenty-nine M.A.'s. Consequently, the Wiley faculty became known as the strongest among the black colleges in Texas.[30]

Steady progress was also made in facilities, alumni relations, and accreditation. Eight major buildings and renovations occurred under Dogan's administration, including the construction of the first Carnegie Library west of the Mississippi River. In an effort to boost alumni support and foster a steady stream of high-quality students, Dogan created Wiley College alumni associations throughout the country. These associations also collected donations, which were forwarded to the college each year.[31] Most importantly, Dogan acquired academic recognition for Wiley. During the 1920s, Wiley achieved accreditation by the Departments of Education in ten states, including Texas. In 1933, Wiley reached another milestone when it became the first black college west of the Mississippi River to receive an "A" rating from the Southern Association of Colleges.[32]

Though an energetic and tough-minded administrator, Dogan evidenced an outward love and concern for his students. He has been characterized as a gentle, loving man who was not feared by his students, but rather loved and respected. George H. Chandler, a former Wiley student, recalled Dogan as a dedicated leader who strove to give each student as much attention as humanly possible and whose goal was to help every Wiley student become a "self-helper." Commenting on Dogan's style of leadership, Effie Kaye Adams noted, "It would grieve the president to learn that the Discipline Committee was about to 'ship' certain students home because of grades or some gross infraction of the college rules, and he was always willing to give them another chance. He believed in the ideals of the Christian

[30] U.S. Department of the Interior, Bureau of Education, *Survey of Negro Colleges and Universities*, prepared by Arthur J. Klein, Bulletin No. 7, p. 831; *Houston Informer*, October 28, 1933; Wiley College, *Catalog*, 1945, pp. 11–12; U.S. Bureau of Education, *Negro Education*, I: 20; Thompson, "Black Religious Colleges in East Texas," pp. 49–51.

[31] E. C. Evans, *The Story of Texas Schools*, p. 220; Adams, *Tall Black Texans*, p. 185.

[32] *Houston Informer*, December 16, 1933; George H. Chandler, interview with author, Wiley College, Marshall, July 20, 1979; Wiley College, *Catalog*, 1928, pp. 28–29.

faith, the brotherhood of man, and in trying to go the 'second mile.'"[33]

Dogan had many interests, and somehow found the time in his busy schedule to be involved in numerous state and national organizations. He remained deeply committed to his faith and led the Texas delegation to the General Conference of the Methodist Episcopal Church on several occasions. Dogan belonged to the National Negro Business League, the Interracial Committee of Texas, the Free and Accepted Masons, the Knights of Pythias, and Phi Beta Sigma fraternity. He served as the president of both the state and the national Association of Colored Teachers and helped organize the Southern Athletic Conference and Oratorical Association, and the Intercollegiate Athletic Association for black colleges in Texas.[34]

The Great Crash of 1929, followed by the depression years, struck individuals and institutions alike with dread. In 1929, Tillotson College was experiencing its own version of the proverbial lean years as it struggled for its institutional life. At this juncture, a bespectacled woman, fiftyish, buxom, self-assured, and possessed of indefatigable strength and courage, came to the capital city of Texas. Her mission was to rescue the small Negro college from the brink of collapse. This woman's life and her performance as president of Tillotson College represent one of the truly noteworthy chapters in black, as well as women's, history.[35]

Mary Elizabeth Branch, one of six children, was born in Farmville, Virginia, on May 20, 1881.[36] She received her high school education in the normal school of Virginia State College in Petersburg. Her career as an English teacher began in the elementary school of Blackstone, Virginia, at the meager salary of $27.50 per month. From this humble beginning, Branch was

[33] Adams, *Tall Black Texans*, p. 186; Chandler interview.

[34] Adams, *Tall Black Texans*, p. 186; Yenser, *Who's Who in Colored America*, p. 161.

[35] Olive D. Brown and Michael R. Heintze, "Mary Branch: Private College Educator," in *Black Leaders: Texans for Their Times*, ed. Alwyn Barr and Robert A. Calvert, p. 114; Olive Durden Brown, interview with author, Austin, May 15, 1980.

[36] *Houston Informer*, July 15, 1944, indicates that Mary Branch was born on May 20, 1882, while Yenser, in *Who's Who in Colored America*, p. 55, and J. M. Cattell, ed., *Leaders in American Education*, p. 111, give her year of birth as 1881.

asked to join the faculty of her alma mater, Virginia State College, where she taught for the next twenty years. Her popularity with the students was unrivaled, and her courses, known as "Branch's English," were always crowded, not because they were easy, but because they proved to be the most challenging and interesting.[37]

In the summers, she pursued undergraduate course work at the University of Pennsylvania, Columbia University, and the University of Chicago. From Chicago she received a bachelor's degree in 1922 and a master's degree in English in 1925. She also began studies toward a doctorate in the School of Education.[38]

In the late 1920s, Branch accepted a position teaching social studies at Sumner Junior College in Kansas City, Kansas. The following year, she became Dean of Girls at Vashon High School in Saint Louis, which was then the largest school of Negro women in the nation. Professionally, she had risen to the very pinnacle of teaching in the world of black female education.[39]

Then, in 1930, Branch received a call from the American Missionary Association to become president of Tillotson College. The decision was difficult, as it would mean giving up the best income she had ever had, as well as another offer from a local community college. On two occasions, she turned down AMA appeals, but in the end she relented, noting:

I thought of the numbers of white teachers who had gone South for years since the Civil War and worked among an alien race for no other reason than a Christian interest in the underprivileged. They had made far greater sacrifices than I would be called upon to make. I thought and prayed over the matter and finally got a definite feeling that I should go to Tillotson.[40]

Branch knew that Tillotson was in a state of decline, but beyond that, she was aware of little else about her new responsibility. On July 1, 1930, Branch got the first glimpse of what awaited

---

[37] Tillotson College, *Catalog*, 1945, p. 3; Mary Jenness, *Twelve Negro Americans*, pp. 85–88.

[38] *Austin American*, July 7, 1944.

[39] William H. Jones, "Tillotson College, From 1930–1940: A Study of the Total Institution" (Mimeographed, Austin, 1940); Jenness, *Twelve Negro Americans*, pp. 92–93.

[40] Jenness, *Twelve Negro Americans*, pp. 93–94.

her. Entering the campus through the pitiful remnants of what used to be a fence, she made her way up a "gullied and scraggly path through underbrush so thick that a fox could—and did— hide in it." The campus contained little more than half a dozen timeworn buildings, surrounded by old, weather-beaten mesquite trees. Touring these structures, she entered the administration building, where she found a cramped room, eight by ten feet, which she discovered to be the president's office.[41]

A weaker person might have turned around and walked away, but Mary Branch remained. For her, the school became a challenge which she accepted with hope and self-assurance. Given a free hand by the AMA, Branch laid out a five-year plan to upgrade the physical plant and attract more college students. The library became one of her first projects. There were barely two thousand volumes in the library suitable for college use. By soliciting donations from friends, local businessmen, and civic groups, Branch expanded the library's holdings over the next fourteen years to more than twenty-one thousand volumes.[42] Through her efforts, old buildings such as the women's dormitory and the industrial shop were renovated, while new ones arose. Under her leadership were built a laundry, a college co-op, a home management house, a men's dormitory, several staff homes, and the gymnasium which now bears her name. The campus also added new trees and shrubs, as well as athletic fields.[43]

In order to attract more students, Branch initiated a number of institutional changes. First, she eliminated the high school program and increased the college budget. Then she doubled the size of the faculty and required that all Tillotson faculty members have at least a master's degree. Teachers went out into all corners of the Southwest to recruit qualified students, while small scholarships were offered to assist the most needy. Students were also attracted to the campus through such events as

[41] Ibid., pp. 94–95; Brown and Heintze, "Mary Branch," in *Black Leaders*, ed. Barr and Calvert, p. 118.
[42] See "Report: Lincoln Memorial Fund 1931–1932, 1932–1933"; and the letters Branch wrote in February, 1934, soliciting donations to the library fund, collected in the Mary E. Branch Papers, Archives, Huston-Tillotson College.
[43] *Austin American*, April 20, 1951.

"play day activities," which brought high school girls from around the state to participate in athletic events.[44] Finally, in 1935, the Branch administration returned Tillotson to a coeducational status. Because of such innovations, the college's enrollment grew steadily from 140 students in 1930 to 362 in 1938, and to 502 in 1944.[45]

Branch was also successful in the field of student affairs. She abolished mandatory chapel, while permitting social fraternities and sororities, and promoted the formation of academic and athletic clubs.[46] Yet her religious training, which had begun in the African Methodist Episcopal Church and later included worship in the Episcopal and Congregational churches, endowed her with many conventional Christian and moral principles which she applied in dealing with students. One such belief was that all students should be willing to work for at least a portion of their educational expenses. Thus, almost every student at Tillotson held some sort of part-time job.[47]

Branch also sought to generate a positive working relationship with the surrounding community. To this end, she involved herself and her students in community affairs. Her interests were many and varied. She supported the work of charity clubs, participated in forums, served on committees, and concerned herself with city politics and public school operations. She established a rapport with faculty members at the University of Texas and at the nearby black college, Samuel Huston, as well as with public school administrators and teachers. She also brought to the campus noteworthy speakers and artists of local, state, and national reputation.[48] Although her frankness, which often approached brusqueness, irritated some, few ever thought of

[44] Brown and Heintze, "Mary Branch," in *Black Leaders*, ed. Barr and Calvert, p. 119.

[45] *Texas Almanac*, 1931, 1939, and 1945.

[46] Jenness, *Twelve Negro Americans*, p. 98. The national Greek letter organizations founded at Tillotson College were Omega Phi Fraternity (1936), Delta Sigma Theta Sorority (1936), Alpha Kappa Alpha Sorority (1939), Alpha Psi Alpha Fraternity (1939), Zeta Phi Beta Sorority (1940), Sigma Gamma Rho Sorority (1945), and Phi Beta Sigma Fraternity (1946) (Tillotson College, *Catalog*, 1949, p. 18).

[47] Brown and Heintze, "Mary Branch," in *Black Leaders*, ed. Barr and Calvert, pp. 119–20.

[48] For example, Branch invited a local white Baptist minister, Reverend Blake

overlooking Branch in civic matters. Her contemporaries frequently sought her for advice and many group decisions hung upon her opinion.

One such civic organization that claimed her interest was the Austin chapter of the National Association for the Advancement of Colored People (NAACP). She served as chapter president in 1943, always encouraged her students to participate, and sponsored a student chapter on campus. She was also a member of the State Interracial Commission of Texas. Her involvement in civil rights activities was linked to the social conditions of the era. Spurred on by the humiliations of Jim Crowism, the Tillotson president supported almost any plan that might improve living conditions for black people. She apparently used her powers as the chief business officer of the college to boycott or close accounts with those businesses which enforced segregation. Many times coworkers would venture to suggest a curtailment of these activities, but such advice only elicited a greater determination on her part to proceed.[49]

During the depression years, Mary Branch also devoted much of her time to working with the New Deal's National Youth Administration (NYA), which provided part-time jobs and vocational training for needy high school and college students. In 1935, the NYA director for Texas, Lyndon B. Johnson, appointed Mary Branch to the state's NYA Negro Advisory Board. Serving with such leading Negro figures as Joseph J. Rhoads, president of Bishop College, and L. V. Williams, principal of Booker T. Washington High School in Dallas, Mary Branch worked to ensure that the federal jobs program would benefit black, as well as white, students. Efforts of the Negro Advisory Board proved reasonably successful. By mid-1936, some 770 students in the black colleges of Texas received assistance from the NYA program.[50]

The 1930s and early 1940s were hard, strange, and often

Smith, and noted black educator Benjamin Mays of Atlanta to serve as commencement speakers (*Austin American Statesman*, May 21, 1944).

[49]William Pickens to B. F. Caruthers, November 30, 1936, NAACP Papers, Library of Congress; Cattell, *Leaders in Education*, pp. 111.

[50]Mary E. Branch to Lyndon B. Johnson, March 11, 1936; Clippings from *Dallas Gazette*, March 7, 1936; *Marshall News Messenger*, March 1, 1936; *Negro Labor News* (Houston), December 31, 1935; *Houston Informer*, January 18, 1936; and "NYA Report,

frightening times, yet through these years Mary Branch revealed a strength and vision which brought recognition to her college. In 1931, Tillotson College received unconditional senior college standing from the Texas Department of Education. During 1933, the Southern Association of Colleges and Secondary Schools approved the college as a class "B" institution. Two years later, Tillotson returned to a coeducational status and in 1936 was admitted to membership in the American Association of Colleges. Finally, in 1943, the college received an "A" rating by the Southern Association. This was an impressive succession of achievements for the Branch administration, and they did not go unrewarded. For her services to the college, Mary Branch was granted two honorary degrees—the first Doctor of Pedagogy bestowed by Virginia State College and a Doctor of Laws degree from Howard University.[51]

Her wish to make Tillotson a successful and respected college for black youth led Branch to encourage effecting a coalition with Samuel Huston College, a Methodist Episcopal school, which was also in Austin. The two colleges were situated less than a mile apart, offered essentially the same curricula, and faced the same need for supplementary funding and increased enrollment. Branch and Karl E. Downs, president of Samuel Huston, entered upon several cooperative programs, such as sharing faculty members and presentations of speakers and artists. Although Branch and Downs both died before the colleges merged in 1952, they played a decisive role in the movement toward the creation of Huston-Tillotson College.[52]

At the height of her career, Mary Branch was struck down by illness. In the summer of 1944, she sought medical consultation at Johns Hopkins University Hospital in Baltimore, concerning a goiter ailment. While in the East, she decided to visit

1936" in National Youth Administration Papers, Box 10, Lyndon B. Johnson Library, Austin.

[51]Chrystine I. Shackles, *Reminiscences of Huston-Tillotson College*, pp. 33, 49; Jenness, *Twelve Negro Americans*, pp. 95–99; Brown and Heintze, "Mary Branch," in *Black Leaders*, ed. Barr and Calvert, p. 122.

[52]"Memorandum Concerning the Proposed Merger of Samuel Huston and Tillotson College," and William H. Jones to Fred J. Brownlee, July 1, 1948, Addendum: Huston-Tillotson College.

her two sisters in New Jersey. During her stay, she again became seriously ill and was rushed to a local hospital, where she died on July 6.[53]

The career of Mary Branch as a college president placed her in an elite group of black women who successfully directed institutions of higher education. During the 1930s and 1940s, Branch had only two comparable contemporaries. One, Mary McLeod Bethune, founded Bethune-Cookman College in Florida and gained national prominence by serving as the director of the Division of Negro Affairs for the National Youth Administration under Franklin D. Roosevelt and as a member of the Committee for National Defense under President Harry S. Truman.[54] The other, Artemisia Bowden, served St. Philip's College in San Antonio as instructor, principal, dean, and president from 1902 to 1954.[55] The contributions of Mary Branch are equally impressive. The impact of her handiwork is clearly visible if one compares enrollment statistics between 1930 and 1944 for the various black colleges in Texas. During this period, ten of the thirteen black colleges experienced declines in their enrollments, and one school, Guadalupe College in Seguin, was forced to close its doors in 1937. Meanwhile, the enrollment at Tillotson soared from 140 in 1930 to 502 in 1944. This 258.5 percent increase in enrollment, coupled with the improvements fostered by Branch in the faculty, staff, and facilities, convinced the Southern Association to award Tillotson an "A" rating in 1943.[56]

Bishop College, one of the oldest private black colleges in Texas, might have closed during the depression years had it not been for the leadership of its first black president, Joseph J. Rhoads. Born in Marshall, Texas, on October 30, 1890, J. J. Rhoads graduated from Bishop College in 1910. He later earned

[53] *Austin American Statesman*, July 7, 1944.

[54] *San Antonio Register*, December 25, 1942; Mary McLeod Bethune, "A College on a Garbage Dump," in *Black Women in White America: A Documentary History*, ed. Gerda Lerner, pp. 134–35.

[55] Clarence W. Norris, Jr., "St. Philip's College: A Case Study of a Historically Black Two-Year College" (Ph.D. diss., University of Southern California, 1975), pp. 68–70, 82, 166, 193, 210.

[56] *Seguin Enterprise*, February 14 and 21, 1936, January 29, 1937; *Texas Almanac*, 1930–40.

advanced degrees at the University of Michigan and Yale University. While pursuing his graduate studies, Rhoads served as assistant principal of Pemberton High School in Marshall from 1910 to 1918, instructor at Tuskegee Institute from 1919 to 1922, and principal of Booker T. Washington High School in Dallas from 1923 to 1929.[57]

In 1929 the American Baptist Home Mission Society selected Joseph J. Rhoads as president of Bishop College. Rhoads inherited an awesome task: the campus was shamefully rundown, the faculty and staff were demoralized, and enrollment was slipping. Rhoads proposed a plan of renovation, which he called the New Development Program. The program called for a vigorous financial campaign, the reorganization of an outdated classical curriculum, and the establishment of a department of public relations.[58]

To his regret, Rhoads discovered a number of hurdles had to be cleared before any progress could be made. First, the administration faced the problems revealed by a study conducted under former president C. H. Maxon. The study investigated the possibility of moving the college to a site in Marion County, some twenty miles away. The fact that the former administration had allowed the physical plant to deteriorate alarmed many Marshallites into believing the school would have to leave the city. This suspicion appeared to be substantiated by a federal government study of black colleges in 1928, which suggested that the Bishop campus was strategically located, but too small to support its needs: "The present campus of Bishop College consists of a tract of valuable real estate located in the heart of the residential section of Marshall. It is small in size and because of the high value of surrounding property the expansion of the institution's physical plant is practically impossible."[59]

The popular belief that the college was leaving Marshall

---

[57] *Austin American Statesman*, October 11, 1951; Melvin J. Banks, interview with author, Bishop College, July 23, 1979; Bishop College, *Catalog*, 1978, p. 6; Fleming and Burckel, *Who's Who in Colored America*, p. 436.

[58] Bishop College, *Catalog*, 1945, p. 17.

[59] U.S. Bureau of Education, *Survey of Negro Colleges and Universities*, p. 822.

had the effect of slowing down or drying up many sources of financial support. This became painfully evident when Rhoads appealed to the General Education Board for funds to begin his development program. The board met his request with two questions. First, the board wondered if it should extend funds to any of the Baptist colleges in Texas, Arkansas, and Louisiana until Baptist supporters could agree on the primacy of one institution. Second, the board wanted to know the future location of Bishop College.[60]

A second source of pressure on Rhoads was the Texas State Board of College Examiners, which was considering the withdrawal of state accreditation from Bishop. A recent examination had shown serious deficiencies in the facilities and programs of the college. President Rhoads understood that Bishop retained its standing only because the examination had occurred during the transition from Maxon to himself and, consequently, the agency wished to give him a chance to rectify the situation. A third obstacle was the national economic collapse of 1929 and the onset of the Depression. In such hard times, raising funds from alumni and friends would be especially difficult.[61]

Between 1929 and 1944, Bishop struggled to survive, while Rhoads forged ahead with a series of moves to improve the institution. In order to enhance the reputation of the college and make it more appealing to serious students, Rhoads toughened entrance and graduation requirements. In describing this institutional shift, Rhoads declared:

This is the beginning of an aggressive movement to select with unusual care our students; to make . . . contacts with the homes from which our students come; and to give some financial aid to the most needy. . . . We deliberately and positively change the nature of our approach to applicants for admission to Bishop College. It is no longer a matter of accepting "whosoever will come." Applications must be made and other evidence presented to convince us that they are fit from a standpoint of character and scholarship.

    . . . we have no scholarships for high school graduates whose only

[60] Toles, "History of Bishop College," p. 83.
[61] Ibid., pp. 80–81.

recommendation is that of a good athlete and whose sole ambition is that of making the varsity or having a good time. We shall direct our appeal only to the serious minded and discriminating—to those who care.[62]

In September, 1933, he established a college guidance department to counsel students in educational, vocational, social, religious, and recreational matters. An effort was also made to assist students in finding jobs. Rhoads also played a central role in working with the New Deal's National Youth Administration (NYA), which funded part-time jobs and industrial training for needy high school and college students. Working with prominent black leaders such as Mary Elizabeth Branch, president of Tillotson College, and L. V. Williams, principal of Booker T. Washington High School in Dallas, Rhoads sought to acquire an appropriate portion of the federal job funds for black students.[63]

In an effort to win renewed confidence from both the General Education Board and area supporters, Rhoads initiated an exhaustive institutional study. The sweeping investigation dealt with such matters as the future location of the college, community support for the New Development Program, the adequacy of the present campus, and the cost of relocating. It also explored the contribution of the college to the education of local students, the influence of Bishop graduates on education, Bishop's interest in agriculture, the possibility of cooperation with other area colleges such as Wiley, and the potential for a college center in Dallas.[64]

The report, which was forwarded to the General Education Board, concluded that Bishop should remain in Marshall. The report made special note of the contributions of the college to blacks in East Texas, the support the college received from the Marshall citizenry, and the specialized mission of Bishop College, to both its students and the community. This last point was significant because the board had wondered about the advisability of having two similar black colleges in the same town. To

[62]*Houston Informer*, January 11, 1930.
[63]*Houston Informer*, September 23, 1933; "NYA Report: 1936," NYA Papers.
[64]Toles, "History of Bishop College," pp. 85–86.

show that Bishop was making a unique contribution, Rhoads pointed out to the board that, unlike Wiley College, Bishop had developed accredited programs in religion, music, and home-making. In addition, he cited the Bishop College–Community Relations Program as an example of distinctive service to the community.[65]

In response, the General Education Board offered Bishop a conditional grant of $61,000 to be applied to Rhoads's proposed $146,000 improvement program. In order to qualify for the grant, the Rhoads administration had to raise the remaining $85,000. With this goal, the New Development Program got under way. By 1948, the new public relations department had collected the required $85,000. At the same time, Rhoads altered the college curriculum from a classical to a liberal arts format with a junior and a senior division. The junior division became a two-year curriculum in general education, while the senior level provided a traditional bachelor's degree program. In addition, Rhoads instituted a broadbased college–community relations program, made up of several projects, the first of which was the Sabine Farms Project. Begun in 1944, this program was a unique rural laboratory located south of Marshall consisting of seventy-five small farms. The program combined education with community service in an effort to improve the standard of living among poor black farmers and to offer a practical application of the courses taught at Bishop. Under this program, a community center was built, courses in agriculture and homemaking were taught, and a full schedule of cooperative college-community activities was offered. From the Sabine Farms Project, Bishop developed a department of agriculture, which used area farms as laboratories in which students could acquire a "practical acquaintance with the natural resources of East Texas and modern methods by which they were developed, utilized, and conserved."[66]

[65] Joseph J. Rhoads, "Interim Report to the Board of Trustees of Bishop College, In Re: College-Community Relations," July 1, 1944, Melvin J. Banks Papers, Bishop College.
[66] Banks interview; Bishop College, *Catalog*, 1945, pp. 58–66; Toles, "History of Bishop College," pp. 98–106, 109.

The college arranged similar projects in the Ebenezer and Antioch-Leigh communities. There college officials helped with basic education, water purification, sanitation, community centers, health programs, and crop and livestock improvement. Shops were also constructed which sponsored canning, tool repair, and homecrafts seminars. In 1946, the college established trade schools for veterans in Texarkana and Kilgore; these schools taught auto mechanics, carpentry, electricity, radio, plumbing, welding, and tailoring.[67]

President Rhoads did not limit his definition of "community" to Marshall or East Texas, for he announced the opening of a college center at Dallas during 1946. The purpose of this center was to meet the educational needs of thousands of returning veterans and other nontraditional students in North Texas. Rhoads took care to prevent the center's becoming just another extension program and made every effort to create in Dallas the atmosphere, ideals, and purposes of the home campus.[68]

In 1951, Joseph J. Rhoads died, after twenty-one years at the Bishop helm. During this period he had succeeded not only in preserving the college, but also in enlarging and enriching it. Aware that education must not be confined to the campus classroom, Rhoads brought the benefits of higher education to the surrounding black community in a degree and manner unmatched among the black private colleges in Texas. The Rhoads administration provided an excellent example of how some black college presidents achieved a wider relevance for their institutions.

At Texas College, W. R. Banks and D. R. Glass established distinguished records by overcoming crises. W. Rutherford Banks, who served from 1915 to 1926 as the sixth president of Texas College, was born on August 8, 1881, in Hartell, Georgia. He received his A.B. degree from Atlanta University and later earned a master's degree from Paul Quinn College (1922). Before coming to Texas College, Banks taught at Fort Valley Industrial School in Georgia from 1909 to 1912, and served as the principal

[67]T. S. Montgomery, *The Senior Colleges for Negroes in Texas*, p. 50; Banks interview; Toles, "History of Bishop College," p. 110.
[68]Toles, "History of Bishop College," pp. 111–13.

of Kowaliga Industrial School in Alabama from 1912 to 1915. Banks also received ordination as a minister in the Colored Methodist Episcopal Church (CME).[69]

Banks became noted for his determination to upgrade the academic quality of Texas College. When he assumed control in 1915, the school hardly qualified as an institution of higher education. Enrollment statistics for 1916 revealed that of 110 students, only 3 were engaged in college courses, while the rest were in elementary, secondary, and industrial classes. By 1926, Banks had increased the number of college students to 107 and had reduced the numbers of elementary and secondary students to 39 and 174 respectively. The quality of instruction, combined with the improved student body, encouraged the Texas State Department of Education to extend junior college accreditation to Texas College in 1924. Similar accreditation was soon offered by Mississippi, Louisiana, and Oklahoma.[70]

Banks also stood out as an administrator who led with charm and concern. As the president of Texas College and later Prairie View A&M, Banks was perpetually under a hectic schedule, yet considered it part of his duty to know as much about his students as possible. Students of the period recalled that Banks knew each of the students by name and frequently took the time to converse at length with them about personal as well as academic concerns. In a letter to Banks in 1946, W. E. B. DuBois commented, "It is hard to find words with which to congratulate you upon what you have done: first of all, your single-hearted devotion to a cause; secondly, your utter indifference to salary and money return; and finally the interest which you always have had in students as human beings."[71]

Overall, however, Texas College's most successful president was Dominion R. Glass. Glass led the college through the Depression to an unprecedented level of academic quality. Born in

[69] *Dallas Times Herald*, October 17, 1969; *Houston Chronicle*, October 17, 1969; Woolfolk, *Prairie View*, pp. 214–18.

[70] U.S. Bureau of Education, *Negro Education*, II: 589; U.S. Bureau of Education, *Survey of Negro Colleges and Universities*, p. 873; Texas College, *Catalog*, 1934, p. 11.

[71] W. E. B. DuBois to W. R. Banks, December 3, 1946, quoted in Thompson, "Black Religious Colleges in East Texas," p. 99.

Forsyth, Georgia, on April 19, 1895, and graduated from Atlanta University in 1917, Glass eventually received an LL.D. degree in 1925 from Miles College in Birmingham, Alabama. He began his career teaching sociology and economics at Paine College in Augusta, Georgia, and was named dean there in 1918. From 1919 to 1928, Glass served as president of Arkansas-Haygood College in Pine Bluff, and from 1929 to 1931 he worked as the registrar of Prairie View State College. In 1931, the CME Church selected Glass to be the president of Texas College.[72]

During the next thirty years, Glass led Texas College to the most prosperous period in its history. In curricula, Glass continued the push toward the modernization and sophistication of courses begun by W. R. Banks. In 1934, Glass phased out the high-school program and limited the vocational offerings to courses in home economics. The Texas Department of Education rewarded his efforts in 1932 by granting Texas College a four-year accreditation. The Southern Association of Colleges gave the Tyler school a "B" rating in 1933 and an "A" rating in 1948.[73]

Although Texas College was never free of financial problems, D. R. Glass acquired a reputation as a skilled fund raiser and financial planner. Mrs. Willie Lee Glass later noted that her husband's warmth and charm, combined with his ingenious public relations projects, netted the college more financial support from blacks, the CME Church, and area whites than had been obtained during any previous administration. Referring to the president's managerial skills, Allen C. Hancock, a former Texas College student, observed that no administrator, white or black, could "stretch a dollar as far as Dr. Glass."[74]

President Glass also displayed a concern that the college should be interrelated with the community. Working with the

[72]*Dallas News*, October 9, 1968; Willie Lee Glass, interview with author, Tyler, April 4, 1981; Fleming and Burckel, *Who's Who in Colored America*, p. 213.

[73]Texas College, *Catalog*, 1934, p. 16, 1975, p. 23; Montgomery, *Senior Colleges for Negroes in Texas*, p. 49.

[74]Glass interview; Hancock interview. Glass was one of the moving forces in the formation of the United Negro College Fund. Allen C. Hancock was president of Texas College from 1967 to 1980.

Community Council of Tyler, the college helped administer programs in home improvement, raised funds for the Red Cross, and established day-care centers and a public library for blacks. Glass assisted the black public schools in the area by organizing teacher workshops at the college and by supplying hundreds of student teachers. Other students went into the community independently to help repair tools, rework furniture, and mend clothes. T. S. Montgomery may have had D. R. Glass in mind when he pointed out in 1944 that black institutions were "conscious not only of the opportunity for valid educative experiences . . . but also the obligation of the college to enrich community life and to furnish leadership to the community."[75]

By 1954, Glass had taken one of the weakest black colleges in Texas and built it into one of the strongest. The rising popularity and reputation of Texas College was evident in the school's increased enrollment. Even though the high-school program had been dismantled and vocationalism deemphasized, the number of students increased from 400 in 1931 to 672 in 1954.[76] In a fitting tribute, the CME Church stated that Texas College expanded with such rapidity largely through the "genius and leadership" of D. R. Glass.[77] Upon Glass's retirement in 1961, Benjamin E. Mays, president of Morehouse College, praised him: "The very fact that you have stayed there thirty years is proof that you are a man of sterling character and that the people in the community and the trustees and C.M.E. Church have faith and confidence in you. I want to congratulate you for the growth of the college, for the inspiration you have given hundreds, yes, thousands, of young men and women, and for the leadership that you have given in education."[78]

Although these individuals represent the most prominent black college presidents in Texas, several others also deserve mention. The fifty-two-year administration of Artemisia Bowden

[75] Glass interview; Montgomery, *Senior Colleges for Negroes in Texas*, p. 49.

[76] *Texas Almanac*, 1931, 1954.

[77] Lloyd R. Thompson, "The Origins and Development of Black Religious Colleges in East Texas" (Ph.D. diss., North Texas State University, 1976), p. 101.

[78] Benjamin E. Mays to D. R. Glass, February 10, 1961, D. R. Glass Papers, in possession of Willie Lee Glass, Tyler.

at St. Philip's College was a picture of determination in the face of overwhelming problems. Bowden was born in Albany, Georgia, on January 1, 1879. A 1900 graduate of St. Augustine's Collegiate Institute, Bowden began her career in education at St. Joseph's Parochial School in Fayetteville, North Carolina. In 1901, she moved to High Point Normal and Industrial School in High Point, North Carolina. The following year, Bishop James Steptoe Johnston invited her to take control of St. Philip's.[79]

Throughout her phenomenal half-century at St. Philip's, Bowden displayed a supreme confidence that she could overcome any obstacle. Her brother, the Reverend Henry J. C. Bowden, recalled one of her favorite mottoes: "Learn to do something, and do it well." A review of her administration indicates that she succeeded in this goal. Throughout most of the twentieth century, St. Philip's remained so impoverished that its tiny staff had to wear many occupational hats. When Bowden established the Normal Department in 1906, she was its only instructor. The normal courses she taught over the next thirty years included geography, Latin, American and English literature, composition, rhetoric, ancient and English history, algebra, geometry, government, botany, philosophy, and pedagogy.[80] Yet such an array of teaching duties represented only one dimension of Bowden's responsibilities. For most of her half-century of service, she served not only as chief executive and instructor, but also as matron of boarding facilities, business manager, fund raiser, public relations agent, and director of curriculum.[81]

Bowden realized her dream of developing St. Philip's into a high-quality junior college very slowly. In 1915, when high school courses were first offered, Bowden used the occasion to seek financial support for additional facilities in order to make St. Philip's a junior college. Although some San Antonio businessmen and local black organizations contributed, Bowden could not establish a college curriculum until 1927.[82]

[79] Fleming and Burckel, *Who's Who in Colored America*, p. 45.
[80] Norris, "St. Philip's College," p. 69; St. Philip's College, *Catalog*, 1906, pp. 10–11.
[81] Norris, "St. Philip's College," p. 82.
[82] Ibid., pp. 114–15.

During the Depression, Bowden managed to keep the college alive through borrowing and the timely donations of friends. She also improved the liberal arts curriculum and eliminated the elementary and junior high school departments. These steps meant, though, that the college was saddled with a debt that threatened to bankrupt it. In 1942, however, Bowden solved these financial problems when she convinced the San Antonio Independent School District to incorporate St. Philip's as a municipal junior college. Finally, in 1951, the Southern Association affirmed her lifelong efforts when it awarded St. Philip's an "A" junior college rating.[83] While St. Philip's never achieved the stature of some of the other private black colleges in Texas, no institution ever possessed a more dedicated servant.

At Mary Allen Seminary, Byrd Randolph Smith won lasting recognition not only as the first black president of the Presbyterian school, but also as the man who brought the greatest recognition to the college. Smith was a native of Virginia, who held Bachelor of Science and Doctor of Divinity degrees from Johnson C. Smith University. Appointed by the Board of National Missions of the Presbyterian Church as the school's president in 1924, Smith is credited with reorganizing Mary Allen as a coeducational institution, establishing an accredited high school program, and, for the first time, gaining junior college accreditation.[84]

In the history of Samuel Huston College, Reuben S. Lovinggood stands out as its most respected president. As the first president of Samuel Huston, serving from 1900 to 1916, Lovinggood became noted for his unselfish efforts to see the college firmly established. When the black educator arrived in Austin in 1900, he found that the entire college "campus" was the basement of an unfinished building.[85] Lovinggood delivered his first lectures in this basement to eight students, who had to sit on

[83] Ibid., pp. 130–38, 168–74, 186, 214; San Antonio Register, August 21, 1931, September 2, 1932.

[84] Houston Informer, July 6, 1940.

[85] Austin American Statesman, June 13, 1948; J. Mason Brewer, An Historical Outline of the Negro in Travis County, p. 47; Waco Messenger, December 14, 1934. When Lovinggood and his wife arrived at the site, they found "chickens roosting and hogs wallowing" in the basement.

trunks and old boxes. The first meal served to these students consisted of a jug of molasses and fourteen loaves of bread.[86]

Even under such dire circumstances, the students exhibited a strong desire to learn, and Lovinggood showed great enthusiasm. Over the next sixteen years, Samuel Huston's enrollment grew to 377. The physical plant improved from a single basement to three brick buildings worth $65,000. The value of books, furniture, and farm and laboratory equipment exceeded $8,000. Courses ranged from elementary school through college and included instruction in blacksmithing, bookkeeping, teaching, and preaching.[87] Lovinggood instilled in his students a burning desire to develop their talents. His favorite motto reflected this attitude:

> Good, better, best
> Never let it rest
> Until good is better
> and better is best.[88]

Reviewing the early history of Samuel Huston College, the *Houston Informer* noted in 1931 that Reuben Lovinggood had literally "worn out his life" building up the college.[89]

Unfortunately, the outstanding characteristics of people like Reuben Lovinggood, Mary Branch, and Joseph J. Rhoads were not displayed by all presidents. The private black colleges in Texas, like all colleges and universities, both white and black, occasionally experienced serious problems caused by ineffective leadership. The administration of J. T. Hodges at Tillotson College serves as an example. A native of Gonzales, Hodges graduated from Atlanta University and held positions at Prairie View and Houston colleges before moving to Tillotson. Appointed in 1925 by the American Missionary Association (AMA), Hodges became Tillotson's first black president. Hodges might have writ-

---

[86] *Houston Informer*, April 18, 1931; Samuel Huston College, *Catalog*, 1948, p. 10.

[87] *Austin American Statesman*, June 13, 1948; U.S. Bureau of Education, *Negro Education*, II: 594; Walter P. Webb and H. Bailey Carroll, eds., *The Handbook of Texas*, II: 539.

[88] *Houston Informer*, April 18, 1931.

[89] *Houston Informer*, August 18, 1931.

ten an important chapter in the history of the college had it not been for his lackluster and nepotistic leadership. By appointing members of his family to high-ranking administrative positions, Hodges quickly lost most of his credibility and community support. He further alienated the Austin community by remaining aloof from civic activities. The impact of Hodges's indifference upon the college was devastating. Enrollment plummeted, and in 1936 Tillotson was converted to a women's junior college. For three more years, the school struggled for existence, until finally the AMA compelled Hodges to resign.[90]

Another example of mediocre leadership can be found in the administration of J. W. Yancy II. Appointed president of Paul Quinn College in 1939, Yancy was apparently unable to cope with the varied responsibilities of his office. Within a year, rumors began to spread that the college was in a state of total confusion. In 1941, the board of trustees and representatives of the African Methodist Episcopal Church (AME) began an investigation that yielded a number of serious charges. Their report disclosed that several faculty members were purchasing personal goods from Waco stores and charging them to the college. AME officials also found that students were forced to accept cornbread, molasses, and bacon for breakfast four or five times a week. In addition, Yancy evidently failed to institute an administrative system for keeping track of school property. Charges arose that faculty and staff loaned out college equipment to friends and that some had stolen college livestock. The report of the board observed that the college truck was at an "unknown location," but gas and oil bills were still being received by the school. The report went so far as to label Yancy a "glorified office boy." To everyone's relief, Yancy stepped down in 1942.[91]

At Wiley College, the administration of E. C. McLeod (1942–48) was characterized by dissent. Following World War II, McLeod became the catalyst for one of the few episodes of student unrest at the black colleges in Texas. The problems arose in

[90] Brown and Heintze, "Mary Branch," in *Black Leaders*, ed. Barr and Calvert, pp. 118, 126.

[91] *San Antonio Register*, June 5, 1942.

1947, when Wiley students petitioned the president to modernize campus rules regarding student life, including allowing them to form a student government. The petition also called for the resignations of four unpopular instructors. McLeod rejected the demands, prompting a student boycott of classes. With the future of Wiley at stake, McLeod relented and announced that reforms were forthcoming, that students would be allowed to elect a council or government, and that three faculty members were resigning. Within weeks, however, word leaked out that McLeod had changed his mind and planned to rehire one of the teachers and abolish the student government. Relations between the students and the administration deteriorated rapidly, precipitating a second strike in 1948. McLeod, frustrated and desperate, called in local police and even the Texas Rangers to patrol the campus. Eventually student interest in the strike waned, and classes resumed. The effect on Wiley, however, was unmistakable, as enrollment slipped from 774 in 1946 to 573 in 1948.[92]

Faculty

Among the issues faced by college presidents, none proved more important than developing strong faculties. Several general observations may be made about them. Wiley, Bishop, Tillotson, Mary Allen, and St. Philip's colleges, which were founded by predominantly white, northern denominations, started with white faculties. Around the turn of the century, as black pressure to replace white instructors with blacks increased and as more black teachers became available, these colleges slowly switched to black personnel. The colleges founded by the AME, CME, and black Baptist denominations, however, had black faculties from the beginning. Like most other black colleges of the period, all the private Texas schools employed significant numbers of instructors without graduate degrees. This situation began to improve in the 1930s with regard to the number of mas-

[92] *Houston Informer*, October 11, 1947, January 10, 1948; *Pittsburgh Courier*, October 11, 1947, January 17, 1948; *Marshall News Messenger*, January 7, 1948; *Texas Almanac*, 1946, 1948.

ter's degrees, but never improved appreciably in terms of doctoral degrees. Because of their meager budgets, black colleges could not maintain faculties of adequate size and consequently tended to overwork their professors. Moreover, the salaries received by teachers in black colleges remained much lower than those white schools offered, and salaries in private black schools were lower than those in public black institutions. Average annual salaries for professors in 1914 ranged from a low of $315 at Texas College to a high of $600 at Bishop. The black public college, Prairie View, paid its teachers an average of $800. While salaries had improved by 1927, ranging from $1,100 per year at Jarvis Christian to $1,500 annually at Wiley, the private schools still lagged behind Prairie View, which gave its professors an average of $1,866. By 1942, the private schools had generally closed the salary gap with Prairie View. The median salary for most of the private schools was $1,000, but Wiley and Tillotson professors earned $1,600 and $1,500, respectively. Meanwhile Prairie View and Houston College offered median pay of $1,338 and $1,300. The salaries of the black private and public colleges were woefully inadequate, however, when compared with those of white Texas colleges, which paid their professors average salaries of $2,700–5,000 during the same period. Because of such difficult conditions, many professors abandoned their institutions each year, either to seek new positions elsewhere or to find a different type of employment.[93]

Perhaps most important, each institution had a small group of dedicated and often outstanding instructors who endured the hardships of their situation and remained with their colleges for extended periods of time. It might be suggested that these men and women provided the academic continuity and intellectual leadership vital to the reputation and appeal of their institutions. Because most studies of black colleges have omitted any mention of teachers, it seems fitting that this chapter should identify several of the most prominent instructors who dedicated their lives to the education of black youth.

[93] Montgomery, *Senior Colleges for Negroes in Texas*, pp. 38–41; "Salary Schedule, Tillotson College, 1940, 1942, 1944, 1946," Addendum: Huston-Tillotson College.

An excellent example of a faculty member who possessed many talents and made a lifelong commitment to Bishop College was Melvin J. Banks. A native of Alabama, Banks received his bachelor's degree at Howard University, master's degree at the University of Colorado, and doctorate at Syracuse University. In 1929, he joined the faculty of Bishop College at the request of his personal friend Joseph J. Rhoads.[94] As associate dean for general studies, Banks taught a variety of courses and played a central role in the modernization of the college curricula. He was chosen for this position because of his strong background in the black college liberal arts tradition. At Howard University, the "Harvard of the Black Race," Banks had studied under many of America's finest black scholars, including Carter G. Woodson, Charles H. Wesley, Leo Hansbury, and Alain Leroy Locke. At Bishop College he made many curriculum revisions based upon the powerful liberal arts education he had received at Howard.[95]

Banks became involved in many other aspects of Bishop life. He was an active figure in the Bishop College–Community Relations Program. In 1944, President Rhoads picked Banks to head the Sabine Farms Project, which became the prototype for other area experiments. Always interested in student affairs, Banks helped sponsor numerous campus organizations and clubs and was an avid supporter of the student government. Banks also became a social activist and outspoken critic of Jim Crowism. In the 1940s he sponsored one of the largest NAACP student chapters in the nation. Banks encouraged Bishop students to speak out on the issues and in one instance, arranged for them to speak before the Texas Legislature in support of desegregating the University of Texas. Perhaps the best testament of his ability and dedication was the fact that he served Bishop College for fifty years, from 1929 to 1979.[96]

Among the outstanding figures to teach at Samuel Huston

---

[94] Banks interview; *Houston Informer*, September 25, 1937. Banks and Rhoads were both working at Booker T. Washington High School in Dallas when Rhoads was offered the presidency. Rhoads accepted the position with the condition that Banks agree to come with him to Bishop College.

[95] Ibid.

[96] Ibid.

College, J. W. Frazier became one of the most "devotedly loved" by the former students of the college. Born in North Carolina and educated at Bennett Seminary, Frazier came to Texas in 1886. After working in the public schools of Victoria for fourteen years, he joined Reuben S. Lovinggood to help transform Samuel Huston from a struggling elementary school into a successful liberal arts college. Regarded as the "most loyal helper" Lovinggood had, Frazier served on the college faculty for twenty-eight years.[97]

Samuel Huston later boasted that it had one of America's finest black folklorists, J. Mason Brewer. A graduate of Wiley College and Indiana University, Brewer produced dozens of articles and ten major works in the fields of history, poetry, and folklore between 1933 and 1965. Theta Sigma Phi honored him in 1954 as one of the twenty-five best authors in Texas.[98]

During the 1930s and 1940s, Melvin B. Tolson, a major Harlem Renaissance poet, became the most renowned professor at Wiley College. A graduate of Lincoln University and Columbia University, Tolson began his career at Wiley by publishing poems in newspapers and magazines such as the *Atlantic Monthly* and *Art Quarterly*. Well-known poets such as Robert Frost and Theodore Roethke praised his work, which included *Rendezvous with America* (1944), *Libretto for the Republic of Liberia* (1953), and *Harlem Gallery* (1965).[99]

One of the most gifted scholars at Texas College was Ira DeA. Reid. A graduate of Morehouse College, the University of Pittsburgh, and Columbia University, Ira Reid served the Tyler school as a professor of sociology during the 1920s. Regarded as an able teacher, Reid later proved to be an outstanding scholar. After leaving Texas College, he produced four major works, entitled *Negro Membership in American Labor Unions* (1930), *Adult Education Among Negroes* (1936), *The Urban Negro*

[97] Brewer, *Negroes in Travis County*, p. 51.

[98] For an excellent biographical sketch of Brewer, see James W. Byrd, *J. Mason Brewer: Negro Folklorist*.

[99] John Hope Franklin, *From Slavery to Freedom: A History of Negro Americans*, 3rd ed., p. 514; Arthur P. Davis and Saunders Redding, ed., *Cavalcade: Negro American Writing From 1760 to the Present*, p. 364.

Worker in the United States (1938), and *Sharecroppers All* (1941).[100]

At Jarvis Christian College, E. W. Rand distinguished himself as both a scholar and an administrator. A Jarvis graduate, Rand completed graduate study in biology at Atlanta University (1941) and in education at Indiana University (1952). Besides teaching biology and education and authoring more than ten articles, Rand served as dean of the college from 1937 to 1942 and from 1957 to 1959.[101] The career of another noteworthy Jarvis faculty member, Venita C. Waddleton, spanned the fifty years from 1929 to 1979. She divided her energies among the positions of instructor of business, secretary to the president, and college registrar.[102]

A review of the administrations and faculties of the private black colleges in Texas makes it clear that the outstanding individuals who served these institutions bore many of the same traits. In an age of racial intolerance, they displayed the courage, imagination, and stamina necessary to overcome most obstacles. They were united by a common goal of expanding the educational horizons for the black youth of the state. Comparing the character and development of academic leaders in the church-related black colleges of Texas with those in the state's public black colleges, as well as those in other black colleges around the nation, makes it evident that their stories are almost identical.

In terms of racial composition, the state schools—Prairie View and Texas Southern—paralleled black-owned private schools such as Paul Quinn, Texas, and Guadalupe colleges by employing black administrators and teachers from the start. Because the other private colleges in Texas represented only a part of a larger national effort by white religious groups, it is not surprising that the racial patterns in these colleges mirrored those in their sister colleges around the country. For example, the Methodist colleges were among the first in Texas to make the

[100] Thompson, "Black Religious Colleges in East Texas," pp. 129–30.
[101] Ibid.
[102] Interview with Venita C. Waddleton, Jarvis Christian College, Hawkins, Texas, July 18, 1979.

transition to black leadership. Wiley College began the process in 1894, while Samuel Huston was founded in 1900 with a black staff already in place. Other denominational bodies such as the Baptist Home Mission Society, the Board of Missions for Freedmen of the Presbyterian Church, and the American Missionary Association were slower to follow suit. While the white denominations began to integrate their staffs during the 1880s and 1890s, the move toward total black faculties and administrations did not occur until after 1900. In Texas, blacks assumed control of St. Philip's shortly after 1902 and of Mary Allen Seminary, Tillotson, and Bishop colleges during the 1920s. Jarvis Christian, which was not founded until 1913, also began with an all-black staff.[103]

Great similarity also existed in the type of presidents found in the black colleges. The uniformity of presidential leadership resulted primarily from the common problems these institutions faced, such as limited funds, a hostile environment, and a scarcity of qualified students and faculty. The ability of black colleges to endure such hardship during their turbulent history reflects in large part the aggressive and pragmatic leadership of their chief executives. Presidents of public and private black colleges alike faced the same awesome task of providing sound educational opportunities, consistent with the mission of their institution, with marginal resources. They accomplished this through strong, careful leadership, in a style of governance characterized as "hardheaded financial management and transcendental spiritualism."[104] Although most black college presidents followed the bureaucratic model, many still gained reputations as warm, caring administrators who related well with their stu-

[103] Graham Blackstock, *Staff Monograph on Higher Education for Negroes in Texas*, p. 8; Alton Hornsby, Jr., "Negro Education in Texas, 1865–1917" (M.A. thesis, University of Texas, 1962), pp. 100–101; Woolfolk, *Prairie View*, pp. 44–46; 144–49; Wesley A. Hotchkiss, "Congregationalists and Negro Education," *Journal of Negro Education* 29 (Summer, 1960): 289–98; Green, "Colleges Maintained by the African Methodist Episcopal Church," pp. 319–22; Thomas, "Support of Negro Colleges by the Methodist Church," pp. 252–59; Ellison, "Colleges Maintained by the Baptist Denominations," pp. 330–38; Coleman, "The Christian Methodist Episcopal Church," pp. 313–18.

[104] Chester M. Hedgepeth, Jr., Ronald R. Edmonds, and Ann Craig, "Overview," in *Black Colleges*, ed. Willie and Edmonds, pp. 97–98.

dents and the community. This combination of traits was apparent in the better private college presidents of Texas like D. R. Glass, M. W. Dogan, Mary Elizabeth Branch, and Reuben S. Lovinggood. Not surprisingly, such traits were not characteristic of all college leaders. Every college, white or black, has at some point experienced the problems caused by perhaps well-meaning, but nevertheless mediocre or even inept administrators. The private black colleges in Texas were no exception. The administrations of presidents such as J. T. Hodges at Tillotson, J. W. Yancy II at Paul Quinn, and E. C. McLeod at Wiley were classic examples of weak leadership, tinged with nepotism, incompetence, insensitivity, and authoritarianism.

Finally, similarities existed in the character and development of black college faculties. Several studies have made it clear that the problems, strengths, and weaknesses of black college faculties in Texas were the same as in other states. Summarizing the nature of these staffs, Daniel C. Thompson noted:

Judged by any set of criteria, black colleges, like other colleges, have had their share of incompetent and mediocre teachers. However, when teachers in these colleges are evaluated according to the relative success of their products or graduates—the final results of their work— it must be agreed that a significant number of them merit the status of great.

Even the most substandard black college is likely to have some truly successful teachers who have made unique contributions to the art and science of teaching.[105]

[105] Daniel C. Thompson, "Black College Faculty and Students: The Nature of Their Interaction," in *Black Colleges*, ed. Willie and Edmonds, pp. 188–89.

4

Finances

THROUGHOUT the late nineteenth century and the first half of the twentieth, the church-related black colleges in Texas faced the problem of inadequate financing. The minimal budgets under which the Texas schools operated adversely affected every aspect of these institutions, including facilities, staff, salaries, and curriculum. This chapter explores the financial development of the private colleges in Texas on four levels. First, the major sources of income for these colleges will be identified and an estimate of their overall significance provided. Second, supplementary sources of income will be surveyed. Third, institutional cooperation as a financial measure will be examined. Finally, the financial trends of these schools will be compared with those of other black colleges across the nation.

Major Sources of Income

There is little doubt that denominational contributions remained among the most significant, as well as consistent, sources of financial support for the church-related black colleges in Texas. This was especially true in the late 1800s and early 1900s when the colleges were first being established. During their formative years, the black colleges relied heavily upon their churches because they had few other outside sources of support and could not collect substantial funds from tuition and fees. The exact amounts of money contributed to the Texas colleges differed according to the assets of each church body and the number, size, and educational level of the colleges it supported. In terms of national donations, however, most religious denominations provided similar amounts of funding for their colleges, with the exception of the Presbyterians, Episcopalians, and black Baptists, who contributed somewhat less to their schools.[1]

A comparison of the amounts of money these colleges received in 1914 and in 1926 reveals the prominent role of church appropriations. Table 8 illustrates that while the amount of money received by each college in 1914 continued to be relatively small, it nevertheless composed a major portion of each school's overall budget. In dollars, Jarvis Christian College received the smallest donation—$1,680—while Paul Quinn College was given the largest grant—$15,537. The other church grants fell between these two extremes and averaged just over $6,000. As percentages of the college budgets, the church appropriations for 1914 varied widely. At Samuel Huston College, a donation of $4,429 by the Freedmen's Aid Society represented 15 percent of the budget. On the other hand, the $1,680 provided to Jarvis Christian by the Christian Women's Board of Missions constituted 98 percent of that institution's income. Again, most of the percentages from the other colleges fell within these limits, averaging slightly over 51 percent.

Comparing the figures in 1914 with those in 1926 yields two important observations. The size of church appropriations increased significantly from an average of $6,000 in 1914, to over $20,000 in 1926. Yet, while the church donations received by these colleges grew, the percentage of the total budget they represented did not change appreciably. For example, Wiley College received $4,950, or 47.5 percent of its income, from the Freedmen's Aid Society in 1914. In 1926, Wiley was given $23,000, which represented 47 percent of the college budget. A similar comparison can be made for Paul Quinn, where AME Church appropriations rose from $15,537 in 1914 to $22,000 in 1926, but the percentage of the total budget increased only slightly, from

[1] Among the white denominations, the Presbyterians had particular difficulty in raising funds for their black colleges. In its annual report for 1892, the Board of Missions for Freedmen lamented that 3,022 of its churches, with a composite membership of over 200,000 had refused to give anything to the Board's educational activities (Board of Missions for Freedmen of the Presbyterian Church in the United States of America, *Annual Report*, 1892, p. 12; James M. McPherson, *The Abolitionist Legacy: From Reconstruction to the NAACP*, pp. 143–60).

TABLE 8
Survey of Church Appropriations to Private Black Colleges in Texas,
1914–15 and 1926–27

	1914–15		1926–27	
Institution	Church Appro- priations	Percent of Total Budget	Church Appro- priations	Percent of Total Budget
Bishop	$12,238	27%	$20,082	16%
Butler	4,000	42		
Guadalupe	4,400*	67.7		
Jarvis Christian	1,680	98	21,000	63
Mary Allen	7,166	47.8		
Paul Quinn	15,537	53	22,000	55.9
St. Philip's	1,800	72		
Samuel Huston	4,429	15	20,000	40.9
Texas	3,500	53.7	22,815	76.7
Tillotson	8,581	42	17,257	69
Wiley	4,950	47.5	23,000	47

SOURCE: U.S. Department of the Interior, Bureau of Education, *Negro Education: A Study of the Private and Higher Schools for Colored People in the United States*, prepared by Thomas Jesse Jones, Bulletin No. 39, II: 567–602; U.S. Department of the Interior, Bureau of Education, *Survey of Negro Colleges and Universities*, prepared by Arthur J. Klein, Bulletin No. 7, pp. 810–81.
* Figure for Guadalupe includes tuition and fees.

53 percent to 55.9 percent. In the cases of Bishop College and Jarvis Christian College, the percentage of the total budget represented by church donations actually declined. At Bishop, while church appropriations rose from $12,238 in 1914 to $20,082 in 1926, the percentage they represented in the budget fell from 27 to 16 percent. At Jarvis Christian, Church donations represented 98 percent of its budget in 1914, but only 63 percent in 1926.

A simple reason accounted for the declining percentages in the face of increasing church funding. By 1926, the budgets of the colleges were growing larger through increased revenues from other sources such as tuition, fees, room, and board. This trend continued through 1954. Consequently, while church support for these colleges remained constant, or even increased, it nevertheless came to represent a smaller percentage of their overall budgets. T. S. Montgomery noted that in 1940 denominational sources accounted for 20 percent of the Texas College budget, 22 percent of the Wiley budget, and slightly more than 30 percent of the Tillotson College budget. Montgomery surmised that during 1940 the four-year private black colleges in Texas derived approximately 30 percent of their total income from denominational sources.[2] By 1949, Tillotson College reported an appropriation of $40,000 from the American Missionary Association, which represented 14.3 percent of its total income. That same year, Wiley College received a grant from the Freedmen's Aid Society of $24,363, which represented only 5.6 percent of its total budget.[3]

Tuition and student fees historically have represented major sources of income for all institutions of higher education. This proved to be especially true for private colleges, both white and black, which operated without the benefit of state support. However, most church-related black colleges, including those in Texas, had great difficulty in securing substantial income from tuition and fees in the late nineteenth and early twentieth centuries. These colleges had very small enrollments and the vast majority of their students came from the poorest levels of American society. Thus, the black colleges were forced to keep their tuition and fees to a minimal level until well into the twentieth century. The 1887 catalog for Wiley College listed tuition as $1.25 per month or $11.25 annually. The Paul Quinn catalog for that same year noted a charge of $2.50 per month. At Guadalupe College in 1892, the combined charges for tuition, room, and board totaled $10.00 per month. In its catalog for 1898, Bishop

---

[2]T. S. Montgomery, *The Senior Colleges for Negroes in Texas*, p. 73.

[3]Tillotson College: Summary of Proposed Budget, 1949," Addendum: Huston-Tillotson College, Temporary Box No. 1, Amistad Research Center, New Orleans; Raphael O'Hara Lanier, "The History of Higher Education for Negroes in Texas: 1930–1955, with Particular Reference to Texas Southern University" (Ph.D. diss., New York University, 1957), p. 100.

College also charged $10.00 per month for tuition, fees, room, and board.[4]

Slowly, as more students attended these colleges and as the standard of living for black Texans gradually improved, the private colleges began to increase their tuition. Comparing the tuition rates for these colleges during the 1920s with those of the earlier period, it is clear that the increase in tuition charges was evolutionary, rather than revolutionary. In 1920, Wiley College charged its students $27.00 per year for college students and $22.50 per year for preparatory or high school students. By 1926, Wiley had gradually increased these figures to $45.00 for college and $36.00 for high school students. The other black colleges put into effect similar tuition schedules during 1926. Paul Quinn charged $45.00; Texas College, $27.00; and Samuel Huston College, $36.00 per year.[5]

By the late 1940s the tuition charged by most of the private colleges approached that of many white private institutions in the state. The annual tuition for eight of these colleges between 1949 and 1952 was as follows:

Austin College	$300.00
Samuel Huston College	168.00
St. Mary's College	240.00
Texas Christian University	240.00
Texas College	180.00
Texas Lutheran College	200.00
Tillotson College	170.00
Wiley College	120.00[6]

Although the black colleges began to increase their tuition, the income they acquired from such fees still represented only a

    [4]Wiley College, *Catalog*, 1887, p. 30; Paul Quinn College, *Catalog*, 1887, p. 26; Guadalupe College, *Catalog*, 1892, p. 16; Bishop College, *Catalog*, 1898, p. 43.

    [5]Wiley College, *Catalog*, 1920, p. 9; U.S. Bureau of Education, *Survey of Negro Colleges and Universities*, pp. 838, 858, 874.

    [6]Austin College, *Catalog*, 1949, p. 18; Samuel Huston College, *Catalog*, 1952, p. 3; St. Mary's College, *Catalog*, 1949, p. 27; Texas Christian University, *Catalog*, 1949, p. 59; Texas College, *Catalog*, 1949, p. 26; Texas Lutheran College, *Catalog*, 1949, p. 23; Tillotson College, *Catalog*, 1949, p. 14; Wiley College, *Catalog*, 1950, p. 14.

TABLE 9

Survey of Tuition and Fee Income for the Private Black Colleges in
Texas, 1914–15 and 1926–27

Institution	1914–15		1926–27	
	Tuition and Fees	Percent of Total Budget	Tuition and Fees	Percent of Total Budget
Bishop	$5,327	11.7%	$28,235	22.6%
Butler	1,500	15.7		
Guadalupe*				
Jarvis Christian	32	1	4,868	14.6
Mary Allen	2,237	14.9		
Paul Quinn	3,285	11	17,000	43
St. Philip's	100	4		
Samuel Huston	4,053	13.9		
Texas	265	4	5,583	18.7
Tillotson	2,693	13	3,150	12.6
Wiley	4,870	21.8	20,540	42

SOURCES: U.S. Department of the Interior, Bureau of Education, *Negro Educa-
tion: A Study of the Private and Higher Schools for Colored People in the United States*,
prepared by Thomas Jesse Jones, Bulletin No. 39, II: 567–602; U.S. Department of the
Interior, Bureau of Education, *Survey of Negro Colleges and Universities*, prepared by
Arthur J. Klein, Bulletin No. 7, pp. 810–81.
*Figures are not available for Guadalupe College.

small part of their overall budgets. Not until the late 1920s did
the combined factors of increased enrollments and tuition lead
to significant financial gains for these colleges. As Table 9 indicates, income from tuition and fees began to climb sharply after
1914. While these fees, on average, were only about 11 percent
of their total budgets in 1914, they averaged more than 25 percent of their incomes by 1926. Among the institutions surveyed,
Wiley and Paul Quinn colleges displayed the greatest increase in
the proportion of the budget derived from tuition income. By
1926, both schools received more than 40 percent of their total
revenues from these sources.

Other colleges, however, also experienced significant increases in tuition revenue. Jarvis Christian College, which re-

ceived only $32.00, or 1 percent of its budget, from tuition in 1914, acquired $4,868, or 14.6 percent of its income, from these fees in 1926. At Paul Quinn, tuition represented 11 percent of the college budget in 1914 and 43 percent in 1926. At Bishop, tuition increased from 11.7 percent of the budget in 1914 to 22.6 percent in 1926. At Texas College, these fees jumped from $265, or 4 percent of the budget, in 1914 to $5,583, or 18.7 percent of the budget, in 1926.

While the exact amount each black college received from tuition and fees, as well as the portion of the budget these sums represented, varied from school to school and was influenced by the size of enrollment, a general pattern became clear by the 1930s. T. S. Montgomery noted that the private black colleges in Texas received approximately 35 percent of their total income from tuition during the 1930s and 1940s.[7] In 1949, Jarvis Christian received $25,079, or 20 percent of its total budget, from tuition. That same year, Wiley College acquired $151,284, or 35 percent of its income, in this manner. As late as 1950, Tillotson College realized $134,565, or about 45 percent of its budget, from these fees.[8] While tuition failed to provide the black colleges with much revenue during their early years, by the 1920s it had come to represent, along with church appropriations, one of the most significant sources of institutional income.

Another source of income each college derived from students was a room and board charge. Like tuition, room and board fees were minimal at first, but were later increased as costs and student income rose. Unlike tuition and church appropriations, however, room and board charges were not normally applied to educational expenses, such as faculty salaries, library books and periodicals, musical instruments, scientific equipment, furniture, supplies, or student aid. Room and board charges also were not directly figured into the planning for any institutional improvements, such as new facilities or staff members. As Thomas Jesse Jones pointed out, revenue from room

[7] Montgomery, *Senior Colleges for Negroes in Texas*, pp. 71–73.
[8] "Tillotson College: Summary of Proposed Budget, 1950," Addendum: Huston-Tillotson College, Temporary Box No. 4; Lanier, "Higher Education for Negroes in Texas," pp. 100–101.

and board was calculated to pay the cost of feeding and housing the college students. It appears that at most schools these fees were structured to try to break even with operating expenses.[9]

By comparing the income the private black colleges got from room and board fees with boarding expenses during 1914, it is clear that none of the schools, with the possible exception of Bishop and Wiley, enjoyed significant surpluses. As Table 10 illustrates, five of the eleven Texas colleges showed surpluses, while four displayed deficits and one broke even. The actual boarding expenses incurred by these colleges probably amounted to more than the table indicates, however, because no figures exist concerning the costs of salaries for dormitory staff, repairs, utilities, or insurance.

Room and board revenue, like tuition, increased during the 1930s and ultimately came to represent approximately 25 percent of the total budgets for these institutions.[10] By the late 1940s, many of the black colleges showed small surpluses, which could be used to refurbish the residence halls or help support other institutional needs. For example, room and board income at Tillotson College exceeded dormitory and dining hall expenses at an increasing rate, resulting in the following surpluses:

1940	$ 492
1942	6,604
1944	16,154
1945	24,021
1950	23,432[11]

Organized philanthropy was another source of financial support for the black colleges in Texas. Large philanthropic foundations received their funds primarily from wealthy northern businessmen who had accumulated vast fortunes during the industrial boom of the late 1800s. The most significant foundations included the George Peabody Education Fund, the John F. Slater Fund, the General Education Board, and the Julius Rosen-

[9] U.S. Bureau of Education, *Negro Education*, II: 576–602.

[10] Montgomery, *Senior Colleges for Negroes in Texas*, p. 73.

[11] "Tillotson College: Summary of Proposed Budget, 1940, 1942, 1944, 1945, 1950," Addendum: Huston-Tillotson College, Temporary Box No. 4.

TABLE 10

Survey of Room and Board Income and Expenses for the Private
Black Colleges in Texas, 1914–15

Institution	Boarding Income	Boarding Expenses	Net Surplus or Deficit
Bishop	$23,044	$14,457	$ +8,587
Butler	4,000	3,000	+1,000
Guadalupe	1,500	3,500*	−2,000
Jarvis Christian †			
Mary Allen	4,000	4,150	−150
Paul Quinn	4,292	3,130	+1,162
St. Philip's ‡			0
Samuel Huston	11,391	11,662	−271
Texas	2,750	3,728	−978
Tillotson	6,635	6,217	+418
Wiley	11,875	4,523	+7,352

SOURCE: U.S. Department of the Interior, Bureau of Education, *Negro Education: A Study of the Private and Higher Schools for Colored People in the United States*, prepared by Thomas Jesse Jones, Bulletin No. 39, II: 567–602.

*No separate figure is available for boarding expenses at Guadalupe College. Jones lists only "other expenses," $3,500.

†No figures are given for Jarvis Christian.

‡No figures were provided for St. Philip's, but it was disclosed that boarding expenses were equal to boarding income.

wald Fund. Considering such assistance their civic and moral responsibility, these wealthy businessmen aided black education in such fields as industrial training, teacher education, endowments, scholarships, and building construction. [12]

Such philanthropy, however, did little to further democratic ideals in black education. The educational foundations seemed willing to support black education only in ways that were compatible with southern attitudes and with the needs of northern

[12] Henry Allen Bullock, *A History of Negro Education in The South*, pp. 117–43; Sherman J. Jones and George B. Weathersby, "Financing the Black College," in *Black Colleges in America: Challenge, Development, Survival*, ed. Charles V. Willie and Ronald R. Edmonds, pp. 107–14; McPherson, *Abolitionist Legacy*, pp. 145–46; Virgil A. Clift, Archibald W. Anderson, and Gordon H. Hullfish, *Negro Education in America*, p. 41.

industry. Donald Spivey has pointed out that following the Civil War prominent northern industrialists, many of whom headed educational foundations, allied themselves with southern whites to channel the freedmen into a second-class status as semiskilled laborers. Spivey argues that this alliance suited northern whites who wished to "harness the blacks' economic potential and to eliminate their political threat," as well as the northern industrialists who wanted the black population developed as an industrial work force.[13]

Considering the prevailing racial attitudes of the post-Reconstruction era, it comes as no surprise that the educational foundations, which were established by northern industrialists and usually administered by southern whites, directed their funds mostly toward promoting either basic or industrial education, rather than classical or liberal arts training.[14] For example, the George Peabody Education Fund, which was founded in 1867, used its $2.3 million budget to support the development of black and white public schools in the South and Southwest. As the Peabody Fund limited its support to public education, no black denominational colleges, including those in Texas, received any direct support. When the Peabody Fund was dissolved in 1914, its assets of $350,000 went to the John F. Slater Fund.[15]

In 1882, millionaire merchant John F. Slater set aside $1 million for the creation of an educational foundation to uplift the "lately emancipated population of the Southern States, and their posterity, by conferring on them the blessings of Christian education." The fund allotted money to all levels of black education, but specialized in supporting black colleges. From the beginning, however, the Slater Fund favored black colleges that offered industrial training. Its first two general agents, Atticus G. Haygood (1882–91) and J. L. M. Curry (1891–1903), set the fu-

[13] Donald Spivey, *Schooling for the New Slavery: Black Industrial Education, 1868–1915*, pp. 76–79.

[14] Clift, Anderson, and Hullfish, *Negro Education in America*, p. 41.

[15] Ullin Whitney Leavell, *Philanthropy in Negro Education*; pp. 59–60; Jabez Lamar Monroe Curry, *A Brief Sketch of George Peabody, and a History of the Peabody Education Fund Through Thirty Years*, pp. 18–22; Dwight Oliver Wendell Holmes, *The Evolution of the Negro College*, pp. 164–65.

ture pattern for the Slater Fund by encouraging private black colleges to develop industrial programs and by lavishing the largest Slater grants upon industrially-oriented schools such as Hampton Institute and Tuskegee Institute.[16]

Because most private black colleges never developed extensive industrial curricula, Slater donations to them remained infrequent and more limited. Seven private colleges in Texas received Slater grants between 1884 and 1936, but only Bishop, Wiley, and Texas colleges became consistent recipients. Bishop College received annual grants between 1893 and 1935. These grants to Bishop ranged from $500 to $2,695 per year, but averaged only about $1,500. Texas College got the second highest number of Slater awards, beginning in 1917 and continuing through 1936. Grants to the Tyler school ranged from $400 to $2,500 and averaged just over $1,100. Wiley College followed as a close third, receiving steady Slater appropriations between 1917 and 1934. These donations varied from $500 to $2,675 and also averaged $1,100.[17]

Four of the other black colleges in Texas received only sporadic support from the Slater Fund. Tillotson College was given small grants of less than $400 in 1884 and 1891 but did not receive further assistance until the early 1930s. Paul Quinn College received $600 from the Slater Fund in 1891 but got no additional support until 1930. Samuel Huston College and St. Philip's College obtained similar support in 1929 and 1930, respectively.[18]

The General Education Board, which was created by John D. Rockefeller in 1902, became another important foundation for black education. The General Education Board (GEB) sought to help finance all forms of black education in America, including black colleges. In its dealings with black higher education, the GEB helped many schools, but favored those which reflected a strong belief in industrial education and demonstrated

[16] Holmes, *Evolution of the Negro College*, pp. 165, 167–72; John F. Slater Fund, *Proceedings of the Trustees*, 1892, p. 16; Jones and Weathersby, "Financing the Black College," in *Black Colleges*, ed. Willie and Edmonds, p. 101.

[17] Slater Fund, *Proceedings*, 1884–1936.

[18] Ibid.

a strong commitment toward self-help. In these situations, the GEB often made large lump-sum gifts to help black colleges achieve specific goals. For example, in 1928, the General Education Board granted (1) $75,000 to Prairie View State Normal and Industrial College toward a permanent improvement goal of $305,500; (2) $100,000 to State Agricultural and Mechanical Institute, Normal, Alabama, for $300,000 in improvements; and (3) $35,000 to the State Normal School at Fayetteville, North Carolina, toward a $70,000 construction and equipment drive.[19] Bishop College was similarly aided in 1944, when the GEB granted $61,000 toward the New Development Program of President Joseph J. Rhoads.[20]

While the GEB had given over $23 million to black colleges by 1932, only limited amounts had gone to the private black colleges in Texas. Early in its work, the Board allotted much of its funding for black higher education to several public and private industrial schools, such as Tuskegee Institute.[21] This resulted from the belief of the GEB's first president, William H. Baldwin, that blacks were a valuable source of labor in the South and ideally suited for industrial training:

The potential economic value of the Negro population properly educated is infinite and incalculable. In the Negro is the opportunity of the South. Time has proven that he is best fitted to perform the heavy labor in the Southern states. The negro and the mule is the only combination so far to grow cotton. The South needs him; but the South needs him educated to be a suitable citizen. Properly directed he is the best possible laborer to meet the climatic conditions of the South. He will willingly fill the more menial positions, and do the heavy work, at less wages, than the American white man or any foreign race which has yet come to our shores. This will permit the Southern white laborer to perform the more expert labor, and leave the fields, the mines, and the simpler trades for the Negro.[22]

At the same time, Dwight Oliver Wendell Holmes pointed out that the GEB also wished to develop a select number of

---

[19] Holmes, *Evolution of the Negro College*, pp. 172–73.

[20] Caesar Francis Toles, "The History of Bishop College" (M.A. thesis, University of Michigan, 1947), pp. 98–106.

[21] Holmes, *Evolution of the Negro College*, pp. 172–74.

[22] Quoted in Spivey, *Schooling for the New Slavery*, pp. 93–94.

black college centers, regionally located in such cities as Atlanta, Washington, D.C., Nashville, and New Orleans. To achieve this goal the GEB vigorously supported the merger of several small black institutions in New Orleans and Atlanta.[23]

It is worth noting, however, that the GEB did continue to extend limited support to many private black colleges, especially to the black colleges sponsored by the American Baptist Home Mission Society. By 1929, the society found that the rapidly increasing costs of supporting its six colleges and many secondary schools were outstripping its assets. In spite of increased student fees, the society was forced to withdraw support from some of its schools. The GEB became interested in helping the Home Mission Society as early as 1908, and by 1917 it had provided $84,413. From 1917 to 1928, the GEB granted the Baptist organization $2,139,772 for its colleges and soon superseded the Home Mission Society as the chief benefactor of Baptist colleges such as Bishop.[24]

The renowned American industrialist Andrew Carnegie established a fund of $10 million in 1902 to build libraries on the campuses of many white and black colleges.[25] Wiley College became the only black college in Texas to receive a library grant. The Wiley College catalog for 1920 described the new Carnegie Library as:

a thoroughly modern structure, two stories high, built of red pressed brick, trimmed with stone. The style of the building is classic with two massive Ionic columns gracefully guarding the beautiful entrance. . . . The library contains about twelve thousand volumes besides pamphlets. Over five thousand splendid reference books are placed at the disposal of the students daily. A large number of magazines and newspapers are received daily.[26]

In the early twentieth century, several other educational foundations were established, but they directed their support toward all levels of black education or to black colleges outside Texas. The Anna T. Jeanes Fund, created in 1907, assisted the

[23] Holmes, *Evolution of the Negro College*, pp. 173–74.
[24] Ibid., p. 127; Montgomery, *Senior Colleges for Negroes in Texas*, p. 73.
[25] Clift, Anderson, and Hullfish, *Negro Education in America*, p. 42.
[26] Wiley College, *Catalog*, 1920, p. 17.

advancement of black rural schools in the South. While it provided indirect benefits to Negro education on all levels, black colleges received no direct assistance from the fund.[27]

The Phelps-Stokes Fund was established in 1910 to further the education of "negroes, both in Africa and the United States, North American Indians and needy and deserving white students, through industrial schools, . . . scholarships, and the erection or endowment of school buildings or chapels."[28] While the chief activities of the Phelps-Stokes Fund did not directly affect most black colleges, the fund spent sizeable amounts of money to support federal government surveys of black education, such as those authored by Thomas Jesse Jones and Arthur J. Klein.[29]

Incorporated in 1917, the Julius Rosenwald Fund administered more than $22 million in the areas of health, education, and race relations. When the fund was finally exhausted in 1948, about 22 percent of its assets had been given to black colleges. The vast majority of the Rosenwald funds, however, had gone to a number of select institutions, which were all outside Texas. These included Howard University, Fisk University, Meharry Medical College, Atlanta University, Spelman College, and Dillard University.[30]

Minor Sources of Income

To supplement the meager funds received from organized philanthropy, church bodies, tuition, and fees the black colleges in Texas developed alternative financial strategies. From their beginnings, these colleges sought additional funds from both black and white individuals, as well as local clubs, fraternal organizations, and civic groups. The methods of appeal to individuals and organizations were varied and usually orchestrated by the

[27] Bullock, *Negro Education in the South*, p. 133; Holmes, *Evolution of the Negro College*, p. 164.

[28] Thomas Jesse Jones, *Educational Adaptations: Report of Ten Years' Work of the Phelps-Stokes Fund, 1910–1920*, p. 16.

[29] Holmes, *Evolution of the Negro College*, pp. 177–78.

[30] Ibid., p. 176; Jones and Weathersby, "Financing the Black College," in *Black Colleges*, ed. Willie and Edmonds, pp. 113–14.

president. In the late nineteenth and early twentieth centuries, many of the colleges published open appeals or lists of needs in their catalogs. These appeals are significant because they provide early clues to the financial condition of the colleges and their plans for the future.

One of the most detailed appeals for assistance appeared in the 1887 catalog of Paul Quinn College. In describing the general needs of the Waco school, the catalog stated:

> We need books of reference on scientific and biographical subjects, and for general reading. We need apparatus in the departments of philosophy, chemistry, and applied mathematics; in the primary department, such as maps, globes and charts. We also need farming implements, sewing machines, and more printer's supplies. We ask our friends to help us in these particulars.
>
> We need other buildings for additional recitation rooms, music room, library, reading room and rooms for the accommodation of a greater number of female students.[31]

The catalog went on to describe the school's inability to provide adequate salaries for its faculty.

> We need that some immediate steps be taken and some sure plan established for the payment of teachers so that the usefulness of the college may be continued and teachers retained. The frequent change of teachers is very unfavorable to the progress of a college. We cannot expect any worthy corps of teachers to remain long with us without a reasonable compensation, and as long as teachers are poorly paid, a school is embarrassed and disrespected.[32]

The 1887 catalog also pleaded for money to expand the industrial department because it provided food and income for the college, as well as training for the students.

> We need money to buy lands and to put our Industrial Department upon a firm basis. In our poverty-stricken state, we are not able to buy the common implements for farm work. And while it is true that our very life depends upon what we make in farming, we must establish other forms of industry. The door of trades and useful training is eternally closed against us unless we do something among ourselves. Upon

[31] Paul Quinn College, *Catalog*, 1887, pp. 24–25.
[32] Ibid., p. 25.

this industrial training depends largely the destiny of our people. So we must ask assistance in securing tools and other material for the establishment of a blacksmith shop, and for the full equipment of our printing office.[33]

The 1887 catalog of Wiley College listed a broad number of "wants," including a desire to see a greater interest in the college among the ministers and laity of the Methodist Episcopal Church. The catalog also asked for help in adding books to the library, constructing new buildings, and attacting five hundred students, "hungering and thirsting for knowledge."[34]

The Wiley College catalog for 1891 listed a number of needs of the college: a printing press, a barn to protect the grain and feed raised on the college farm, a carpentry shop to facilitate needed repairs and train students, and several new buildings. The catalog noted that 425 students were cramped into quarters designed for 200 and that there were more students waiting to get in. The catalog closed by asking, "Who will honor God and build a monument here by coming to our help?"[35]

In 1892, the Guadalupe College catalog designated a new laundry and industrial building as the greatest need and offered the following entreaty: "Who will open his or her hearts and send in a donation small or great? We shall anxiously await a reply. The building is needed."[36]

In a straightforward manner, the Texas College catalog for 1918 listed the needs of the college as

$25,000   Administration Building
 1,500   Equipping Farm
 7,500   Heating Plant
 5,000   Library and Laboratory
 3,000   Fifty Scholarships for worthy students[37]

It is clear from such statements that the major sources of income for these colleges did not meet all their monetary needs. As a result, the presidents of the private black colleges frequently

[33] Ibid.
[34] Wiley College, *Catalog*, 1887, p. 32.
[35] Wiley College, *Catalog*, 1891, p. 60.
[36] Guadalupe College, *Catalog*, 1892, p. 2.
[37] Texas College, *Catalog*, 1918, p. 9.

invented new devices for raising money. For example, they often traveled around the state visiting their constituencies and soliciting additional donations. Another method was to devise special short- or long-range projects. In 1881, Bishop Richard H. Cain, president of Paul Quinn College, led the previously mentioned "Ten Cents a Brick" campaign to raise money for the first permanent college building. Cain succeeded in raising the needed funds by getting families in the Southwest Conference of the African Methodist Episcopal Church to pledge ten cents each for the new structure.[38] When Samuel Huston College was established in 1900, Reuben S. Lovinggood helped equip the college by sponsoring "Chair Socials," "Pillow Case Entertainments," and "Laundry Equipment Fairs" in the Austin community.[39] A. S. Jackson helped rescue Paul Quinn during the depression years partly through his special fund-raising group, the Progressive Club. Made up of alumni and college boosters, the Progressive Club raised funds, coordinated weekly college radio broadcasts, sponsored library book drives and campus beautification projects, and campaigned for state accreditation.[40] In an effort to revitalize Bishop College in the 1930s and 1940s, Joseph J. Rhoads designed and implemented the New Development Program.[41]

The musical talents of the choirs and quartets of these colleges also became valuable development tools. Virtually every black college president used them on fund-raising drives around the state, as well as for numerous campus concerts and picnics. Like the Jubilee Singers of Fisk University, the choirs of Jarvis Christian, Paul Quinn, Samuel Huston, Wiley, and Bishop colleges performed regularly on statewide radio programs, usually to promote development projects.[42]

In addition to organized projects, the presidents of the church-related colleges also spent much of their time searching for money independently. In some cases, presidents took on a specific project, which they handled largely on their own. The

[38] Paul Quinn College, *Catalog*, 1978, p. 19.

[39] Alton Hornsby, Jr., "Negro Education in Texas, 1865–1917" (M.A. thesis, University of Texas, 1962), p. 145.

[40] *Waco Messenger*, June 23, 1933, July 14, 1933, July 21, 1933, February 8, 1935.

[41] Bishop College, *Catalog*, 1945, p. 17.

[42] *Waco Messenger*, May 14 and 21, 1937, November 2, 1934; Venita C. Waddleton, interview with author, Jarvis Christian College, Hawkins, July 18, 1979.

efforts of Mary E. Branch to improve the Tillotson College library serve as an example. By writing hundreds of personal letters to friends, alumni, Austin civic groups, and businessmen, Branch succeeded in collecting a large number of small donations—most less than ten dollars each—and scores of second-hand books. Over her fourteen-year administration, Branch elevated the holdings of the library from 2,000 volumes in 1930 to over 21,000 by 1944.[43]

While it is impossible to estimate the exact amount of money raised by such means during a given period, it appears that significant sums were realized, but only intermittently. Thomas Jesse Jones noted that individual or private contributions were registered by seven of the eleven black private colleges in Texas during 1914. The contributions averaged $2,240 per school and represented roughly 12 percent of the total budgets.[44]

One of the best indicators of the financial problems faced by the black denominational colleges in Texas was the fact that none of them received significant incomes from institutional endowments. In 1914, the United States Bureau of Education found that none of the Texas colleges reported productive endowments. In a similar survey of black colleges in 1928, the federal government reported some change, noting that Bishop, Wiley, and Jarvis had developed small endowments. The report, however, revealed that these funds were so meager that the interest from them remained insignificant.[45] By the late 1930s, several of the other colleges began to establish endowments, but theirs too were usually too small to produce meaningful returns. Tillotson College was typical. Between 1937 and 1950, the AMA institution had an average annual endowment income of just eighty-one dollars.[46]

[43]"Report: Lincoln Memorial Fund, 1931–1932, 1932–1933," Mary Elizabeth Branch Papers, Huston-Tillotson College, Austin; Mary Jenness, *Twelve Negro Americans*, pp. 96–98.

[44]U.S. Bureau of Education, *Negro Education*, II: 574–601.

[45]Ibid.; Baptist Missionary State Convention of Texas, *Minutes*, 1887, pp. 23–24; U.S. Bureau of Education, *Survey of Negro Colleges and Universities*, pp. 810–80.

[46]"Tillotson College: Summary of Proposed Budget, 1937," Addendum: Huston-Tillotson College, Temporary Box No. 4.

Institutional Cooperation

The persistent shortage of endowment income and other funds encouraged a variety of cooperative relationships between the private and public black colleges in Texas. While inter-denominational cooperation faced some limitations, several of the institutions that were located in the same city or nearby locations devised a number of ways to reduce operating costs. Bishop College, a Baptist school, and Wiley College, a Methodist institution, began sharing faculty members as early as 1932. In 1934, Paul Quinn College, an African Methodist Episcopal school, announced that the state's black public college, Prairie View, would be allowed to offer several junior- and senior-level courses on the Waco campus. During 1936, Jarvis Christian College, a Disciples of Christ institution, and Wiley College started sharing the cost of bringing speakers and special entertainment to their campuses.[47]

The strongest example of cooperation, however, existed in Austin between Samuel Huston College and Tillotson College. The two schools were situated less than a mile apart, offered essentially the same curricula, and shared the same difficulties in securing sufficient funding and enrollment. During 1930, Tillotson president Mary E. Branch and the leader of Samuel Huston, Karl E. Downs, entered upon several cooperative ventures, including sharing faculty and the presentations of speakers and artists.[48]

Recognizing the benefits of an even closer relationship, Fred L. Brownlee, General Secretary of the American Missionary Association (AMA), took the lead in proposing that the two schools merge. In light of the rising costs of operation, Brownlee felt it was socially as well as financially unwise for two schools of similar character to continue to operate competitively, rather

[47] *Houston Informer,* October 3, 1931; *Waco Messenger,* September 14, 1934; William R. Davis, *The Development and Present Status of Negro Education in East Texas,* p. 112; Douglas Barnes Taylor, "Negro Education in Texas" (M.A. thesis, University of Texas, 1927), p. 42.

[48] "Memorandum Concerning the Proposed Merger of Samuel Huston and Tillotson Colleges," Addendum: Huston-Tillotson College, Temporary Box No. 1; *Waco Messenger,* September 8, 1933.

than cooperatively, in the Austin community. Brownlee discussed the idea with I. Garland Penn of the Methodist Board of Education, and together they made proposals to their respective denominations. As time passed, the trustees, denominational boards, officials, and alumni of the two institutions carried on informal discussions. Subsequently, a series of meetings commenced in 1944 which began to formulate concrete plans for the proposed union.[49]

Progress toward the merger proved to be slow and often laborious. Although the proposed marriage of the two colleges required much deliberation, the two church bodies worked diligently to effect a general agreement. On July 27, 1945, the AMA gave its official support to the merger, while the Methodist Board of Education extended its approval on February 25, 1947.[50] In a memorandum concerning the merger, Fred L. Brownlee of the AMA and M. S. Davage of the Board of Education agreed on six general principles in bringing about a union of the colleges:

1. The pooling of the present and potential resources of the two colleges in a united effort to do better what each is now doing inadequately and insecurely.
2. The incorporation of a new college under the direction of its own trustees, representative of the alumni and patrons as well as the church boards now responsible for the separate colleges.
3. The adoption of a new name for the united college.
4. The selection of an adequate site.
5. The conservation of the interest of the churches represented by the two missions boards.
6. The securing of reasonably adequate financial aid for buildings and endowments for a bona fide, A-rated, liberal arts college of possibly 1,000 students. (At present there are slightly over 1,000 students in the combined enrollments of the two colleges.)[51]

Between 1947 and 1952, the problems arising from this general outline were resolved. Many well-intentioned but often

[49] Huston-Tillotson College, *Catalog*, 1952, p. 9.

[50] M. S. Davage to Fred L. Brownlee, March 3, 1947, Addendum: Huston-Tillotson College, Temporary Box No. 1; Huston-Tillotson College, *Catalog*, 1952, p. 9.

[51] "Memorandum Concerning the Proposed Merger of Samuel Huston and Tillotson Colleges," Addendum: Huston-Tillotson College, Temporary Box No. 1.

conflicting proposals had to be settled before the merger would be accepted by the officials, students, and alumni of the two institutions. For example, there were several suggestions for the new name for the college. Leaders of the AMA and the Methodist Episcopal Church toyed with the idea of naming it Lovinggood-Tillotson University in honor of the first president of Samuel Huston College, Reuben S. Lovinggood, and Reverend George Jeffrey Tillotson, who founded Tillotson College. In a spirit of give and take, the two church bodies also considered using the title Lovinggood College, provided the old campus of Tillotson College were selected as the site for the new institution. In the end, both sides decided to adopt the name Huston-Tillotson College.[52]

Other considerations involving the future location and finances of the new institution were equally important. In 1947, Fred L. Brownlee and M. S. Davage suggested that the campus of Tillotson offered the best location for the new school, but left the final decision to a committee made up of faculty and staff from the two colleges.[53] The following year, however, William H. Jones, president of Tillotson College, wrote Brownlee to suggest that the merger should follow the pattern of the Atlanta University System, in which each school maintained its own campus, but shared faculty, staff, and certain facilities:

There has been developed some very strong sentiment behind these respective institutions, and it asserts its power whenever the proposal of destroying the individuality of the traditional college comes up for discussion. I believe that the affiliated plan would gain the whole-hearted support of the Methodist constituency . . . our own denominational interest . . . alumni, students, staff . . . [and] community.[54]

Brownlee and Davage pointed out that approximately $1,750,000 would be required to establish the new college on

[52] Ibid.; Fred L. Brownlee to Jackson Davis, February 18, 1947, Addendum; Huston-Tillotson College, Temporary Box No. 1; Huston-Tillotson College, *Preliminary Bulletin*, 1952, p. 1.

[53] "Memorandum Concerning the Proposed Merger of Samuel Huston and Tillotson Colleges," Addendum: Huston-Tillotson College, Temporary Box No. 1.

[54] William H. Jones to Fred L. Brownlee, July 1, 1948, Addendum: Huston-Tillotson College, Temporary Box No. 1.

another site, but perhaps $550,000 less if it were set up on the Tillotson campus. While recognizing that a merger remained more dream than reality, Brownlee and Davage also pointed out that pooling the resources of the two schools would result in a much sounder budget and proposed the following as a list of real and potential revenue:

$35,000   from AMA, to be credited as income in $1,000,000 endowment
17,500   from Methodist Board and Methodist churches, to be credited as income on $550,000 endowment
35,000   income on general endowment of $1,000,000 to be secured from outside sources
35,000   from United Negro College Fund
200,000   from students in fees, tuition and living expenses
25,000   from individual gifts.[55]

The merger was further complicated by local Samuel Huston alumni and supporters, who apparently ignored the wishes of the Methodist Church and opposed the union. Unlike Tillotson, which was run by a centralized authority (the AMA), Samuel Huston was controlled by local supporters through a representative board of trustees. President William H. Jones observed that the board members were almost "unanimously hostile" to the merger and openly sought to "squelch it."[56] In the summer of 1948, rumors surfaced that Samuel Huston might merge with its sister school, Wiley College, and relocate it in Dallas or Austin.[57]

In spite of alumni grumblings and rumors of a Wiley–Samuel Huston merger, William H. Jones believed that the position of President Karl E. Downs would be decisive: "I do not believe his [Downs'] board is going to force anything on him that he does not want. If he recommends the merger, it will be approved; if he does not recommend it, it will not be approved. I do not be-

---

[55]"Memorandum Concerning the Proposed Merger of Samuel Huston and Tillotson Colleges," Addendum: Huston-Tillotson College, Temporary Box No. 1.

[56]William H. Jones to Fred L. Brownlee, February 28, 1947, Addendum: Huston-Tillotson College, Temporary Box No. 1.

[57]William H. Jones to Fred L. Brownlee, July 1, 1948, Addendum: Huston-Tillotson College, Temporary Box No. 1; *Austin American Statesman*, June 13, 1948.

lieve Methodist officials can or will out flank him and let him 'die on the vine.'"[58] Not surprisingly, Downs, who had enjoyed a good working relationship with Tillotson College for more than ten years, remained a staunch supporter of merging with the AMA school and used his influence to bring the Methodist trustees to his point of view.[59]

Finally, on January 26, 1952, the trustees of Tillotson and Samuel Huston College met and agreed that the merger should proceed at once. Subsequently, merger plans based upon those proposed by the AMA and the Methodist Board of Education were adopted on April 16, 1952. While details would be worked out over the next few years, the new college began operation under the following guidelines:

(a) the pooling of the present and potential tangible assets of the two colleges . . . ; (b) the creation of a joint and thoroughly representative board of trustees . . . ; (c) the formation of a new charter; (d) a building program which will involve a minimum cost of $1,500,000 and the ultimate location on one campus . . . ; (e) preservation of the supporting constituencies of both denominations.[60]

The permanent plant would be located on the Tillotson campus, but until additional classroom and living facilities could be constructed, the activities of the new college would be conducted on both campuses. The former Samuel Huston campus was renamed the West Campus, while the Tillotson campus became known as the East Campus. The first catalog of Huston-Tillotson College proudly proclaimed that the union of "these two historical colleges will make available to Negro youth in Texas and the Southwest, one of the largest and strongest private Negro colleges in the nation."[61]

An even broader expression of cooperation among the private black colleges in Texas and around the nation was the formation of the United Negro College Fund in 1943. The fund was

[58] Jones to Brownlee, February 28, 1947, Addendum: Huston-Tillotson College, Temporary Box No. 1.

[59] "Memorandum Concerning the Proposed Merger of Samuel Huston and Tillotson Colleges," Addendum: Huston-Tillotson College, Temporary Box No. 1.

[60] Huston-Tillotson College, *Catalog*, 1952, pp. 10–11.

[61] Huston-Tillotson College, *Preliminary Bulletin*, 1952, pp. 1–2.

inspired by a newspaper article that appeared in the *Pittsburgh Courier*. The article, by Frederick D. Patterson, president of Tuskegee Institute, described the general financial crisis faced by black private colleges and called for the creation of a cooperative fund-raising effort. Later that year, presidents of twenty-seven black private colleges met in Atlanta, Georgia, and established the United Negro College Fund (UNCF).[62]

The fund primarily sought to acquire money for the member colleges by pooling their limited finances to publicize their financial needs and appeal to organized philanthropy. The founders of the UNCF became reasonably successful in raising significant sums from major foundations such as the Rockefeller-backed General Education Board and the Julius Rosenwald Fund. In its first year of operation, the UNCF raised $765,000, far more than could have been collected had each school conducted its own fund-raising campaign.[63] The member colleges agreed to share the income and the expense of the UNCF campaign in proportion to each college's income for current expenses. The receipts of the UNCF were distributed in the following manner: (1) 50 percent divided among the colleges regardless of size; (2) 40 percent divided in proportion to a college's church support or its annual income from endowment; and (3) 10 percent on the basis of enrollment.[64]

Several of the Texas colleges, including Samuel Huston, Texas, Tillotson, and Wiley, became charter members of the UNCF. Bishop College joined in 1945. As Table 11 illustrates, the member colleges in Texas received substantial incomes, which represented a major source of revenue. Between 1944 and 1954, the UNCF extended a total of $1,035,582.60 to the Texas colleges for operating expenses. Beginning in 1952, the UNCF also launched a separate "capital funds" drive to help the colleges finance a variety of institutional improvement and mod-

[62] United Negro College Fund, *Annual Report*, 1975, p. 6.

[63] Ibid.; Frederick Patterson, "Cooperation Among the Predominantly Negro Colleges and Universities," *Journal of Negro Education* 35 (Fall, 1966): 480–81.

[64] "Report on the Meeting of the Representatives of Private Colleges Held in Atlanta, Georgia, September 27, 1943," Addendum: Huston-Tillotson College, Temporary Box No. 1; Patterson, "Cooperation Among Negro Colleges and Universities," p. 481.

TABLE 11
United Negro College Fund, Distribution of Net Proceeds to Member Colleges in Texas, 1944–54

Year	Bishop	Huston-Tillotson	Samuel Huston	Texas	Tillotson	Wiley
1944	—		$14,308.34	$13,145.76	$16,822.04	$16,790.63
1945	$16,832.24		17,871.55	17,193.74	20,447.22	21,034.66
1946	15,206.36		14,896.70	16,403.76	18,310.58	17,666.76
1947	16,207.79		17,129.06	17,966.08	19,685.84	18,959.03
1948	16,170.78		19,282.17	17,017.49	19,274.49	19,804.80
1949	20,649.58		24,760.74	22,012.25	23,203.41	24,014.50
1950	20,510.39		25,057.11	23,113.85	22,915.74	23,599.65
1951	22,467.51		26,306.49	24,522.73	23,972.86	24,906.77
1952	23,559.82	$51,637.20*	—*	25,924.73	—*	25,555.53
1953	24,673.92	42,338.82	—	27,310.87	—	26,229.94
1954	25,454.36	38,732.29	—	28,193.38	—	27,530.87
TOTAL	201,732.75	132,708.31	159,612.16	232,804.64	164,632.18	246,093.14

SOURCE: "United Negro College Fund, Inc. Distribution of New Proceeds to Member Colleges in Texas, 1944–1954," United Negro College Fund Archives, New York.

*Samuel Huston and Tillotson College merged in 1952.

ernization projects. Between 1952 and 1954, the member colleges in Texas received the following total allocations:

Bishop	$314,880
Huston-Tillotson	478,016
Samuel Huston	89,000
Texas	326,040
Tillotson	84,576
Wiley	326,576[65]

Conclusion

Financing black higher education has always been a risky business in the United States. According to most contemporary authors, the financial characteristics of the private black colleges in Texas were similar to those of black colleges elsewhere. In the late nineteenth and early twentieth centuries, colleges generally received 70 to 90 percent of their budgets from denominational and private sources. Income from tuition and fees for most black private colleges did not become a substantial part of their revenues until the 1920s. Organized philanthropy provided badly needed funding for many black colleges, but tended to be biased in favor of those institutions specializing in industrial training. Consequently, the lure of philanthropic support led many black private institutions to offer at least limited industrial or vocational courses. In developing alternate or supplemental sources of income, black college presidents have played the leading role in creating special fund-raising schemes. Finally, inadequate financing forced many of the black colleges to join together in a variety of cooperative ventures.[66]

Because adequate funds were difficult to secure, only a few black colleges succeeded in building substantial financial bases. The best-financed institutions were those that offered industrial arts courses and, therefore, attracted significant philanthropic

[65]"United Negro College Fund, Inc., Distribution of Net Proceeds to Member Colleges in Texas, 1944–1954," United Negro College Fund Archives, New York.

[66]Jones and Weathersby, "Financing the Black College," pp. 106–14; Charles V. Willie and Marlene Y. MacLeish, "The Priorities of Presidents of Black Colleges," pp. 132–33, and Prezell R. Robinson, "Effective Management of Scarce Resources: Presidential Responsibility," pp. 162–63, all in Black Colleges, ed. Willie and Edmonds.

support. By 1915, Hampton Institute and Tuskegee Institute emerged as the two most heavily endowed black colleges, with endowments of $2,709,344 and $1,942,112 respectively. Added together, the endowments of these two schools were as large as the endowments of all the other black colleges combined.[67]

None of the Texas colleges was able to raise enough capital to establish a significant endowment, and the majority were hard-pressed to meet the expenses of operating and minor improvements. Most private black colleges in Texas functioned from one year to the next by juggling a shifting combination of denominational gifts, tuition and fee revenue, and philanthropic grants. Dorms usually faced overcrowding, while older buildings remained in use for lengthy periods and could not be replaced easily if struck by fire. Administrators found faculty difficult to recruit as a result of low salaries and heavy teaching loads and the best faculty hard to retain because of raids by the few well-endowed black colleges.

A review of the physical and financial assets of these colleges in the late 1930s and early 1940s indicated that Wiley, Bishop, Texas, and Tillotson colleges were the most skillful of the Texas schools in acquiring and managing their meager resources. By 1937, each of the four colleges had an annual income exceeding $100,000. This was almost double the incomes of the other schools, Paul Quinn, St. Philip's, Mary Allen, and Jarvis Christian. Only the black public schools, Prairie View and Houston, with budgets of more than $500,000 each, had larger incomes. Tillotson, Bishop, Wiley, and Prairie View were the only black colleges with libraries of more than 10,000 volumes with Tillotson's the largest of all black colleges in the state (18,853 volumes). Wiley, Tillotson, and Bishop paid the highest faculty salaries of the private colleges; by 1942, their salaries rivaled those of the black public colleges. The five institutions paying the highest median salaries for professors during 1942 were Wiley, $1,600; Tillotson, $1,500; Prairie View, $1,338; Houston, $1,300; and Bishop, $1,125.[68]

[67] Jones and Weathersby, "Financing the Black College," in *Black Colleges*, ed. Willie and Edmonds, pp. 111–12.

[68] Montgomery, *Senior Colleges for Negroes in Texas*, pp. 39–41, 62–65, 71.

Reviewing the finances of black colleges makes it apparent that institutional cooperation has been common among many black colleges, ranging in degree from limited arrangements, such as those which existed between Bishop and Wiley, to full-scale mergers. Three examples of extensive cooperation were the creation of the Atlanta University Center in 1929, which first involved Atlanta University and Morehouse and Spelman colleges, and later included Clark and Morris Brown colleges, as well as the Interdenominational Theological Center; the establishment of Dillard University in 1930, by joining Straight University and New Orleans University; and the union of Samuel Huston and Tillotson colleges in Austin in 1952.[69]

Institutional cooperation among black colleges has been motivated primarily by financial need, the desire to reduce operating costs, and the wish to improve the quality of instruction and the cultural and extracurricular experiences of students. The formation of the United Negro College Fund resulted in perhaps the most far-reaching cooperative effort among black colleges prior to 1954. Twenty-seven colleges, including Samuel Huston, Texas, Tillotson, and Wiley, established the fund-raising organization to combat these financial problems. Bishop College became an active member in 1945. As equal members of the UNCF, the private black colleges of Texas received annual grants based upon the size and income of the institution.[70]

It is clear that the church-related black colleges in Texas were faced with a variety of financial obstacles. Because the leaders of these schools were able to handle most of these problems through skillful management and imaginative development projects, these institutions not only survived, but expanded and improved. Consequently, in the age of Jim Crow, the private black colleges in Texas were able to make vital contributions, both qualitatively and quantitatively, to the advancement of black Texans.

[69] Holmes, *Evolution of the Negro College*, pp. 192–97; McPherson, *Abolitionist Legacy*, p. 151; Patterson, "Cooperation Among Negro Colleges and Universities," pp. 477–83.

[70] United Negro College Fund, *Annual Report*, 1975, p. 6; Patterson, "Cooperation Among Negro Colleges and Universities," pp. 477–83.

5

Student Life

THE extracurricular activities of their students offer additional insights into the character and development of the black denominational colleges in Texas. In this chapter we shall explore these activities as they existed from 1872 to 1954. First, the religious atmosphere and theological requirements of these schools will be compared. Second, a review of the college rules and regulations, as well as student activism, will be offered. Third, the development of academic and social organizations, as well as intercollegiate sports, will be surveyed.

Religious Emphasis

All the church-related black colleges in Texas displayed distinctly, and often strict, religious atmospheres. This was not surprising because two of the principal purposes for their founding were to provide Christian-oriented education for all freedmen and to train young men for the ministry.[1] The Bishop College catalog for 1881 appears typical of this attitude, stating:

No system of education can properly be considered complete that does not provide for religious culture. Bishop College has a distinctly religious design, which is kept steadily in view in the daily educational work. It is desired that they who come to receive the benefits of the school should not only acquire a thorough education in secular knowl-

[1] *Methodist Review*, 1886, p. 329; Freedmen's Aid Society, *Annual Report*, 1875, pp. 13–14; Board of Missions for Freedmen of the Presbyterian Church in the United States of America, *Annual Report*, 1888, pp. 20–21, and 1892, p. 10; *Journal of the Texas Annual Conference of the Methodist Episcopal Church*, 1928, p. 32; Melvin J. Banks, interview with author, Bishop College, Dallas, July 23, 1979; Allen C. Hancock, interview with author, Texas College, Tyler, July 18, 1979.

edge, but that they should leave it intelligent, sensible and earnest Christian men and women.[2]

Similar statements can be found in the records of the other colleges. The catalog of Guadalupe College in 1892 remarked that the Seguin school was established to "awaken a warm educational interest among the Colored people of the South West, giving special prominence to the Normal and Theological training." The 1918 Texas College catalog listed as a goal the opportunity for "negro youths to have the advantages of a liberal Christian education." The 1929 Jarvis Christian College catalog noted that the Hawkins school sought to "set such standards of scholarship, of high idealism [and] of Christian character, . . . that will enable them to become citizens of honor."[3] The 1945 Paul Quinn College catalog described the college not only as a Christian school of the African Methodist Episcopal Church, but also as a "college extending Christian communion to all faith." The 1950 Wiley College catalog listed as its first purpose the desire to "aid youth in attaining a Christian basis for life or a Christian philosophy of life." In its initial catalog in 1952, Huston-Tillotson College declared its desire to "develop within the student a character definitely Christian and to sensitize him to the need for sustained spiritual growth."[4]

These colleges coupled their strong commitment to religiously-oriented education with stern expectations of student participation in campus religious activities. In addition to daily convocations, prayer meetings, or vesper services, each college also provided regular Sunday worship services. Student attendance at these events was mandatory or at least "strongly urged."[5] Samplings from several college catalogs indicate that

[2]Quoted in William R. Davis, *The Development and Present Status of Negro Education in East Texas*, p. 104.

[3]Guadalupe College, *Catalog*, 1892, p. 1; Texas College, *Catalog*, 1918, p. 6; Jarvis Christian College, *Catalog*, 1929, p. 10.

[4]Paul Quinn College, *Catalog*, 1945, p. 12; Wiley College, *Catalog*, 1950, p. 17; Huston-Tillotson College, *Catalog*, 1952, p. 12.

[5]*American Missionary* 49 (1895): 102; Guadalupe College, *Catalog*, 1892, p. 15; Texas College, *Catalog*, 1926, p. 9; Paul Quinn College, *Catalog*, 1937, p. 13; Samuel Huston College, *Student Handbook*, n.d., pp. 15–16, 20.

this attitude continued during the late nineteenth and early twentieth centuries. The 1892 Guadalupe College catalog reported that "Bible and chapel services form part of the daily work" and explained that "familiar acquaintance with the Bible and its teachings hurt no one, but lifts all." The Wiley College catalog for 1906 listed three separate and mandatory church services for students each Sunday. According to the catalog, these opportunities provided: "the means of bringing all of the students in close touch with the Bible. Teachers and pupils received practical application from each lesson to their everyday life, and the critical study of the Holy Scriptures tends to make all wiser unto salvation." In a similar vein, the 1935 Tillotson College catalog declared that a systematic effort was made to "stimulate in every student high moral and spiritual idealism . . . through the medium of Chapel Exercises, Sunday School, Y.M.C.A., Y.W.C.A., Sunday Vesper Services, and Christian Endeavor."[6]

Between 1930 and 1954, changing social attitudes encouraged several of the colleges to relax or modify their attendance requirements. The 1937 Paul Quinn College catalog pointed out that "chapel exercises, attendance at which is expected, though voluntary on the part of the student, are held three times each week. . . ." The catalog went on to point out, however, that attendance for convocation and prayer services was required. During the 1940s Samuel Huston College urged its students to attend religious activities because they were "vital to the development of Christian character" and were conducted as a "medium of inter-cultural development, for announcements, and matters of general interest." By 1954, Huston-Tillotson College and Wiley College had simply dropped from their catalogs any mention of required attendance.[7]

[6]Guadalupe College, *Catalog*, 1892, p. 15; Wiley College catalog quoted in Lloyd Kay Thompson, "The Origins and Development of Black Religious Colleges in East Texas" (Ph.D. diss., North Texas State University, 1976), p. 31; Tillotson College, *Catalog*, 1935, p. 19.

[7]Paul Quinn College, *Catalog*, 1937, p. 13; Samuel Huston College, *Student Handbook*, n.d., p. 19; Huston-Tillotson College, *Catalog*, 1952, pp. 13–14; Wiley College, *Catalog*, 1950, p. 27.

Not all the colleges, however, followed this approach. Jarvis Christian College remained steadfast in demanding student participation in campus religious activities. The Jarvis catalog for 1950 declared:

The college accepts the responsibility for creating an atmosphere conducive to the development of and appreciation for the fundamental moral tenants, which spring from the Judeo-Christian tradition. In this regard, the college administration expects both the faculty and student personnel to make articulate in their own lives, both in the class room and otherwise a functional appreciation and adherence to the Christian philosophy of life.

Religious opportunities at Jarvis included weekly chapel services, Sunday school, and Wednesday evening vespers. Student attendance was described as "imperative."[8]

In addition to offering a variety of religious activities and requiring attendance, most of the black colleges also required course work in theology. In the late nineteenth century, such classes were offered on the college, secondary, and elementary grade levels. In many instances, the study of religion coincided with the study of Greek or Latin. During the late 1800s, Bishop, Wiley, and Guadalupe colleges offered required courses in Greek which focused on translations of the New Testament.[9] During the twentieth century, the colleges shifted away from classical studies toward formal theology courses, which showed an evangelical bent, except in the Presbyterian and Episcopal schools. While the number of credit hours varied, most of the black colleges in Texas asked their students to take from three to six semester hours of religion. The following survey of theology requirements between the years 1942 and 1950 illustrates this near uniformity:

Bishop	nine quarter hours
Butler	three quarter hours
Jarvis Christian	three semester hours
Paul Quinn	no hours required

[8] Jarvis Christian College, *Catalog*, 1950, p. 20.
[9] Bishop College, *Catalog*, 1897, pp. 8–32; Wiley College, *Catalog*, 1887, pp. 22–23; Guadalupe College, *Catalog*, 1892, p. 305.

Samuel Huston	six semester hours
Texas	nine quarter hours
Tillotson	three semester hours
Wiley	five quarter hours [10]

Rules and Regulations

In light of the strong religious emphasis found at these colleges, it is not surprising that they also observed strict codes of social and educational conduct. Statements of disciplinary procedures appeared in the catalogs of all the schools. In the late nineteenth century, the tone of these statements revealed a stern and regimented attitude. The 1892 catalog of Guadalupe College noted that discipline was "strict and firm," requiring that students "bring testimonials of good moral character, and . . . expect to abide by the rules and regulations of the school, or take the consequent results that follow disobedience." The Bishop College 1897 catalog noted that discipline was "mild, but firm," and administered with a "view to the best culture of students in manners and morals." The catalog went on to warn that "the best government is self-government; but in cases where self-indulgence disregards wholesome rules, it must be met by inflexible governmental firmness." In the 1887 catalog of Paul Quinn College, the following note was made: "Wholesome regulations are instituted, designated to promote the prosperity and happiness of the student. . . . A disposition to evade just and salutary rules will meet with the special disapprobation of the faculty and good students. . . . Every student is placed on his honor. A record is made daily of every student's conduct, general deportment and recitations. A monthly report is sent to the parent or guardian of each pupil. . . ."[11]

[10] Jarvis Christian College, *Catalog*, 1946, p. 19; Paul Quinn College, *Catalog*, 1949, p. 40; Samuel Huston College, *Catalog*, 1942, p. 5; Texas College, *Catalog*, 1949, p. 35; Tillotson College, *Catalog*, 1950, p. 27; Wiley College, *Catalog*, 1950, p. 46; Raphael O' Hara Lanier, "The History of Higher Education for Negroes in Texas: 1930–1955, With Particular Reference to Texas Southern University" (Ph.D. diss., New York University, 1957), pp. 122, 126–27.

[11] Guadalupe College, *Catalog*, 1892, p. 14; Bishop College, *Catalog*, 1897, p. 41; Paul Quinn College, *Catalog*, 1887, p. 26.

The rules and regulations imposed by the private schools in Texas were quite similar and affected every aspect of the student's life. Students in these colleges were forced to attend weekly religious activities and Sunday worship services. They could not leave campus or go home without the written permission of the president. Female students leaving campus had to be escorted by a faculty member. Students were not permitted to visit the room of another student without permission. Most of the colleges closed their campuses on Sunday to outside visitors and expected their students to observe the Sabbath in quiet meditation. The possession of liquor, tobacco, or firearms was strictly forbidden. Loud or boisterous behavior in the dormitories, dining hall, or classrooms was also prohibited. Communications of any type between the sexes, except at approved school functions, were also taboo. Incoming and outgoing mail was often censored by college officials and students were expected to write their parents regularly. A variety of rules also dealt with school conduct, such as whispering or sleeping in class, tardiness, and the reading of unrelated materials.[12]

In the early years, several of the colleges also made their students wear uniforms. In 1891, female students at Wiley College wore blue flannel dress goods, trimmed around the collar and cuffs with gold braid, while male students wore blue flannel cloth sack coats with brass buttons. The Wiley catalog noted that dress regulations were not compulsory, but urged they be observed in the interest of economy, uniformity, and the "appearance of the students as a body."[13] At St. Philip's College during 1903, uniforms for women students in the fall and spring terms included a navy blue skirt, white waists, and blue mortar-boards; and during the winter term, navy blue suits with mortar-boards. The few male students at the San Antonio school wore navy blue pants and white shirts.[14] During the 1920s, Jarvis Christian Col-

---

[12] Paul Quinn College, *Catalog*, 1887, pp. 26–27; Wiley College, *Catalog*, 1901, pp. 19–20; Jarvis Christian College, *Catalog*, 1922, pp. 15–16; Tillotson College, *Catalog*, 1935, pp. 18–19; Guadalupe College, *Catalog*, 1892, pp. 14–15; Texas College, *Catalog*, 1930, pp. 8–9; *American Missionary* 45 (1891): 324.

[13] Wiley College, *Catalog*, 1891, p. 52.

[14] Clarence W. Norris, Jr., "St. Philip's College: A Case Study of a Historically Black Two-Year College" (Ph.D. diss., University of Southern California, 1975), p. 72.

lege asked its female students to dress in "blue skirts and inexpensive waists." Jarvis officials justified this requirment, saying "school uniforms should be used by girls, especially where the temptation to dress beyond one's means is noticeable."[15] While not mandating a particular color or style, the Texas College catalog of 1926 specified that "girls are required to wear uniforms. Each girl makes her own uniform in the sewing room under the supervision of the sewing instructor. Each girl must provide herself with two work aprons. Each young man must provide himself with overalls or work clothes."[16]

Regulations requiring uniforms vanished during the 1920s, but rules demanding formal attire continued down through the mid-1940s. In most of the colleges, women could not attend classes in anything but dresses. Men were expected to wear white shirts and ties and, in some cases, dress coats.[17]

Regimented time schedules also formed a part of early student life at these colleges. The average day usually began around six o'clock in the morning and ended with "lights-out" at ten or ten-thirty in the evening. A typical day at Bishop College during the 1890s involved the following schedule:

6:00 A.M.	rising bell;
7:00 A.M.	breakfast;
8:00–8:45 A.M.	study hall;
9:00–9:20 A.M.	assembly consisting of Bible reading, a hymn and a short talk;
9:20–12:20 P.M.	classes;
12:20–1:00 P.M.	lunch;
1:00–4:00 P.M.	classes;
4:00–5:30 P.M.	relaxation and work;
5:30 P.M.	dinner;
6:00–7:00 P.M.	relaxation;
7:00–9:45 P.M.	supervised study;
10:00 P.M.	bell for retiring;
10:30 P.M.	lights out[18]

[15] Jarvis Christian College, *Catalog*, 1922, p. 15.

[16] Texas College, *Catalog*, 1926, p. 11.

[17] Interview with George H. Chandler, Wiley College, Marshall, July 20, 1979; Banks Interview.

[18] Melvin J. Banks, "Bishop Students—Then, As Now—'In Quest of the Best,'" *Bishop Herald*, Fall, 1977, pp. 10–11.

Although the Victorian rules of these colleges went largely unchallenged, there is little doubt that some students found the atmosphere too restrictive and either withdrew or were expelled. It is also realistic to believe that college students could and did circumvent many of the rules, especially those limiting socialization with the opposite sex.[19]

Students began to voice opposition to strict rules and regulations at the close of World War II. The first signs appeared as thousands of black veterans returned from duty and enrolled in black colleges around the nation. Many of these young men were beyond the normal age for college students, had experienced other cultures, and were accustomed to being self-reliant. To many of these young men, the prim and proper rules of conduct in black colleges seemed outdated. At the same time, social attitudes in the nation were changing. Many of the white colleges and universities already had begun to modify some of their rules. Consequently, during the 1940s students voiced demands for reforms on many black college campuses, including the church-related institutions in Texas.[20]

Students wished to see reforms in almost every aspect of student life, including an end to regimented time schedules, segregation of the sexes, mandatory church and vesper services, room inspections, formal attire, and restrictions on social activities such as dancing. Students on some campuses also wanted to have a voice in the formulation of social and academic policy. While a few of the Texas schools experienced periods of tension and frustration, acceptable reforms were usually developed. At Bishop College, President Joseph J. Rhoads skillfully avoided any student unrest during the 1940s by quietly working out a series of modest reforms, including an end to surprise room checks, nightly curfews, and formal dress codes. In addition, Dean Melvin J. Banks helped in the creation of the first student government, which represented the student body and served as a line of communication to the staff and faculty.[21]

[19]Venita C. Waddleton, interview with author, Jarvis Christian College, Hawkins, July 18, 1979; Chandler interview.

[20]John P. Jones, interview with author, Texas College, Tyler, July 19, 1979; Banks interview; Chandler interview.

[21]Chandler interview; Banks interview.

Evans Industrial Building, Tillotson College, circa 1920. This building, completed in 1912, was used primarily for home economics classes. Courtesy Huston-Tillotson College.

Paul Quinn College printing shop, 1914. Courtesy Paul Quinn College.

Tillotson College faculty, 1924. Until the mid-1920s, the Tillotson faculty was staffed exclusively by white instructors. Courtesy Huston-Tillotson College.

Paul Quinn College faculty, 1927. Black denominations, such as the African Methodist Episcopal Church, employed black staffs and faculties from the beginning. Courtesy Paul Quinn College.

Left: Bishop Richard H. Cain, circa 1880, the second president of Paul Quinn College. Courtesy Paul Quinn College. *Right*: Matthew Winfred Dogan, circa 1930. As president of Wiley College from 1896 to 1942, Dogan guided the school through almost a half-century of diverse problems. Courtesy Wiley College.

Left: Mary Elizabeth Branch, circa 1940, one of a handful of black women ever to achieve the rank of college president. Branch served Tillotson College from 1930 to 1944. Courtesy Huston-Tillotson College. *Right*: Joseph J. Rhoads, circa 1930, the first black president of Bishop College. Courtesy Bishop College.

Left: Dominion R. Glass, circa 1945. Glass led Texas College to the most prosperous period in its history. Courtesy Texas College. *Right*: Artemisia Bowden, circa 1950. Bowden served St. Philip's College for fifty-two years in a variety of positions, including president of the school. Courtesy St. Philip's College.

Reuben S. Lovinggood, circa 1916, the first president of Samuel Huston College. Courtesy Huston-Tillotson College. *Right*: Melvin B. Tolson, circa 1935. At one time a professor at Wiley College, Tolson was recognized as a major Harlem Renaissance poet. Courtesy Wiley College.

Wiley College library, circa 1947. Wiley was the only black college in Texas to receive a Carnegie library grant. This building, completed in the early 1900s, originally housed a collection of more than seventeen thousand volumes. Courtesy Wiley College.

A view of the Wiley College campus in 1945. Courtesy Wiley College.

Bishop College homecoming dance, 1950. Some social activities, such as dancing, were not allowed at black colleges in Texas until the mid-1940s. Courtesy
Bishop College.

Flo Mills Drama Society at Samuel Huston College, 1928. Some of the first
social and cultural organizations to appear at black colleges were drama and
debating clubs. Courtesy Huston-Tillotson College.

Bands, choirs, and quartets, such as the Wiley College Quartet of 1936 shown here, were a popular part of campus life. Courtesy Wiley College.

Texas College voice recital, circa 1940. Courtesy Texas College.

Intercollegiate sports at these schools included football, baseball, track, tennis, and basketball. Pictured here is the 1928 Samuel Huston College men's basketball team. Courtesy Huston-Tillotson College.

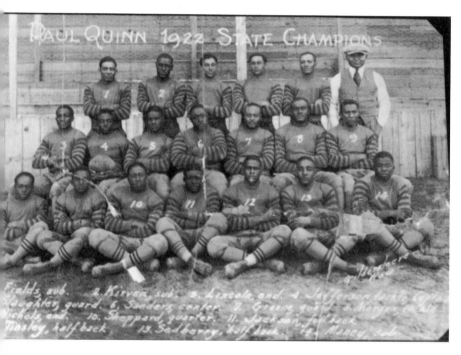

The 1922 Paul Quinn College football team. In terms of interest and emphasis, the premier sport at the black colleges was unquestionably football. Courtesy Paul Quinn College.

The only overt example of student unrest in Texas occurred at Wiley College during late 1947 and early 1948. The confrontation began on October 2, 1947, when Wiley students delivered a petition, signed by 548 students, to President E. C. McLeod demanding several reforms. The petition called for changes in campus rules concerning segregation of the sexes, academic rules for athletes, and limitations on Greek letter organizations. Furthermore, it demanded that Wiley students have a voice in "governing themselves according to the standards of moral codes, and the right to be represented in disciplinary matters."[22] Finally, the petition called for the resignations of four professors who, students claimed, were guilty of "unorthodox failures" of students, refusal to discuss student expulsions with parents, and moral misconduct.[23]

When McLeod refused the petition, student leaders called for a strike. For five days (October 2–6), the Wiley campus was paralyzed, as a majority of the student body boycotted classes. Though Marshall officials and the McLeod administration expressed concern, the students refrained from any acts of violence. The strike essentially involved students staying away from classes and posting signs and placards around campus. In the meantime, student leaders Joseph R. Willie and Fred Jones, both veterans and seniors, conducted ongoing discussions with the administration. In order to bring additional pressure upon Wiley officials, student representatives traveled to New Orleans to meet with leaders of the Methodist Episcopal Church who were attending a convention. Subsequently, Executive Secretary M. S. Davage came to Marshall to investigate the situation and to attempt a resolution of the crisis.[24]

With the campus deserted and the future of the college in doubt, President McLeod announced on October 10 that several reforms were forthcoming. The Wiley president promised that social privileges would be broadened, that student failures would be closely examined, and that students would be allowed

[22] *Houston Informer*, October 11, 1947.

[23] *The Call* (Kansas City), October 17, 1947; *Pittsburgh Courier*, October 11, 1947; *Houston Informer*, October 11, 1947.

[24] Ibid.; *San Antonio Register*, October 10, 1947; *Negro Labor News* (Houston), October 11, 1947.

to form a student government or "council" in order to have a voice in the making of academic and social regulations. McLeod also disclosed that three faculty members, including Dean Irving J. Scott, R. G. Lloyd, head of the social science department, and J. H. Dixon, chairman of the physical education department, had submitted resignations.[25]

Although the strike brought about some changes, problems at the college persisted through the fall term. On November 17, 1947, the newly-organized student government called for the resignation of President McLeod. Leaders of the student government were convinced that McLeod planned to dissolve the student organization and reinstate the ousted dean, Irving J. Scott.[26]

Again the Methodist Church intervened, by sending Bishop R. N. Brooks to Marshall to confer with Wiley trustees. On December 17, Brooks attempted to deliver an address before the Wiley student body concerning the crisis. As the Methodist official told the audience that the trustees and the Methodist Church fully supported President McLeod and stated that the student government had acted irresponsibly and would be disbanded, most of the students rose and walked out of the meeting. The following day, tension increased as McLeod expelled fifty-three student government members.[27]

The confrontation culminated in a second student strike as the spring semester began. During January, students paraded in front of the administration building with signs denouncing McLeod and urging all students to join in a general boycott. Expecting violence, McLeod called upon local law enforcement officials to protect the faculty and staff and requested intervention by the Texas Rangers. State officials responded on January 7 by sending Captain M. T. (Lone Wolf) Gonzales and another Ranger to patrol the Marshall campus.[28]

Although no violence occurred and less than half the stu-

[25]Negro Labor News (Houston), October 11, 1947; The Call (Kansas City), October 17, 1947; San Antonio Register, October 10, 1947.

[26]Houston Informer, January 10, 1948.

[27]Ibid.; Pittsburgh Courier, January 17, 1948.

[28]Marshall News Messenger, January 7, 1948; Pittsburgh Courier, January 17, 1948.

dent body supported the second strike, the future of the college was nevertheless threatened. The bad publicity spawned by the walkout increased when students retained the services of Chicago attorney and former Wiley student Herbert J. Dotson to seek the reinstatement of the fifty-three ousted students. Consequently, as colleges officials and students moved their battle into the courts, McLeod began a series of closed meetings with students in an attempt to end the crisis. At the same time, he moved to quiet the campus by asking police to keep all expelled students off campus. By the end of the month, student interest in the strike waned, as approximately three hundred students returned to classes. Most Wiley students felt the student government had been excessive in its criticism of McLeod and had overstepped its rights as a student organization. On February 3, lawyers for both sides agreed that twenty-nine of the fifty-three students expelled by McLeod would be readmitted. The remaining twenty-four would be eligible for reinstatement pending interviews with the administration. By mid-February, the whole affair had blown over and the campus was back to normal, with the exception of the student government, which was dissolved.[29]

The student strikes at Wiley were virtually isolated incidents. Although administrators of the other private black colleges resisted sweeping change, they usually worked out their differences with students peacefully. Bishop College administrator Melvin J. Banks noted that the problems experienced at Wiley College profoundly impressed black college administrators around the state. Banks observed that the desire to avoid similar unpleasant situations prompted many colleges to respond to student proposals for reform more readily. By 1954, most of the colleges had modified their rules governing student behavior, allowing more student interaction and freedom. Only Bishop and Huston-Tillotson colleges, however, allowed their students to form student governments.[30]

---

[29] *New Orleans Informer Sentinel,* January 24, 1948; *Marshall News Messenger,* January 11 and 18, 1948; *Pittsburgh Courier,* January 17, 1948; *The Call* (Kansas City), February 13, 1948.

[30] Banks interviews; Huston-Tillotson College, *Catalog,* 1952, p. 13.

Organizations and Sports

The conservative religious atmospheres and limited budgets of the church-related black colleges in Texas also slowed the development of student organizations. In the late 1800s and early 1900s, only a few academic and social organizations existed. The most common of these included debating and literary societies, musical and choral groups, and local chapters of the YMCA and YWCA.[31]

Music became another important early feature of student life. Each of the schools formed a choir and band almost immediately. Throughout the history of these colleges, piano and organ recitals were common events. In addition to their local performances, college quartets and choirs toured the state, enchanting crowds with their classical and religious repertoires. The spirited brass bands of these schools blared the strains of religious hymns, as well as popular composers. Like black and white colleges around the nation, the Texas schools developed a variety of school songs expressing the love and loyalty of their students. For example, two Bishop College cheerleaders, W. R. Bledsoe, Jr., and Ola Fowler, introduced a pep song during 1910 that became the Bishop alma mater:

There's a color I love, 'tis the azure above
The good old Bishop Blue.
There's nothing quite like it, the others don't strike it.
The good old Bishop Blue.

Chorus

The good old Bishop Blue, the good old Bishop Blue.
A little piece will make a man feel just as good as new.
We'll put a strip up here you see
To show our hearts beat true;
The best school in the Union is—
The good old Bishop Blue.

[31] Bishop College, *Catalog*, 1897, p. 42; Wiley College, *Catalog*, 1901, p. 21; Texas College, *Catalog*, 1918, p. 7; Jarvis Christian College, *Catalog*, 1916, pp. 12–13; Banks interview; *Journal of the Texas Annual Conference of the Methodist Episcopal Church*, 1929, p. 18.

As long as we live, the best we will give
To the good old Bishop Blue.
Be loyal forever; Dishonor it never
The good old Bishop Blue.[32]

While most of the schools had alma maters built around similar pep songs, Samuel Huston College exhibited an alma mater much broader in scope:

There's a College down in Austin,
Where the morning glories twine,
Where sugar cane is sweetest,
And the sun shines all the time:
I am now in this old slow town,
But I won't be here for long.
For my heart is gladly turning
To my old Sam Huston Home.

It's the only growing College,
Down here in this Lone Star State,
It would like to be with others,
But it has no time to wait.
And no matter where I roam;
I can hear the fulsome praises
Of my old Sam Huston Home.

I can see them in the Chapel,
Just before the hour of noon,
Making all those great big speeches,
'Hitch your chariot to the moon:
I can see them in the kitchen,
Making bread that rises like foam,
And I want to go, I tell you,
To my old Sam Huston home.

We will not be here forever,
For they tell us we must go,

[32] Melvin J. Banks, "Our Heritage in Song: Bishop Music Through the Years," *Bishop Herald*, Spring, 1977, p. 10.

Up to Heaven to live with Jesus,
But I tell you I don't know.
I am going to ask St. Peter
When I reach that Heavenly shore:
"Will you please, Oh, please do send me
To my old Sam Huston Home."—*Repeat.*[33]

Debating also proved quite popular in the late nineteenth and early twentieth centuries. Numerous contests pitting the skills of students from Bishop, Wiley, Paul Quinn, Texas, Tillotson, and Samuel Huston college were staged each year. Students from schools like Virginia Union College, Fisk University, Morehouse College, and Howard University also crossed wits with the Texas students.[34]

During the 1920s and 1930s, a wider variety of academic and social clubs emerged as college enrollments grew and elementary and secondary courses were eliminated. Academic clubs and honor societies were formed for students in mathematics, science, English, history, foreign languages, home economics, and theology. The 1935 Tillotson College catalog listed twelve academically-oriented student organizations, including the Delvers Dramatic Club, Carver Science Club, Descartes Mathematics Club, Glee Club, YMCA, YWCA, E. E. Just Biology Club, Franco Hispanic society, Education Club, Home Economics Club, Interracial Forum, and Debating Society.[35]

Between 1930 and 1954, several of the colleges organized local honor societies and formed chapters of national honorary organizations. Texas College created the Phi Delta Psi Honor Society in 1932 as the official scholarship society of the college. Membership was open to all students maintaining a "B" average. Other honorary groups at Texas College included Mu Chi Sigma for outstanding students in science and Phi Delta Chi for leading students in education. At Wiley College, the Sigma Rho Sigma

[33] "Samuel Huston College Commencement Invitation," May 13, 1928.
[34] *Waco Messenger*, May 5, 1933; *Houston Informer*, April 5, 1930; Banks interview.
[35] Paul Quinn College, *The Tiger* (Annual), 1927, pp. 38–39; Paul Quinn College, *Catalog*, 1937, pp. 13–15; Wiley College, *Catalog*, 1928, pp. 24–26; Jarvis Christian College, *Catalog*, 1922, p. 17; Texas College, *Catalog*, 1934, pp. 13–14; Tillotson College, *Catalog*, 1935, pp. 16–17.

honor society accepted students majoring or minoring in the social sciences who maintained a "B" average.[36] Wiley, Texas, Jarvis Christian, and Huston-Tillotson College were among the first to organize chapters of Alpha Kappa Mu, a national honor society for juniors and seniors displaying a 2.5 grade point average (on a 3.0 scale); Beta Kappa Chi, a national honor group for students majoring in mathematics, science, home economics, and physical education; and Zeta Sigma Pi, a national social science society.[37]

Fraternities and sororities became the most common type of social organizations to develop on these campuses. Because of the restrictive nature of college life in the late nineteenth century, these clubs did not begin to appear until after 1915. Wiley College became the first black college in Texas to permit such social organizations when it allowed its students to found Phi Beta Sigma Fraternity in 1916. By 1946, a total of four fraternities and four sororities had been established at Wiley. As time passed, the other schools also permitted chapters of national black fraternities and sororities on their campuses. At Tillotson College, three fraternities and four sororities were founded between 1936 and 1946. A similar trend occurred at Texas College, where three fraternities and three sororities appeared between 1937 and 1945.[38]

Some of the other colleges were more reluctant. Paul Quinn College officials did not allow fraternities on their campus until 1951. Neither fraternities nor sororities were established at Bishop College until 1954. Bishop administrator Melvin J. Banks noted that college leaders were concerned that such groups might create a "class element" on campus, which would be harmful to the growth of the school.[39] Jarvis Christian College also remained wary of fraternal societies. The 1954 catalog listed only two quasi-social clubs for its students:

[36] Texas College, *Catalog*, 1950, pp. 17–18; Wiley College, *Catalog*, 1950, p. 24.

[37] Ibid.; Huston-Tillotson College, *Catalog*, 1952, p. 14; Jarvis Christian College, *Catalog*, 1966, p. 43.

[38] Wiley College, *Catalog*, 1950, p. 24; Paul Quinn College, *Catalog*, 1978, p. 42; Texas College, *Catalog*, 1949, p. 17; Mabel Crayton Williams, "The History of Tillotson College, 1881–1952" (M.A. thesis, Texas Southern University, 1967), pp. 105–106.

[39] Banks interview.

Tau Gamma: This is an organization of eighteen young women. The members regard themselves as comrades of culture and conduct. They feel that it is their duty to foster the best possible conduct by practical examples throughout the entire college community.

The Tidy Teens: This organization limits its membership to nineteen. The club has high ideals as to scholarship and life goals.[40]

The most common fraternities found at these colleges were Phi Beta Sigma, Kappa Alpha Psi, Alpha Phi Alpha, and Omega Psi Phi. The most popular sororities included chapters of Alpha Kappa Alpha, Delta Sigma Theta, Zeta Phi Beta, and Sigma Gamma Rho. Each had its own constitution, secret ceremonies, and reputation. Like the fraternities and sororities on other black and white college campuses, each group engaged in traditional initiation activities involving stunts, pranks, physical exercise, and paddling. More importantly, however, when properly led and supervised, these organizations served a significant function as mechanisms for social interaction, personal fulfillment, and school pride.[41]

By 1900, intercollegiate sports also had become an integral part of student life. Sports offered for men included football, basketball, baseball, track, and tennis. Sports opportunities for women were limited primarily to intramural basketball and softball. By 1920, however, predominantly female institutions such as Mary Allen, Tillotson, and St. Philip's colleges did manage to field intercollegiate teams in basketball and tennis. The majority of students who competed were nonscholarship athletes. With their limited budgets, none of the black colleges could offer more than partial or token athletic scholarships. Outstanding athletes commonly competed in more than one sport.[42]

In terms of interest and emphasis, football always ranked as the premier sport. Basketball and baseball were popular, but

[40] Jarvis Christian College, *Catalog*, 1954, p. 14.

[41] William H. Ammons, interview with author, Texas College, Tyler, July 17, 1979; Chandler interview; Texas College, *Catalog*, 1949, p. 17; Wiley College, *Catalog*, 1950, p. 24; Huston-Tillotson College, *Catalog*, 1952, p. 14.

[42] *Houston Informer*, March 21, 1936, April 4, 1936; Ammons interview; Hancock interview.

football seemed to elicit the greatest interest among students
and in the community and the press. In 1901, Wiley College
proudly announced:

> The athletic sports are not only allowed, but encouraged. It is thought
> that the best education is that which develops a strong, robust body as
> well as other parts of the human makeup. Football, as it is played at
> Yale and other Eastern colleges was introduced this year; and Wiley's
> prowess in baseball is well known. . . . Roughness and rowdyism,
> which have brought these games into disrepute in many places, are not
> allowed at Wiley.[43]

The glamor and appeal of college football encouraged most
of the other black colleges in Texas to introduce the sport. From
1900 to 1954, nearly every college fielded a team for at least limited periods. Wiley, Bishop, Texas, Samuel Huston, and Jarvis
Christian colleges competed on a fairly regular basis through the
mid-1930s in what was called the Texas Conference, Southern
Athletic Conference, or Big Five Conference, depending on
how many of the colleges participated at the time. Paul Quinn
and Butler College had difficulties in supporting football programs and consequently were involved only infrequently. As
Mary Allen, Tillotson, and St. Philip's colleges were mostly
women's schools, they did not have football programs. Prairie
View State Normal and Industrial College, a conference member, had spirited rivalries with Wiley and Texas colleges. In
1938, the black colleges in Texas adopted the title Southwestern
Athletic Conference.[44]

The gridiron campaigns of these colleges attracted widespread interest in the black community. Fans traveled hundreds
of miles to the college towns of Hawkins, Marshall, Waco, and
Austin to cheer on their favorite teams. Interest was so strong in
Dallas that some games were played there. During the 1930s
and 1940s, Wiley and Prairie View played their annual grudge
match in the Dallas Cotton Bowl before crowds of more than
20,000.[45]

[43] Wiley College, *Catalog*, 1901, pp. 16–17.

[44] *Houston Informer*, January 18, 1930.

[45] Ibid., October 17, 1936; Ammons interview; Chandler interview.

Spectators who followed these teams were constantly amazed at the quality of play exhibited by these small-college players. In spite of the shoestring budgets, which often kept players in threadbare uniforms and prevented most of the schools from lighting their fields or building bleachers, fans flocked to these games to see the black athletic heroes of their day. Outstanding players such as James Cottrell and Pat Walker of Texas College, Gerald "Speed" Alexander of Paul Quinn College, and Shellye Ross, Henry Carroll, and "Satch" Turner of Wiley College were among the many stars who thrilled crowds with their gridiron talents.[46]

During the 1930s and 1940s, the Texas schools gained national prominence when Wiley and Texas College earned invitations to post-season bowl games to battle for the mythical national championship of black college football. Between 1926 and 1933, the Wiley Wildcats won the Texas Conference seven times in eight years. The Wiley dynasty was ended, however, by the Texas College Steers, who ran roughshod over the conference from 1934 through 1942. In 1936, Texas College won its first national championship by defeating Alabama State College, 9-0, in the so-called Chocolate Bowl. The Steers of Tyler followed this in 1942 with another national title. Then, in 1945, the Wiley Wildcats regained the conference crown and went on to capture their first national title by defeating Florida A&M, 32-6, in the Orange Blossom Classic Bowl held in Orlando, Florida.[47]

Comparison of the evolution of student life at the black church-related colleges in Texas with that of other black institutions, shows that most of these colleges followed similar patterns of development. Nearly all black colleges and universities, including the public institutions, displayed strict, religious atmospheres during their early years. Mandatory chapel and Sunday worship services formed a part of life at Prairie View from 1878 through the 1920s. Nondenominational chapel sessions at Prai-

[46] Wiley College, *The Wildcat* (Annual), 1949; Paul Quinn College, *The Tiger* (Annual), 1927, p. 19; Ammons interview.

[47] *Houston Informer*, December 6, 1930, January 4, 1936, February 16, 1938, December 9, 1939; Wiley College, *The Wildcat* (Annual), 1946, n.p.

rie View were led by faculty members selected by their peers. Local black ministers who volunteered their services conducted Sunday worship. George R. Woolfolk has argued that such an atmosphere of strict morality was necessary to escape the "sniping of the denominational schools," which accused the secular institution of being a "den of iniquity" and warned God-fearing parents not to send their children there.[48]

Similar religious requirements existed at the best black public and private colleges throughout the South.[49] For example, religious rules regulated the lives of public and private black college students in Georgia from "dawn to moonlight." Most black denominational colleges, as previously noted, also required their students to take courses in theology.[50]

Rules regulating student life in the Texas schools were similar to those in other colleges, although the regulations at some schools appear to have been more detailed than at others. Black colleges in Georgia went so far as to post rules against dueling, possessing indecent pictures, and reading irreligious books. Fisk, Straight, and Howard universities announced rules against card playing, betting, gambling, dancing, and "whatever is immoral or opposed to true culture."[51]

The regimented time schedules of students in the Texas colleges fit patterns in other quarters of the nation. In the public as well as the private black colleges in Georgia, the students:

were hustled out of bed at five or six o'clock in the morning. They washed in tin basins and some took up the fastidious practice of brushing their teeth. Then came breakfast to be followed by an hour of study or devotions. . . . The rest of the morning was given over to classes. After dinner, other recitations were held or students went off to trade

[48] George R. Woolfolk, *Prairie View: A Study in Public Conscience, 1876–1946*, pp. 92–93, 183, 247.

[49] Willard Range, *The Rise and Progress of Negro Colleges in Georgia, 1865–1949*, pp. 136–37; Rayford W. Logan, *Howard University: The First Hundred Years, 1867–1967*, p. 220; James M. McPherson, *The Abolitionist Legacy: From Reconstruction to the NAACP*, pp. 190–91; Addie Louise Joyner Butler, *The Distinctive Black College: Talladega, Tuskegee, and Morehouse*, pp. 22, 68–69.

[50] Range, *Negro Colleges in Georgia*, pp. 136–37, 129; McPherson, *The Abolitionist Legacy*, p. 190.

[51] McPherson, *The Abolitionist Legacy*, p. 191; Range, *Negro Colleges in Georgia*, p. 138.

shops, farm labor, or the usual "duties,". . . . Supper about six o'clock was followed by evening prayers and a study period. . . . At nine-thirty or ten o'clock lights went out. . . .

Well into the twentieth century many of the schools also required their students to wear uniforms.[52]

Rigid social rules were common in all black colleges and remained virtually untouched for nearly half a century. There were scattered incidents of student protests at some black colleges such as Fisk, Howard, and Wilberforce, during the 1920s, in opposition to accommodationist administrations, white faculty, overemphasis on vocational education, and outdated rules of conduct. Yet the black colleges in Texas were not affected.[53] Most black college students in Texas apparently accepted or learned to live with institutional rules. In addition, black college administrators momentarily deflected much student opposition to strict regulations by allowing a wider range of campus activities. This liberalization included permitting the formation of fraternities, sororities, and academic clubs and organizations, as well as emphasizing intercollegiate sports. Not until the end of the Second World War did both black and white college students finally begin pressing for reforms in student regulations regarding hours, personal freedom, socializing, dress, and discipline. Recognizing the changing attitudes of students, most black colleges worked out their differences quietly, first by ignoring violations of minor rules and later by revising regulations concerning more serious matters. In almost all cases, however, black college administrators carefully maintained the upper hand in their dealings with students. Student organizations which pushed too hard or irresponsibly, as did the Wiley student government in 1947, quickly felt the wrath of administrators.[54]

Finally, the development of black academic and social organizations in Texas also paralleled national trends. Social opportunities at black colleges during the late nineteenth and early

[52] Range, *Negro Colleges in Georgia*, pp. 124, 140.

[53] Logan, *Howard University*, pp. 220–21; Woolfolk, *Prairie View*, pp. 207–208.

[54] Woolfolk, *Prairie View*, pp. 207–208; Raymond Wolters, *The New Negro on Campus: Black College Rebellions of the 1920's*, pp. 1–28, 45, 78–82, 283–96; Range, *Negro Colleges in Georgia*, p. 219.

twentieth centuries were limited to religious clubs like the
YMCA and YWCA and academic organizations such as bands,
choirs, debating societies, and literary clubs. Local and national
academic honor societies first appeared in the 1920s and quickly
spread to most campuses. Sports such as basketball, baseball,
and football began to appear around 1900, while fraternities and
sororities sprang up after World War I. Within a relatively short
span of time, the black colleges began to offer their students a
way of life very similar to their white counterparts.[55]

[55] Woolfolk, *Prairie View*, p. 247; Benjamin Brawley, *History of Morehouse College*, pp. 129–31; Butler, *The Distinctive Black College*, pp. 44–45; Range, *Negro Colleges in Georgia*, pp. 219–20.

6

Conclusion

IT is evident from this study that the church-related black colleges in Texas were vital sources of education and advancement for black people across the Southwest. White and black religious denominations began to establish these institutions shortly after the Civil War in an effort to provide religious education for the freedmen. White organizations such as the American Missionary Association, the Freedmen's Aid Society, and the Baptist Home Mission Society, along with black denominations like the African Methodist Episcopal Church and the Colored Methodist Episcopal Church, committed sizeable sums of money and human energy for the creation of schools that would mold young blacks into enlightened, responsible, and valued members of society. The importance of their efforts was magnified by the fact that most of the southern states, including Texas, were reluctant to provide their black citizens with adequate opportunities in elementary, secondary, or college education. As a result, during the late nineteenth and early twentieth centuries, the denominational colleges in Texas shouldered much of the responsibility for all levels of black education. Had it not been for the early efforts of the northern missionaries and the black denominations, a majority of the black youth in Texas would have remained completely illiterate. Even in later years, after the Texas legislature established two black public colleges, the black church-related schools still produced a majority of the state's black college graduates. Between 1930 and 1954, an average of 43 percent of the black college students in Texas attended either Prairie View or Houston colleges, while 57 percent attended black denominational colleges such as Bishop, Wiley, Texas, Tillotson, Samuel Huston, and Paul Quinn.[1]

---

[1]The exact percentage of students attending black private colleges was actually probably higher than 57 percent because consistent enrollment figures for several of the

The curricula of the church-related black colleges in Texas changed significantly between 1872 and 1954. Like other black colleges, the Texas institutions found themselves involved in the national debate concerning the proper direction that black college curricula should take. Although the private black schools were first established to offer classical training, especially for prospective ministers and teachers, the missionary leaders soon realized that few of the freedmen were qualified for college instruction. When the southern states refused to establish enough public schools to alleviate this problem, the denominational black colleges responded by offering their own elementary and secondary classes along with their collegiate courses. These preparatory courses represented a large portion of their academic curricula until the mid-1920s.

During the 1880s, the curricula of the Texas schools were also affected by the rising tide of vocationalism, popularized by the deeds of Samuel Chapman Armstrong and Booker T. Washington. This rival educational model, which stressed practical vocational schooling over so-called abstract classical instruction, was supported for a number of reasons by most southern whites, many influential businessmen, and numerous educational foundations. Although considerable financial and governmental pressure forced many black land-grant colleges to adopt predominantly vocational curricula, most private colleges, including those in Texas, resisted and developed only limited vocational programs. Vocational courses common to all the private schools in Texas included agriculture, woodwork, and metalwork for men, and a variety of classes in domestic service or home economics for women. While the Tuskegee approach to black higher education was desirable to most whites and some blacks, the black denominational colleges judged vocational courses too expensive to maintain and a threat to the advancement of their liberal arts curricula. Black college leaders in Texas and elsewhere feared that if all black colleges emphasized industrial training, their race would be barred from achieving equality and possibly condemned to a second-class status as semiskilled factory and agricultural laborers.

---

private schools including Guadalupe, St. Philip's, and the Butler colleges are not available (*Texas Almanac*, 1930–54).

Without dedicated administrators and instructors, the church-related black colleges could not have survived. In an era of segregation and racial hostility, these men and women displayed the courage and ingenuity to overcome almost any problem that confronted their institutions. In dealing with the issue of racial composition, the leaders of the private schools in Texas followed national trends. The faculties and staffs of the colleges founded by the northern denominational boards were white at first, while the black church organizations utilized black personnel from the beginning. Exhibiting a somewhat paternalistic attitude, northern missionary entities such as the Freedmen's Aid Society and the American Missionary Association were reluctant to admit that blacks were capable of running institutions of higher education. They honestly felt that white teachers and administrators were needed because there were not enough qualified black educators available during the late nineteenth century. The black denominations, however, were much more conscious of the need for racial identity and therefore were determined to use black personnel. In order to demonstrate their own independence, the black churches felt it was imperative to set their own goals and rely upon their own people.

Blacks were divided on the issue of racial composition. Arguments for black control of the northern denominational schools were supported by the fact that black denominations such as the AME and CME were already operating colleges. Other blacks, especially black parents, may have approved of the concept, but opposed any radical shift to black control on the grounds that white teachers were better trained and more experienced than most black instructors. Many of these people favored gradual rather than immediate change. In the end, each denomination made the transition to black control at its own pace. Generally speaking, the northern denominations began relinquishing control of their black colleges during the late 1880s and finished the process during the 1920s. This was also true in Texas, where the transition began at a Methodist school, Wiley College, in 1894, and was completed at a Baptist institution, Bishop Collge, in 1929.

Reviewing the administrators of these schools, it is clear

that the individuals who made noteworthy contributions shared certain personality and leadership traits. Although some authors, such as Christopher Jencks and David Riesman, have depicted black college presidents as being authoritarian or even tyrannical, it is evident from this work that most of these men and women did not deserve such a negative description. In reality, the presidents of the private black colleges in Texas were generally aggressive and pragmatic leaders, who governed with a strong but careful, hand. The uniformity of presidential leadership found in most black colleges resulted, in large measure, from the universal problems these administrators faced, such as marginal resources, a hostile environment, and a scarcity of qualified teachers and students.

Maintaining an adequately trained faculty was a problem common to all black colleges. Because their faculties were usually overworked and underpaid, the black denominational colleges in Texas experienced an unusually rapid turnover in their teaching staffs. This did not mean, as some scholars have suggested, that black college faculties were entirely lacking in effective and well-trained instructors. Fortunately, each college had a few individuals who served for extended lengths of time and who excelled as instructors and scholars. In most cases, these teachers had a special link with their school. Some felt loyalty and remained because they were graduates of these schools; some had personal friends on the staff; some were staunch supporters of their denominations and saw their service as an act of stewardship; and others were inspired by idealism, believing that their efforts would benefit their race. Consequently, these men and women provided the academic continuity and intellectual leadership vital to the reputation and appeal of their institutions.

Throughout the late nineteenth and first half of the twentieth centuries the private black colleges in Texas faced the persistent problem of inadequate financing. The minimal budgets under which the Texas schools operated adversely affected every function of these institutions. This lack of funds often delayed needed renovations or new construction, hampered the acquisition of library materials and research and musical equipment, prevented the payment of adequate salaries, necessitated heavy workloads for administrators and instructors, and prohibited the development of significant endowments and scholarship programs.

Not surprisingly, much of the criticism that has been leveled at black colleges has stemmed from their inability to establish strong financial bases. What most authors have overlooked is the fact that black colleges drew most of their support from the most impoverished segment of American society. As most whites were either apathetic or hostile toward the concept of black higher education, white financial support remained limited and usually directed toward schools specializing in vocational training. Only through skillful management, countless sacrifices, and dogged determination were these colleges able to offer their students meaningful educational opportunities.

The major sources of income for the private black colleges in Texas were denominational contributions, tuition and fees, room and board charges, organized philanthropy, and special development projects. Denominational contributions were among the most significant and consistent sources of revenue for these colleges. This was especially true in the late 1800s and early 1900s when the schools were very new. During their early years, the colleges relied upon church support because they had few outside sources of income and their students could not afford to pay substantial tuition charges. The amounts of money received by these colleges varied depending upon the size, wealth, and attitude of the denomination. Among the northern churches, the Baptists, Methodists, and Congregationalists were traditionally more generous than the Presbyterians or Episcopalians. The black denominations, while desiring to invest great sums in their colleges, were hard-pressed to do so. Because they drew their financial support from the least well-to-do group in American society, the AME and CME churches found it difficult to contribute consistently to their colleges.

The combined factors of small enrollments and relatively impoverished students kept tuition and room and board charges from becoming major sources of income until the mid-1920s. Slowly, as more students attended these colleges and as the standard of living improved, the private colleges began to increase their charges. Consequently, by the 1930s, these schools were acquiring about 35 percent of their total income from tuition and fees. Room and board charges also were minimal at first, but were later increased. Initially, room and board charges were designed to cover the cost of feeding and housing the students. By the 1940s, however, these fees came to represent about 25 percent of the total budgets for these schools and several colleges even showed small surpluses which were used to refurbish residence halls and help pay the salaries of dormitory staff.

Organized philanthropy was not a major source of income for most of the private black colleges in Texas. Educational foundations such as the Slater Education Fund, the General Education Board (GEB), and the Phelps-Stokes Fund favored institutions such as Hampton and Tuskegee Institute, which stressed vocational training. Because the church-related black colleges in Texas viewed vocational training as only a small part of their mission, they received only minor and often sporadic grants. Only the General Education Board gave substantial gifts to any of the Texas schools. This was probably because John D. Rockefeller was a devout Baptist and supporter of black colleges. Beginning in 1908, the GEB assisted the financially weak Baptist Home Mission Society in supporting several black colleges and secondary schools. By 1929, the GEB had replaced the Home Mission Society as the chief benefactor of Bishop College.

In developing alternate sources of income, black college presidents played the leading role in creating special fund-raising schemes. Direct appeals to black and white individuals, local clubs, fraternal organizations, and civic groups were perhaps the most common of their methods. Black college presidents also formed varieties of special alumni clubs and fund-raising projects. The choirs and quartets of these colleges contributed their musical talents in performances that garnered both goodwill and financial support for the institutions.

The persistent shortage of money led to a wide range of co-operative relationships between the private and public black colleges in Texas. By the 1930s, several of the colleges, including Bishop, Wiley, Paul Quinn, Prairie View, and Jarvis Christian, had begun sharing the costs of faculty, speakers, and special entertainment. In Austin, Samuel Huston and Tillotson colleges, similar in design and curricula and with the same difficulties in securing adequate financing, merged in 1952. The broadest expression of cooperation among the private black colleges in Texas and elsewhere was the formation of the United Negro College Fund (UNCF) during 1943. The UNCF was designed to assist the black colleges in raising money from organized philanthropy by pooling portions of their development budgets in order to publicize collectively their financial needs.

In spite of all their efforts, none of the Texas colleges was able to raise enough capital to establish a serious endowment, and the majority were hard pressed just to stay in operation. In most cases, these schools managed from one year to the next by juggling a shifting combination of denominational gifts, tuition and fee revenue, and philanthropic grants. Almost any unusual or unexpected financial crisis could place the very existence of the institution in jeopardy. For example, when the administration building of Guadalupe College burned in 1936, the Guadalupe Baptist Association was unable to raise enough money to rebuild the structure and consequently was forced to close the college in 1937.[2]

Student life at the church-related black colleges in Texas was similar to that at other black institutions. Strict religious and behavioral regulations were common at all these schools. During the 1920s, some black colleges around the nation experienced incidents of student opposition to rules that established dress codes, separated the sexes, and required attendance at religious events. The black colleges in Texas, however, did not seem affected. Most black college students in Texas apparently accepted or learned to work around institutional rules. In addition, black college administrators wisely allowed for a wider range of campus activities, including fraternities, sororities, academic clubs, and intercollegiate sports. It was not until after World War II that student pressure for change prompted the Texas colleges to relax many of their Victorian regulations.

In spite of their small budgets, overworked faculties, lim-

---

[2] *Seguin Enterprise*, February 14 and 21, 1936, January 29, 1937.

ited facilities, and strict student regulations, the private black colleges in Texas provided their students with educational opportunities similar to those found in other church-related black institutions in the South. While these colleges specialized in training teachers and ministers, they also prepared hundreds of students to become lawyers, physicians, dentists, and other professionals. A brief review of several of the Texas colleges indicates that many of their graduates went on to make significant contributions not only to their fields or professions, but also to the black community in general.

For example, prominent graduates from Texas College included Mildred Jefferson, who became the first woman graduate of Harvard Medical School; Allen C. Hancock, who served as dean of Jarvis Christian College, director of graduate studies at Hampton Institute, and later president of Texas College; and the Reverend Joseph H. Johnson, who was the first black to enter and to receive a Ph.D. from Vanderbilt University. A noted clergyman, Johnson also served on the boards of trustees of Mississippi Industrial College, Texas College, Phillips School of Theology, and Vanderbilt University.[3]

Bishop College had an especially distinctive record in preparing leaders in the field of education. Five Bishop graduates, for example, went on to become presidents of other black colleges. These included David Abner, Jr., the first graduate of Bishop College, who served Guadalupe College; J. R. E. Lee, who taught at Tuskegee Institute before becoming the chief executive of Florida Normal and Industrial College (Florida A&M); J. A. Bacotes, who headed Leland College in Baker, Louisiana; J. B. Watson, who directed Arkansas Normal and Industrial College (Arkansas State College); and Joseph J. Rhoads, who headed Bishop College. Other notable Bishop graduates were novelist Sutton E. Griggs, singer and composer Jules Bledsoe, nationally recognized clergyman L. K. Williams, and NAACP activist John H. Wells.[4]

[3] Allen C. Hancock, interview with author, Texas College, Tyler, July 18, 1979; William H. Ammons, interview with author, Texas College, July 17, 1979; *Ebony Magazine, 1,000 Successful Blacks*, vol. I of *The Ebony Success Library*, pp. 138, 178.

[4] Interview with Melvin J. Banks, Bishop College, Dallas, July 23, 1979; Effie Kay

Emmett J. Scott, Nolan H. Anderson, J. Mason Brewer, James Farmer, and Heman Sweatt were among the well-known graduates of Wiley College. Emmett Scott was a noted educator, serving for years on the faculty of Tuskegee Institute. Scott also functioned as a personal secretary and confidante for Booker T. Washington. In 1909, he was asked by President William Howard Taft to join a three-man committee to investigate conditions in Liberia. Scott also served as the Secretary of the National Negro Business League for twenty years, from 1902 to 1922. In 1919, Scott joined Howard University as its business manager and remained there until 1932. After graduating first in his class at MeHarry Medical College, Nolan Anderson returned to Marshall, Texas, in 1948 to become one of the leading black physicians in East Texas. A staunch supporter of Wiley College, Anderson also found time to be an active member of the NAACP. J. Mason Brewer became one of America's most renowned black writers, producing dozens of articles and ten major works in the fields of history, poetry, and folklore.[5]

After leaving Marshall in 1941, James Farmer became deeply interested in a variety of Christian movements such as the Council of Methodist Youth and the Christian Youth Council of America. In 1942, Farmer and a group of Chicago students organized the Congress for Racial Equality (CORE) as a nonviolent protest organization to confront racism and segregation. Under Farmer's leadership, CORE pioneered the use of "sit-in" demonstrations in Chicago's segregated department stores and cafes and introduced the idea of "freedom rides" in segregated transportation and terminal facilities throughout the South.[6]

Heman Marion Sweatt was perhaps the most famous Wiley graduate of all. Sweatt gained national attention in 1946 when he

Adams, *Tall Black Texans: Men of Courage*, pp. 75–77, 227–29; James G. Fleming and Christian E. Burckel, *Who's Who in Colored America: An Illustrated Directory of Notable Living Persons of African Descent in the United States*, 7th ed., p. 436.

[5]Alwyn Barr, *Black Texans: A History of Negroes in Texas, 1528–1971*, pp. 227–28; Adams, *Tall Black Texans*, pp. 157–59, 205–207; James W. Byrd, *J. Mason Brewer: Negro Folklorist*, pp. 1–3.

[6]George H. Chandler, interview with author, Wiley College, July 20, 1979; Sociological Resources for the Social Sciences, *Leadership in American Society: A Case Study of Black Leadership*, pp. 44–45; Adams, *Tall Black Texans*, pp. 243–44.

attempted to register in the law school of the University of Texas. After being denied admission on the basis of his race, Sweatt filed suit in the Texas courts to desegregate the state institution. Backed by the NAACP, Sweatt's legal challenge was ultimately carried before the United States Supreme Court. In June, 1950, the Supreme Court ruled that Sweatt must be admitted to the law school in Austin as no separate institution of equal quality and academic reputation existed. The Sweatt decision proved to be a decisive blow to the doctrine of "separate but equal" and opened the way for the integration of undergraduate, graduate, and professional schools across the nation.[7]

The private black colleges in Texas made vital, unique, and lasting contributions to the advancement of black Texans. In the age of Jim Crow, these colleges provided many black Texans with their only chance for an education and a better way of life. These schools also displayed a special concern for their communities by developing a wide range of service programs designed to bring the benefits of higher education to everyone. More important, these colleges provided their race with the black leaders of yesterday, today, and tomorrow.

[7] Michael L. Gillette, "Herman Marion Sweatt: Civil Rights Plaintiff," in *Black Leaders: Texans for Their Times*, ed. Alwyn Barr and Robert A. Calvert, pp. 163–84; Barr, *Black Texans*, pp. 213–15.

Bibliography

Primary Sources

Manuscripts and Collections

Austin, Texas. Huston-Tillotson College. Archives. Mary Elizabeth Branch Papers. "Reverend Gustave D. Pike to Reverend E. B. Wright," February 8, 17, 24, 1876.

Austin, Texas. Lyndon B. Johnson Library. National Youth Administration Papers. Box 10.

Crockett, Texas. Crockett Public Library. "History of Mary Allen Junior College," n.d. (mimeographed).

Dallas, Texas. Melvin J. Banks Papers (in the possession of Melvin J. Banks).

Houston, Texas. Houston Public Library. Houston Metropolitan Research Center. John Henry Kirby Collection, Box 38, File R-1.

Marshall, Texas. Wiley College. Archives. W. H. Davis, "Wiley University, Marshall, Texas," November 9, 1878.

New Orleans, Louisiana. Amistad Research Center. Addendum: Huston-Tillotson College, Temporary Box No. 1-5. American Missionary Association Manuscripts: Texas (microfilmed).

New York, New York. United Negro College Fund. Archives. "Distribution of Net Proceeds to Member Colleges in Texas, 1944–1954."

Tyler, Texas. Dominion R. Glass Papers (in the possession of Mrs. Willie Lee Glass).

Tyler, Texas. Allen C. Hancock Papers (in the possession of Allen C. Hancock).

Waco, Texas. Paul Quinn College. Archives of the A.M.E. Church and Ethnic Cultural Center. J. W. Yancy Papers.

Washington, D.C. Library of Congress. NAACP Papers, Box G-200.

Government Documents

Blackstock, Graham. *Staff Monograph on Higher Education for Negroes in Texas.* Austin: Texas Legislative Council, 1950.

Guadalupe County. 25th Judicial District Court Records. Courthouse. Seguin, Texas.

Texas Attorney General's Office. *Heman Marion Sweatt* v. *Theophilus Shickel Painter*, et al., respondents. Brief of Respondents. Austin: n.p., 1950.

Texas Department of Education. *The Certification of Teachers in Texas.* Bulletin No. 43, 1915.

———. *Education in Texas, Source Materials.* Bulletin no. 1824. Austin: University of Texas Press, 1918.

———. *Vocational Education in Texas.* Bulletin No. 204. Austin: State Board of Vocational Education, 1926.

———. *Negro Education in Texas.* Bulletin No. 212. Austin: State Department of Education, 1926.

———. *Education in Texas, 1927–1928.* Bulletin No. 251. Austin: Von Boeckmann–Jones Co., 1929.

———. *Negro Education in Texas.* Bulletin No. 294. Austin: State Department of Education, 1931.

———. *Laws, Rules and Regulations Governing State Teachers Certificates.* Bulletin No. 289, 1923, and No. 299, 1932.

Texas Secretary of State. Charter Division. *Charter of Tillotson Collegiate and Normal Institute.* Charter No. 803. Austin, February 10, 1877.

U.S. Bureau of Refugees, Freedmen and Abandoned Lands. *Report of Brevet Major General J. B. Kiddoo, Assistant Commissioner for Texas, for the Year Ending December 31st, 1866.* Washington, D.C.: Government Printing Office, 1866.

U.S. Commission on Civil Rights. *Freedom to be Free: A Century of Emancipation, 1863–1963.* Washington, D.C.: Government Printing Office, 1963.

U.S. Department of the Interior. Bureau of Education. *History of Education in Texas,* by J. J. Lane. Circular of Information No. 2. Washington, D.C.: Government Printing Office, 1903.

———. Bureau of Education. *Negro Education: A Study of the Private and Higher Schools for Colored People in the United States,* by Thomas Jesse Jones. Bulletin No. 39. 2 vols. Washington, D.C.: Government Printing Office, 1916.

———. Bureau of Education. *Report of the United States Commissioner of Education for 1900–1901,* by Kelly Miller. 2 vols. Washington, D.C.: Government Printing Office, 1902.

———. Bureau of Education. *Statistics of Education of the Negro*

Race, 1925–1926, by David T. Blose. Bulletin No. 19. Washington, D.C.: Government Printing Office, 1928.

————. Bureau of Education. *Survey of Negro Colleges and Universities*, by Arthur J. Klein. Bulletin No. 7. Washington, D.C.: Government Printing Office, 1928.

U.S. Office of Education. *Accredited Higher Institutions, 1952*, by Theresa Birch Wilkins. Bulletin 1952, No. 3.

————. Federal Security Agency. *College Salaries, 1939–1940*. Circular No. 196. Washington, D.C.: Government Printing Office, 1940.

Church Records and Publications

American Missionary. 1877–1932.

American Missionary Association. *Annual Report*. 1877–1954.

Baptist Missionary State Convention of Texas. *Minutes*. 1887, 1889.

Board of Missions for Freedmen of the Presbyterian Church in the United States of America. *Annual Report*. 1888–1912.

Freedmen's Aid Society. *Annual Report*. 1866–1878.

Guadalupe Baptist District Association. *Centennial, 1873–1973*. San Antonio, 1973.

Journal of the General Conference of the African Methodist Episcopal Church. 1872, 1876, 1880.

Journal of the National Baptist Convention. 1898, 1916, 1917.

Journal of the Texas Annual Conference of the Methodist Episcopal Church. 1928–1935.

Methodist Review. 1886, 1925.

Missionary Baptist General Convention of Texas. *Annual Report*. 1916, 1917, 1919, 1920–23.

Mt. Olive Missionary Baptist Association. *Minutes*. 1921.

Palestine Missionary Baptist Association. *Minutes*. 1920.

St. John Regular Missionary Baptist Association. *Minutes*. 1904, 1906, 1913, 1915, 1919.

Second Episcopal District of the Christian Methodist Episcopal Church. *A Pattern of Progress*. n.p., n.d.

Texas and Louisiana Baptist Association. *Proceedings*. 1908.

Women's Home and Foreign Mission Society. *Constitution and By-Laws*. Ft. Worth: Star Publishing, 1940.

College Records and Publications

Austin College. *Catalog*. 1949.

Bishop College. *The Bear* (Annual). 1926.

————. *Catalog.* 1881, 1882, 1896, 1897, 1912, 1921, 1924, 1926, 1930, 1941–54, 1978.

Bishop Herald. 1976–79.

Guadalupe College. *Catalog.* 1892, 1920.

————. *Prospects and General Outlook: The Guadalupe College as Others See It.* Seguin: Guadalupe College, n.d.

Huston-Tillotson College. *The Alumnus (Special Souvenir Edition).* Austin: Huston-Tillotson College, 1953.

————. *Catalog.* 1952.

————. *Preliminary Bulletin.* 1952.

Jarvis Christian College. *Catalog.* 1913, 1916, 1922, 1929, 1938, 1941, 1944, 1946, 1950.

————. *The Inauguration of Earl Wadsworth Rand, Seventh President of Jarvis Christian College.* Hawkins: Jarvis Christian College, 1976.

Paul Quinn College. *Catalog.* 1887, 1888, 1891, 1937, 1938, 1945–49, 1978.

————. *The Tiger* (Annual). 1896, 1927.

Paul Quinn Weekly. 1915.

Phillips University. *Catalog.* 1909.

St. Mary's College. *Catalog.* 1949.

St. Philip's College. *Catalog.* 1906, 1935–54.

Samuel Huston College. *Catalog.* 1942, 1948, 1952.

————. "Commencement Invitation." 1928.

————. *Student Handbook.* n.d.

San Antonio College. *Catalog.* 1954.

Texas Christian University. *Catalog.* 1949.

Texas College. *Catalog.* 1916–50.

————. *The Criterion* (Annual). 1927.

————. *86th Anniversary.* Tyler, 1980.

Texas Lutheran College. *Catalog.* 1949.

Texas State University. *Herald.* 1948.

Tillotson College. *Catalog.* 1934–52.

————. *Student Handbook.* n.d.

Wiley College. *Catalog.* 1887, 1891, 1892, 1901, 1902, 1919–50.

————. *The Wildcat* (Annual). 1926, 1946.

Newspapers

Austin American, 1946–55.
Austin American Statesman, 1944, 1948, 1952, 1953.
Austin Herald, 1916–18.

Bastrop Advertiser, July 10, 1885.
Brenham Weekly Banner, February 6, 1880, September 15, 1881, July 8, 1882.
City Times (Galveston), 1904–1905.
Dallas Gazette, March, 1936.
Dallas Morning News, March 28, 1954, October 17, 1960.
Dallas News, 1936, 1945, 1947, 1948, 1950–54, 1961, 1964, 1968, 1975.
Dallas Times Herald, December 19, 1965, October 17, 1969.
Houston Chronicle, October 17, 1969.
Houston Defender, 1935, 1946.
Houston Informer, 1930–54.
Houston Post, May 7, 1905, May 20, 1965.
Marshall News Messenger, 1936, 1947, 1948.
Marshall Tri-Weekly Herald, March 31, 1877, 1881.
Negro Labor News (Houston), 1935, 1937–40, 1947.
New Orleans Informer Sentinel, January 24, 1948.
Pittsburgh Courier, January, 1948.
San Antonio Register, 1930–54.
Seguin Enterprise, 1891–1937.
Taborian Banner (Galveston), 1906.
Texas Examiner (Houston), 1946.
The Call (Kansas City), October 17, 1947, February 13, 1948.
The Herald (Austin), 1916–19.
Waco Messenger, 1933–54.

Interviews and Correspondence

Ammons, William H. Interview with author. Texas College, Tyler, Texas. July 17, 1979.
Banks, Melvin J. Interview with author. Bishop College, Dallas, Texas. July 23, 1979.
Brown, Olive D. Interview with author. Huston-Tillotson College, Austin, Texas. May 15, 1980.
Chandler, George H. Interview with author. Wiley College, Marshall, Texas. July 20, 1979.
Fuller, E. N. Interview with author. Wiley College, Marshall, Texas. July 20, 1979.
Glass, Willie Lee. Interview with author. Tyler, Texas. April 4, 1981.
Hancock, Allen C. Interview with author. Texas College, Tyler, Texas. July 19, 1979.
Jones, John P. Interview with author. Texas College, Tyler, Texas. July 19, 1979.

McKnight, Eugenia. Autobiographical sketch. Obtained in correspondence with Anne Brawner, April, 1981.

Terrell, Barbara. Interview with author. Tyler, Texas. April 4, 1981.

Waddleton, Venita C. Interview with author. Jarvis Christian College, Hawkins, Texas. July 18, 1979.

Wilson, Henry F. Autobiographical sketch. Obtained in correspondence with Anne Brawner, April, 1981.

Wood, Lavern C. Interview with author. Paul Quinn College, Waco, Texas. July 13, 1979.

Books

Armitage, Thomas. *A History of the Baptists.* New York: Bryan Taylor and Co., 1886.

Curry, J. L. M. *Education of the Negro Since 1860.* Baltimore: John F. Slater Fund, 1894.

Federal Writers' Project. *Slave Narratives: A Folk History of Slavery in the United States from Interviews with Former Slaves.* 17 vols. 1938. Reprint ed., St. Clair Shores, Mich.: Scholarly Press, 1976.

Hagood, L. M. *The Colored Man in the Methodist Episcopal Church.* 1890. Reprint ed., Westport, Conn.: Negro University Press, 1970.

John F. Slater Fund. *Proceedings of the Trustees.* 1884–1936.

Kealing, H. T. *History of African Methodism in Texas.* Waco, 1885.

Kroeger, William H. *Isaac W. Wiley: Late Bishop of the Methodist Episcopal Church, A Monograph.* New York: Cranston and Stowe, 1885.

Morton, Lena. *My First Sixty Years.* New York: Philosophical Library, 1965.

Phillips, C. H. *The History of the Colored Methodist Episcopal Church in America: Comprising Its Organization, Subsequent Development and Present Status.* Jackson, Tenn.: Publishing House of the AME Church, 1898.

Rust, Richard S., ed. *Isaac W. Wiley.* Cincinnati: Cranston and Stowe, 1885.

Simmons, William J. *Men of Mark: Eminent, Progressive and Rising.* 1887. Reprint ed., New York: Arno Press, 1968.

Texas Almanac. Dallas: A. H. Belo Corporation, 1900–55.

United Negro College Fund. *Annual Report.* 1975–79.

Yancy, J. W. *History of the Connectional Departments.* Nashville: Sunday School Union Building, n.d.

Secondary Sources

Manuscripts

Allen, Jewell. "The History of Negro Education at Wiley College." M.A. thesis, East Texas State Teachers College, 1940.

Baker, Orestes Jeremiah. "A Study of Senior College Library Facilities for Negroes in Texas." M.A. thesis, Columbia University, 1936.

Banks, Melvin J. "The Pursuit of Equality: The Movement for First Class Citizenship Among Negroes in Texas, 1920–1950." Ph.D. diss., Syracuse University, 1962.

Barth, Shell. "A History of the Negro Presbyterian Church." Ph.D. diss., University of Texas, 1965.

Batts, William Malcolm. "What the General Baptists of Texas (Negro) Want Educationally With Suggestions for Improvement of the Educational Program." M.A. thesis, Prairie View A&M University, 1946.

Brawner, Anne. "Guadalupe College: A Case History in Negro Higher Education, 1884–1936." M.A. thesis, Southwest Texas State University, 1980.

Chambers, Bill. "The History of the Texas Negro and His Development in Texas." M.A. thesis, North Texas State Teachers College, 1940.

Debes, Robert Randolph. "A Sociological Study of Paul Quinn College, Waco, Texas." M.A. thesis, Baylor University, 1949.

Gee, Ruth Ella. "The History and Development of the Prairie View Training School, 1916–1946," M.A. thesis, Prairie View A&M University, 1946.

Glasrud, Bruce Alden. "Black Texans, 1900–1930." Ph.D. diss., Texas Tech University, 1969.

Hornsby, Alton, Jr. "Negro Education in Texas, 1865–1917." M.A. thesis, University of Texas, 1962.

Jones, William H. "Tillotson College From 1930–1940: A Study of the Total Institution." Austin, 1940. (mimeographed.) Copy held at Huston-Tillotson College, Austin.

LaGrone, Cyrus W. "A Sociological Study of the Negro Population of Marshall, Texas." M.A. thesis, University of Texas, 1932.

Lanier, Raphael O'Hara. "The History of Higher Education for Negroes in Texas: 1930–1955, With Particular Reference to Texas Southern University." Ph.D. diss., New York University, 1957.

Lanier, Roy H. "Church-Related Colleges for Negroes in Texas." M.A. thesis, Hardin-Simmons University, 1950.

Lewis, Elmer Clifford. "A History of Secondary and Higher Education in Negro Schools Related to the Disciples of Christ." Ph.D. diss., University of Pittsburg, 1960.

Long, John Cornelius. "The Disciples of Christ and Negro Education." Ph.D. diss., University of Southern California, 1960.

Norris, Clarence W., Jr. "St. Philip's College: A Case Study of a Historically Black Two-Year College." Ph.D. diss., University of Southern California, 1975.

Patterson, Joseph Lorenzo. "A Study of the History of the Contribution of the American Missionary Association to the Higher Education of the Negro—With Special Reference to Five Selected Colleges Founded by the Association." Ph.D. diss., Cornell University, 1956.

Platt, Hazel. "Negro Education in Texas." M.A. thesis, University of Texas, 1917.

Rodgers, Virginia. "A Survey of Presbyterian Education in Texas." Ph.D. diss., University of Texas, 1941.

Smallwood, James M. "Black Texas During Reconstruction, 1865–1874." Ph.D. diss., Texas Tech University, 1974.

Taylor, Clifford H., Jr. "Jarvis Christian College: Its History and Present Standing in Relationship to the Standards of the Texas State Department of Education and the Southern Association of Colleges and Secondary Schools." B.D. thesis, Texas Christian University, 1946.

Taylor, Douglas Barnes. "Negro Education in Texas." M.A. thesis, University of Texas, 1927.

Thompson, James E. "A History of Negro Colleges of East Texas." M.A. thesis, Stephen F. Austin State College, 1951.

Thompson, Lloyd K. "The Origins and Development of Black Religious Colleges in East Texas." Ph.D. diss., North Texas State University, 1976.

Timmins, Richard Haseltine. "A Study of Three National Efforts in Fund Raising for Colleges and Universities." Ed.D. diss., Columbia University, 1962.

Todd, William Clyde. "Attitudes of the Negroes of Texas Toward Higher Education." M.A. thesis, University of Texas, 1929.

Toles, Caesar Francis. "The History of Bishop College." M.A. thesis, University of Michigan, 1947.

Urquhart, George Richard. "The Status of Secondary and Higher Education of Negroes in Texas." M.A. thesis, University of Texas, 1931.

Williams, Lea Ester. "The United Negro College Fund: Its Growth and Development." Ed.D. diss., Columbia University, 1977.

Williams, Mabel Crayton. "The History of Tillotson College, 1881–1952." M.A. thesis, Texas Southern University, 1967.

Willingham, William Oliver. "Progress of Negro Education in Texas." M.A. thesis, Texas Technological College, 1932.

Books

Adams, Effie Kay. *Tall Black Texans: Men of Courage.* Dubuque, Iowa: Kendall-Hunt Publishing Company, 1972.

Aldrich, Armistead Albert. *History of Houston County.* San Antonio: Naylor Company, 1943.

Aptheker, Herbert, ed. *The Correspondence of W. E. B. DuBois,* 3 vols. Amherst: University of Massachusetts Press, 1973.

————. *A Documentary History of the Negro People in the United States.* New York: Citadel Press, 1951.

Armstrong, Samuel Chapman. *The Founding of Hampton Institute.* Boston: Directors of the Old South Work, 1904.

Ballard, Allen B. *The Education of Black Folk: The Afro-American Struggle for Knowledge in White America.* New York: Harper & Row, 1973.

Banks, William L. *The Black Church in the United States.* Chicago: Moody Press, 1972.

Barber, Jesse B. *Climbing Jacob's Ladder.* New York: Board of National Missions, Presbyterian Church in the United States of America, 1952.

Barr, Alwyn. *Black Texans: A Study of Negroes in Texas, 1528–1971.* Austin: Jenkins Publishing Company, 1973.

Barr, Alwyn, and Robert A. Calvert, eds. *Black Leaders: Texans for Their Times.* Austin: Texas State Historical Association, 1981.

Berglund, Ernest. *History of Marshall.* Austin: Steck Company, 1948.

Berry, L. L. *A Century of Missions of the African Methodist Episcopal Church, 1840–1940.* New York: Gutenberg Printing Co., 1942.

Bond, Horace Mann. *The Education of the Negro in the American Social Order.* New York: Prentice-Hall, 1934.

Bontemps, Arna. *100 Years of Negro Freedom.* New York: Dodd, Mead and Company, 1961.

Bowles, Frank, and Frank A. DeCosta. *Between Two Worlds: A Profile of Negro Higher Education*. New York: McGraw-Hill Book Company, 1971.

Brawley, Benjamin. *History of Morehouse College*. 1917. Reprint ed., College Park, Md.: McGrath Publishing Company, 1970.

Brawley, James P. *Two Centuries of Methodist Concern: Bondage, Freedom and Education of Black People*. New York: Vantage Press, 1974.

Brewer, J. Mason. *Negro Legislators of Texas and Their Descendants*. Dallas: Mathis Publishing Co., 1935.

————. *A Pictorial and Historical Souvenir of Negro Life in Austin, Texas, 1950–1951; Who's Who and What's What*. Austin, 1951.

————, ed. *An Historical Outline of the Negro in Travis County*. Austin: Samuel Huston College, 1940.

Broderick, Francis L. *W. E. B. DuBois: Negro Leader in a Time of Crisis*. Stanford: Stanford University Press, 1959.

Brown, Hugh V. A. *History of the Education of Negroes in North Carolina*. Raleigh: Irving Swain Press, 1961.

Brown, Lawrence L. *A Brief History of the Church in West Texas*. Austin: Seminary of the Southwest, 1959.

Brownlee, Fred L. *New Day Ascending*. Boston: Pilgrim Press, 1946.

Bryant, Ira B. *Texas Southern University: Its Antecedents, Political Origin, and Future*. Houston: privately printed, 1975.

Bucke, Emory S., ed. *The History of American Methodism*. 3 vols. New York: Abindgon Press, 1964.

Bullock, Henry Allen. *A History of Negro Education in the South*. Cambridge, Mass.: Harvard University Press, 1967.

Butler, Addie Louise Joyner. *The Distinctive Black College: Talladega, Tuskegee, and Morehouse*. Metuchen, N.J.: Scarecrow Press, 1977.

Branda, Eldon Stephen. *The Handbook of Texas: A Supplement*. Austin: Texas State Historical Association, 1976.

Byrnum, E. B. *These Carried the Torch: Pioneers of Christian Education in Texas*. Dallas: Walter F. Clark Company, 1946.

Byrd, James W. *J. Mason Brewer: Negro Folklorist*. Southwest Writers Series, no. 12. Austin: Steck-Vaughn Company, 1967.

Carnegie Commission on Higher Education. *From Isolation to Mainstream: Problems of the Colleges Founded for Negroes*. New York: McGraw Hill Book Company, 1971.

Carroll, J. M. *A History of Texas Baptists*. Dallas: Baptist Standard Publishing Company, 1923.

Cattell, J. M., ed. *Leaders in American Education*. New York: New Science Press, 1941.

Chalk, Ocania. *Pioneers of Black Sports*. New York: Dodd, Mead and Company, 1976.

Chambers, Frederick. *Black Higher Education in the United States: A Selected Bibliography on Negro Higher Education and Historically Black Colleges and Universities*. Westport, Conn.: Greenwood Press, 1978.

Christopher, Maurine. *Black Americans in Congress*. New York: Thomas Y. Crowell Company, 1971.

Clift, Virgil A.; Archibald W. Anderson; and H. Gordon Hullfish. *Negro Education in America*. New York: Harper & Brothers, 1962.

Commission on Higher Educational Opportunity in the South. *The Negro and Higher Education in the South*. Atlanta: Southern Regional Education Board, 1967.

Crossland, Fred E. *Minority Access to College*. New York: Schocker Books, 1971.

Crum, Mason. *The Negro in the Methodist Church*. New York: Methodist Church, 1951.

Curry, Jabez Lamar Monroe. *A Brief Sketch of George Peabody, and a History of the Peabody Education Fund Through Thirty Years*. New York: Negro University Press, 1969.

Curry, William H. *A History of Early Waco*. Waco: Library Binding Company, 1968.

Davis, Arthur P., and Saunders Redding, eds. *Cavalcade: Negro American Writing from 1760 to the Present*. Boston: Houghton Mifflin Company, 1971.

Davis, William R. *The Development and Present Status of Negro Education in East Texas*. New York: Bureau of Publications, Teachers College, Columbia University, 1934.

Disciples of Christ. *Survey of Service: Organizations Represented in the International Convention of Disciples of Christ*. St. Louis: Christian Board of Publications, 1928.

DuBois, W. E. B. *The College Bred Negro*. Atlanta: Atlanta University Publications, 1900.

————. *The Education of Black People: Ten Critiques, 1906–1960*. Edited by Herbert Aptheker. Amherst: University of Massachusetts Press, 1973.

————. *The Souls of Black Folk*. 1903. Reprint ed., New York: New American Library, 1969.

————. *What the Negro Has Done for the United States and Texas*. Washington: Government Printing Office, 1936.

Ebony Magazine. 1,000 Successful Blacks. Vol. I of *The Ebony Success Library.* Chicago: Johnson Publishing Co., 1973.

Eby, Frederick. *The Development of Education in Texas.* New York: Macmillan Company, 1925.

———. *The Development of Modern Education.* Englewood Cliffs, N.J.: Prentice-Hall, 1952.

Edwards, Harry. *Black Students.* New York: Free Press, 1970.

Evans, E. C. *The Story of Texas Schools.* Austin: Steck Company, 1955.

Federal Writers' Project. *Houston: A History and Guide.* American Guide Series. Houston: Anson Jones Press, 1942.

Fischel, Leslie H., Jr., and Benjamin Quarles. *The Negro American: A Documentary History.* Glenview, Ill.: Scott, Foresman, 1967.

Fleming, G. James, and Christian E. Burckel. *Who's Who in Colored America: An Illustrated Directory of Notable Living Persons of African Descent in the United States.* 7th ed. Yonkers, N.Y.: Christian E. Burckel & Associates, 1950.

Franklin, John Hope. *From Slavery to Freedom: A History of Negro Americans.* Third ed. New York: Vintage Books, 1967.

Frazier, E. Franklin. *The Negro Church in America.* New York: Schocken Books, 1963.

Frazier, Thomas R., ed. *Afro-American History: Primary Sources.* New York: Harcourt, Brace and World, 1970.

Fredrickson, George M. *The Black Image in the White Mind: The Debate on Afro-American Character and Destiny, 1817–1914.* New York: Harper & Row, 1971.

Gammel, Hans Peter Nielsen. *Laws of Texas, 1822–1897.* 10 vols. Austin: State Printers, n.d.

Garrison, Winfred Ernest. *Religion Follows the Frontier: A History of the Disciples of Christ.* New York: Harper and Brothers, 1931.

———, and Alfred T. DeGroot. *The Disciples of Christ, A History.* St. Louis: Christian Board of Publication, 1948.

Guzman, Jesse Park, ed. *Negro Yearbook.* 11 vols. Tuskegee, Ala.: Tuskegee Institute, 1947.

Haller, John S., Jr. *Outcasts from Evolution: Scientific Attitudes of Racial Inferiority, 1859–1900.* Chicago: University of Illinois Press, 1971.

Harlan, Louis R. *Booker T. Washington: The Making of a Black Leader, 1856–1901.* New York: Oxford University Press, 1972.

———. *Separate and Unequal: Public School Campaigns and Racism in the Southern Seaboard States, 1901–1915.* Chapel Hill: University of North Carolina Press, 1958.

Harris, Eula Wallace, and Macie Harris Craig. *Christian Methodist Episcopal Church Through the Years.* Jackson, Tenn.: Christian Methodist Episcopal Publishing House, 1965.

Harrison, Ida Withers. *A History of the Christian Woman's Board of Missions, 1877–1914.* Indianapolis: Christian Woman's Board of Missions, 1914.

Hart, Katherine, et al. *Austin and Travis County: A Pictorial History, 1839–1939.* Austin: Encino Press, 1975.

Harvey, McClennon Phillip, ed. *A Brief History of Paul Quinn College, 1872–1965.* Waco: privately printed, 1965.

Henri, Florette. *Black Migration: Movement North, 1900–1920.* Garden City, N.Y.: Anchor Press, 1976.

Holmes, Dwight Oliver Wendell. *The Evolution of the Negro College.* 1934. Reprint ed., New York: AMS Press, 1970.

Jackson, Luther Porter. *Negro Officeholders in Virginia, 1865–1895.* Norfolk, Va.: Guide Quality Press, 1945.

Jencks, Christopher, and David Riesman. *The Academic Revolution.* Garden City, N.Y.: Doubleday and Company, 1968.

Jenness, Mary. *Twelve Negro Americans.* New York: Friendship Press, 1936.

Johnson, Charles S. *The Negro College Graduate.* 1938. Reprint ed., College Park, Md.: McGrath Publishing Co., 1969.

Jones, Ann. *Uncle Tom's Campus.* New York: Praeger Publishers, 1973.

Jones, Edward Allen. *A Candle in the Dark: A History of Morehouse College.* Valley Forge: Judson Press, 1967.

Jones, Everett H. *Bishop James Steptoe Johnston: A Biographical Sketch.* San Antonio: Diocese of West Texas, 1923.

Jones, Lance G. E. *The Jeanes Teacher in the United States, 1908–1933.* Chapel Hill: University of North Carolina Press, 1937.

———. *Negro Schools in the Southern States.* Oxford: Clarendon Press, 1926.

Jones, Thomas Jesse. *Educational Adaptations: Report of Ten Years' Work of the Phelps-Stokes Fund, 1910–1920.* New York: Phelps-Stokes Fund, 1920.

Jordan, Robert L. *Two Races in One Fellowship.* Detroit: United Christian Church, 1944.

Kealing, H. T. *History of African Methodism in Texas.* Waco, 1885.

Lakey, Othel Hawthorne. *The Rise of Colored Methodism: A Study of* the *Background and the Beginnings of the Christian Methodist Episcopal Church.* Dallas: Crescendo Book Publications, 1972.

Leavell, Ullin Whitney. *Philanthropy in Negro Education.* 1930. Reprint ed., Westport, Conn.: Negro University Press, 1970.

LeMelle, Tilden J., and Wilbert J. LeMelle. *The Black College: A Strategy for Achieving Relevancy.* New York: Frederick A. Praeger, 1969.

Lerner, Gerda, ed. *Black Women in White America: A Documentary History.* New York: Vintage Books, 1972.

Lester, Julius, ed. *The Seventh Son: The Thought and Writings of W. E. B. DuBois.* 2 vols. New York: Vintage Books, 1971.

Lewis, Grant K. *The American Christian Missionary Society and the Disciples of Christ.* St. Louis: Christian Board of Education, 1937.

Logan, Rayford W. *Howard University: The First Hundred Years, 1867–1967.* New York: New York University Press, 1969.

————., ed. *W. E. B. DuBois: A Profile.* New York: Hill and Wang, 1971.

Loud, I. B. *History of Texas Methodism, 1900–1960.* Austin: Capital Printing Company, 1961.

McCuistion, Fred. *Higher Education of Negroes.* Nashville: Southern Association of Colleges and Secondary Schools, 1933.

McGrath, Earl J. *The Predominantly Negro Colleges and Universities in Transition.* New York: Bureau of Publications, Teachers College, Columbia University, 1965.

McPherson, James M. *The Abolitionist Legacy: From Reconstruction to the NAACP.* New Jersey: Princeton University Press, 1975.

Mathews, Basil. *Booker T. Washington, Educator and Interracial Interpreter.* College Park, Md.: McGrath Publishing Company, 1969.

Mays, Benjamin E. *Born to Rebel: An Autobiography.* New York: Charles Scribners, 1971.

Montgomery, T. S. *The Senior Colleges for Negroes in Texas.* Austin: Bi-Racial Conference for Negroes in Texas, 1944.

Moton, Robert Russa. *Finding a Way Out: An Autobiography.* 1920. Reprint ed., New York: Negro University Press, 1969.

Ridgely, Torrence. *The Story of John Hope.* New York: Macmillan Company, 1948.

Rudwick, Elliot M. *W. E. B. DuBois: A Study in Minority Group Leadership.* Philadelphia: University of Pennsylvania Press, 1960.

Shackles, Chrystine I. *Reminiscences of Huston-Tillotson College.* Austin: Best Printing Company, 1973.

Sherer, Robert G. *Subordination or Liberation? The Development and*

Conflicting Theories of Black Education in Nineteenth Century Alabama. University, Ala.: University of Alabama Press, 1977.

Sibley, Marylin. *George W. Brackenridge: Maverick Philanthropist.* Austin: University of Texas Press, 1973.

Smith, James H. *Vital Facts Concerning the African Methodist Episcopal Church; Its Origins, Doctrines, Government, Usages, Polity, Progress (A Socratic Exposition).* N.p., 1939.

Sociological Resources for the Social Sciences. *Leadership in American Society: A Case Study of Black Leadership.* Episodes in Social Inquiry Series. Boston: Allyn & Bacon, 1969.

Sowell, Thomas. *Black Education: Myths and Tragedies.* New York: David McKay Company, 1972.

Spivey, Donald. *Schooling for the New Slavery: Black Industrial Education, 1868–1915.* Contributions in Afro-American and African Studies, no. 38. Westport, Conn.: Greenwood Press, 1978.

Stampp, Kenneth M. *The Era of Reconstruction, 1865–1877.* New York: Vintage Books, 1965.

———. *The Peculiar Institution.* New York: Random House, 1956.

Swint, Henry Lee. *The Northern Teacher in the South, 1862–1870.* Nashville: Vanderbilt University Press, 1941.

Talbot, Edith Armstrong. *Samuel Chapman Armstrong: A Biographical Study.* 1904. Reprint ed., New York: Negro University Press, 1969.

Thompson, Daniel C. *Private Black Colleges at the Crossroads.* Contributions in Afro-American and African Studies, no. 13. Westport, Conn.: Greenwood Press, 1973.

Thrasher, Max Bennett. *Tuskegee: Its Story and Its Work.* 1901. Reprint ed., New York: Negro University Press, 1969.

Tolson, Melvin B. *The Curator.* Vol. 1 of *The Harlem Gallery.* New York: Twayne Publishers, 1965.

Washington, Booker T. *The Future of the American Negro.* 1899. Reprint ed., New York: Negro University Press, 1969.

———. *Tuskegee and Its People: Their Ideals and Achievements.* 1905. Reprint ed., New York: Negro University Press, 1969.

———. *Up From Slavery: An Autobiography.* 1901. Reprint ed., New York: Bantam Books, 1975.

———. *Working With the Hands.* 1904. Reprint ed., New York: Negro University Press, 1969.

———, et al. *The Negro Problem.* 1903. Reprint ed., New York: Arno Press, 1969.

Washington, E. David, ed. *Selected Speeches of Booker T. Washington.* New York: Doubleday, Doran and Company, 1932.

Washington, Roosevelt, Jr. *Texas Association of Developing Colleges Interinstitutional Cooperative Study.* Dallas: Texas Association of Developing Colleges, 1978.

Webb, Walter Prescott, and H. Bailey Carroll, eds. *The Handbook of Texas.* 2 vols. Austin: Texas State Historical Association, 1952.

Willie, Charles V., and Ronald R. Edmonds, eds. *Black Colleges in America: Challenge, Development, Survival.* New York: Teachers College Press, 1978.

Wolters, Raymond. *The New Negro On Campus: Black College Rebellions of the 1920s.* Princeton: Princeton University Press, 1975.

Woodson, Carter G. *The History of the Negro Church.* Washington, D.C.: Associated Publishers, 1945.

Woolfolk, George R. *Prairie View: A Study in Public Conscience, 1876–1946.* New York: Pageant Press, 1942.

Yenser, Thomas, ed. *Who's Who in Colored America: A Biographical Dictionary of Notable Living Persons of African Descent in America, 1933—1934—1935—1937.* 4th ed. New York: Thomas Yenser, 1933–37.

Articles

"All Around Training at Jarvis." *World Call* (September, 1932): 18.

Alphin, Mrs. William. "The Opening of Jarvis Christian Institute." *Missionary Tidings* (May, 1913): 13.

"Bishop. Huston-Tillotson. Jarvis. Paul Quinn. Texas. Wiley." *Premise* (1975): 14.

Boykin, Leander L. "The Survival and Function of the Negro College in a Changing Social Order." *Journal of Negro Education* 12 (Fall, 1943): 589–99.

Bond, Horace Mann. "The Origin and Development of the Negro Church-Related College." *Journal of Negro Education* 29 (Summer, 1960): 217–26.

Brownlee, Fred L. "Heritage and Opportunity: The Negro Church-Related College: A Critical Summary." *Journal of Negro Education* 29 (Summer, 1960): 401–407.

Chambers, Frederick. "Histories of Black Colleges and Universities." *Journal of Negro History* 57 (July, 1972): 270–75.

Coleman, C. D. "The Christian Methodist Episcopal Church: The Rationale and Policies upon Which Support of Its Colleges Is Predicated." *Journal of Negro Education* 29 (Summer, 1960): 313–18.

Cools, Victor G. "Why Negro Education Has Failed." *Educational Review* 68 (December, 1924): 254–59.

Craighead, James B. "The Future of the Negro in the South." *Popular Science Monthly* (November, 1884): 39–46.

Curtis, Florence Rising. "The Library of the Negro College." *Southern Workman* 55 (September, 1926): 472–74.

———. "The Contribution of the Library to Negro Education." *Southern Workman* 56 (September, 1927): 373–78.

Davis, Jackson. "The Outlook for Negro Colleges." *Southern Workman* 57 (September, 1928): 26–35.

"Desegregating Black Public Colleges: What Will It Mean?" *Civil Rights Digest* 7 (Winter, 1975): 26–35.

Dillard, J. H. "The Negro Goes to College." *World's Work* 55 (January, 1928): 337–40.

DuBois, W. E. B. "Education and Work." *Journal of Negro Education* 1 (April, 1932): 105–12.

———. "Negroes in College." *Nation* 122 (March, 1926): 228–30.

———. "Thomas Jesse Jones." *The Crisis* 22 (October, 1921): 252–56.

Dykes, Eva B. "Higher Training of Negroes." *The Crisis* 22 (July, 1921): 105–12.

Eby, Frederick. "Reorganization of Higher Education." *Texas School Journal* 44 (December, 1926): 17.

"Editorial Comment." *Quarterly Review of Higher Education Among Negroes* 4 (April, 1936): 103.

Ellison, John M. "Policies and Rationale Underlying the Support of Colleges Maintained by the Baptist Denomination." *Journal of Negro Education* 29 (Summer, 1960): 330–38.

"Fire at Jarvis." *World Call* (1913): 46.

Gloster, Hugh M. "The Black College—Its Struggle for Survival and Success." *Journal of Negro History* 63 (April, 1978): 101–107.

Greene, Sherman L., Jr. "The Rationale Underlying the Support of Colleges Maintained by the African Methodist Episcopal Church." *Journal of Negro Education* 29 (Summer, 1960): 319–22.

Harlan, Louis. "Booker T. Washington in Biographical Perspective." *American Historical Review* 75 (October, 1970): 1581–99.

———. "The Secret Life of Booker T. Washington." *Journal of Southern History* 37 (August, 1971): 393–416.

Harris, John J.; Cleopatra Figgures; and David G. Carter. "A Historical Perspective of the Emergence of Higher Education in Black Colleges." *Journal of Black Studies* 6 (Spring, 1975): 55–68.

Hemphill, J. C. "Problems of Negro Education." *North American Review* (July, 1886): 436–45.

Holmes, Dwight Oliver Wendell. "The Beginnings of the Negro College." *Journal of Negro Education* 3 (April, 1934): 167–92.

Hornsby, Alton J., Jr. "The Freedmen's Bureau Schools in Texas, 1865–1870." *Southwestern Historical Quarterly* 76 (April, 1973): 397–417.

Hotchkiss, Wesley A. "Congregationalists and Negro Education." *Journal of Negro Education* 29 (Summer, 1960): 289–98.

Jarvis, Ida. "A Black Cloud of Witnesses." *Missionary Tidings* (February, 1915): 413–14.

———. "Why We Gave the Land—The Evolution of an Idea." *Missionary Tidings* (April, 1913): 464–66.

Jenkins, Martin D. "The National Survey of Higher Education and Post-War Reconstruction: The Resources of Negro Higher Education." *Journal of Negro Education* 11 (Fall, 1942): 382–90.

Johnson, Tobe. "The Black College as System." *Daedalus* 100 (Summer, 1971): 798–812.

Jordan, Vernon E. "Blacks and Higher Education—Some Reflections." *Daedalus* 104 (Winter, 1975): 160–65.

Kirke, Edmund. "How Shall the Negro be Educated?" *North American Review* (November, 1886): 421–26.

Lane, David A., Jr. "The Junior College Movement Among Negroes." *Journal of Negro Education* 2 (July, 1933): 272–83.

Lewis, Ronald L. "Cultural Pluralism and Black Reconstruction: The Public Career of Richard H. Cain." *The Crisis* (February, 1978): 57–65.

Little, Monroe H. "The Extra-Curricular Activities of Black College Students, 1868–1940." *Journal of Negro History* 65 (Spring, 1980): 135–45.

Lloyd, R. Grann. "Some Problems of Graduate Schools Operated Primarily for Negroes." *Journal of Negro Education* 25 (Winter, 1956): 83–86.

McCuistion, Fred. "The South's Negro Teaching Force." *Journal of Negro Education* 1 (April, 1932): 16–24.

McNeely, J. H. "Higher Education of Negroes is Making Marked Progress." *School Life* 14 (October, 1928): 37.

Mays, Benjamin E. "The Significance of the Negro Church-Related College." *Journal of Negro Education* 29 (Summer, 1960): 245–51.

Meier, August. "Notes and Documents: Toward a Reinterpretation of Booker T. Washington." *Journal of Southern History* 23 (May, 1957): 220–27.

Miller, Kelly. "The Higher Education of the Negro is at the Cross-roads." *Educational Review* 72 (December, 1926): 272–78.

———. "The Practical Value of the Higher Education of the Negro." *Education* 36 (December, 1915): 234–40.

Morris, Eddie. "The Contemporary Negro College and the Brain Drain." *Journal of Negro Education* 41 (Fall, 1972): 209–19.

Oak, V. V. "Commercial Education in Negro Colleges." *Journal of Negro Education* 1 (Fall, 1932): 400–407.

Patterson, Frederick D. "Cooperation Among the Predominantly Negro Colleges and Universities." *Journal of Negro Education* 35 (Fall, 1966): 477–84.

———. "Duplication of Facilities and Resources of Negro Church-Related Colleges." *Journal of Negro Education* 29 (Summer, 1960): 368–76.

Phares, Mrs. W. W. "Mrs. Ida Jarvis—An Appreciation." *World Call* (June, 1937): 29.

Rabinowitz, H. N. "Half a Loaf: The Shift from White to Black Teachers in the Negro Schools of the Urban South, 1865–1890." *Journal of Southern History* 40 (November, 1974): 565–94.

Redd, George N. "Better Utilization of the Resources of the Negro Church-Related College Through Curriculum Revision." *Journal of Negro Education* 29 (Summer, 1960): 377–87.

Sherman, Charles. "Jarvis Christian College." *Christian Plea* (October, 1947): 1–2.

Sly, Virgil A. "Between Dawn and Dusk at Jarvis." *World Call* (April, 1934): 6–7.

Smith, Herman B. "New Roles for Black Colleges." In *Effective Use of Resources in State Higher Education*. Atlanta: Southern Regional Education Board, 1970.

Taylor, Joy. "Clearing the Way for the Advance of a Race." *World Call* (May, 1931): 8.

Thomas, James S. "The Rationale Underlying Support of Negro Private Colleges by the Methodist Church." *Journal of Negro Education* 29 (Summer, 1960): 252–59.

Thompson, Charles H. "The Present Status of the Negro Private and Church Related College." *Journal of Negro Education* 29 (Summer, 1960): 227–43.

———. "The Prospect of Negro Higher Education." *Journal of Educational Sociology* 32 (1958–59): 306–16.

Thorpe, Marion D. "The Future of Black Colleges and Universities in the Desegregation and Integration Process." *Journal of Black Studies* 6 (September, 1975): 100–12.

Thurmond, David. "Should Black Colleges Survive?" *Essence* (August, 1972): 40–41.

Washington, P. C. "Jarvis College and Its Needs." *World Call* (April, 1942): 28.

Weaver, Robert C. "The Negro Private and Church-Related College: A Critical Summary." *Journal of Negro Education* 29 (Summer, 1960): 394–400.

Wright, Stephen J. "Some Critical Problems Faced by the Negro Church-Related College." *Journal of Negro Education* (Summer, 1960): 339–44.

Index